HOLLYWOOD BAD BOYS
Loud, Fast, and Out of Control

JAMES ROBERT PARISH

Contemporary Books

Chicago   New York   San Francisco   Lisbon   London   Madrid   Mexico City
Milan   New Delhi   San Juan   Seoul   Singapore   Sydney   Toronto

Library of Congress Cataloging-in-Publication Data

Parish, James Robert.
    Hollywood bad boys : loud, fast, and out of control / James Robert Parish.
       p.   cm.
    Includes bibliographical references and index.
    ISBN 0-07-138137-6
    1. Motion picture actors and actresses—United States—Biography—
Dictionaries.   2. Male actors—United States—Biography—Dictionaries.
I. Title.

PN1998.2 .P365   2002
791.43′028′09227303—dc21
[B]   2002019310

To the memory of
David Fritz, Richard Gruber, Les Schwartz,
and Donald Weinblatt

Contemporary Books

A Division of The **McGraw·Hill** *Companies*

1 2 3 4 5 6 7 8 9 0 AGM/AGM 1 0 9 8 7 6 5 4 3 2

ISBN 0-07-138137-6

This book was set in Sabon
Printed and bound by Quebecor Martinsburg

Cover and interior design by Nick Panos
Cover photographs, top to bottom, left to right: Johnny Depp © Pacha/Corbis; Robert
Downey Jr. © Reuters NewMedia Inc./Corbis; Steve McQueen © Bettmann/Corbis; Hugh
Grant © Rufus F. Folkks/Corbis; movie reel © Paul Eekhoff/Masterlife; Jack Nicholson
© Mitchell Gerber/Corbis; Eddie Murphy © Mitchell Gerber/Corbis; Marlon Brando
© CinemaPhoto/Corbis; Charlie Sheen © Reuters NewMedia Inc./Corbis

McGraw-Hill books are available at special quantity discounts to use as premiums and
sales promotions, or for use in corporate training programs. For more information, please
write to the Director of Special Sales, Professional Publishing, McGraw-Hill, Two Penn
Plaza, New York, NY 10121-2298. Or contact your local bookstore.

This book is printed on acid-free paper.

CONTENTS

ACKNOWLEDGMENTS

Academy of Motion Picture Arts and Sciences: Margaret Herrick Library; Billy Rose Theater Collection of the New York Public Library at Lincoln Center; John Cocchi (JC Archives); Ernest Cunningham; Michael Danahy; Echo Book Shop; Jane Klain (Museum of Television and Radio–New York); Alvin H. Marill; Doug McClelland; Jim Meyer; Albert L. Ortega (Albert L. Ortega Photos); Michael R. Pitts; Barry Rivadue; Brenda Scott Royce; Arleen Schwartz; Allan Taylor (editorial consultant and copyeditor); Vincent Terrace.

Special thanks to my agent, Stuart Bernstein, and to my editor, Matthew Carnicelli.

INTRODUCTION

In studying the privileged lives of Hollywood's famous—past and present—for *Hollywood Bad Boys*, I found one of the most intriguing aspects of their colorful histories to be their enviable, charmed existences. When they are at their peak of popularity they are well paid, pampered by their fawning employers, and lauded by their adoring fans. Nothing is too good for them, no whim too difficult to be satisfied, no personality trait so negative that it cannot be overlooked. As such they *appear* to be above it all, living in a rarified atmosphere where anything they might do (drunken brawling, seducing underage females, snorting coke, and so forth) is without serious consequences—at least until such behavior becomes too explosively destructive to themselves and others and too public to be ignored.

During Tinseltown's Golden Age in the pre-1950s, the studios promoted their roster of indulged movie stars as paragons of talent, striking looks, and supposedly impeccable moral behavior. If those celebrities committed indiscretions, their studio bosses had a smooth-functioning system in place to hide their follies, whether it be drunken driving, a girlfriend's abortion, homosexuality, or, occasionally, a major crime. To protect their investments, film companies did whatever it took to keep the misdeeds of the luminaries from public scrutiny, or if the incident became public knowledge, to give it a proper positive spin. (There were some exceptions, however, as with Roscoe "Fatty" Arbuckle in the 1920s, when both his studio and the film industry chose to throw the victim to the wolves.)

Usually it was not until years after the Golden Age celebrities had slipped from power and the public eye, or had died, that previously undisclosed aspects of their pasts were sometimes revealed in memoirs, oral histories, or investigative biographies. Even then, the "facts" had to be pieced together from several sources to discover the full "story." (One such example was the officially unsolved murder of silent film director William Desmond Taylor in 1922, which even today remains something of a mystery.) The challenge of researching, evaluating, and presenting the often unknown or forgotten notorious facts in past stars' lives was a key factor for my writing this book.

By the time the Hollywood studio system broke down in the 1950s and movie stars became independent contractors, it was more difficult for these bigger-than-life celebrities to hide their indiscretions (although the worst offenders seem to commit these reckless acts on a grander scale and more frequently than the average person who would not be given so many opportunities to reform). In the post–Golden Age Tinseltown there was no longer a studio factory to protect miscreants from snooping reporters, determined law enforcers, or the overly curious public. The famous wrongdoers also now had to contend with the proliferation of the supermarket tabloids—as well as the later advent of tabloid television and Internet websites. These sources thrived on uncovering the "hidden" activities of these "big" folk in movies and on television.

No longer could a major celebrity count on keeping quiet a drinking or drug problem, an illicit affair (while married, or otherwise), or other such behavior. Unlike decades before, and thanks to changing moral standards, it almost became a public ritual for the trouble-plagued notable to hold a media conference. In these public forums the person often acknowledged his or her current problem (substance abuse about to be treated, a no-longer-viable romantic relationship, and so forth) and then would ask for public forgiveness (a cycle that became a repeated behavior for some celebrities).

But in the tell-all new Hollywood where such "negative" revelations about, and by, celebrities became almost commonplace, there was soon too much information for most celebrity watchers to absorb fully. As such it became difficult for the public to sort out—let alone remember—who did what to whom or to form a perspective on how the disclosed problem(s) impacted the celebrity's life. After parsing through the clutter of "documented" events in contemporary male stars' lives, putting the information into the perspective of their careers and personal lives was also a major reason for undertaking this investigative volume.

Hollywood Bad Boys covers a range of intriguing Hollywood personalities from the past and present. Just as these vivid subjects have led or now lead exaggerated existences in front of the cameras, so their off-screen lives seem in many cases to have been or be far more intensely lived than that of average persons. Being pop idols, they often have been given a license, both by their studio employers and their adoring public, to indulge themselves without the moral or legal restraints that typically control the noncelebrity.

Included herein are accounts of the fantastic lives of seventy of Tinseltown's privileged male stars, revealing their indulgent escapades and misadventures. Some are leading men of old Hollywood such as John Barrymore, Charlie Chaplin, Errol Flynn, Clark Gable, and Rudolph Valentino. Other narratives focus on contemporary actors like Ben Affleck, Alec Baldwin, Russell Crowe, Robert Downey Jr., and Brad Renfro. Because of their quite unordinary and often amazing, free-wheeling lifestyles—which are detailed—they all qualify as charter members of *Hollywood Bad Boys*.

Ben Affleck

[Benjamin Geza Affleck]
AUGUST 15, 1972–

"I'm really bad at moderation," unassuming Affleck insisted in 1998, referencing his penchant for heavy-duty partying, his sudden and incessant motorcycle road trips, and for doing "something stupid." The six-foot, three-inch movie hunk acknowledged, "I have a lot of alcoholism in my family, but I seem to have dodged that particular bullet." At the time the likeable actor claimed to have his act under control; others apparently agreed. But there was Ben's well-known thirst for (Guinness) beer, gambling, and playing the dating game—all in an increasingly nonstop manner. The Hollywood hotshot who had won a Best Screenplay Oscar with pal Matt Damon for coscripting *Good Will Hunting* (1997) was on the fast track, wisely making a blend of big and little pictures.

He was born in Berkeley, California, in 1972, the son of a social worker (Tim) and a teacher (Chris). The family relocated to Cambridge, Massachusetts, in 1974 where Tim, a jack-of-all-trades got involved in a Boston theater company while supporting his family as a janitor at Harvard University. In 1975 the Afflecks' second son, Casey, was born. Tim had a self-admitted drinking problem that led to the couple divorcing, although the sons remained supportive of their father as he battled his addiction. By then Ben had begun an acting career, first in commercials, then with roles in such projects as the PBS-TV series *The Voyage of the Mimi*, which he did from age eight to fourteen. Also at age eight Affleck first met a Cambridge neighbor, ten-year-old Matt Damon. Both shared a passion for acting and Little League and began a lifelong friendship. As a teenager, Affleck tried pot smoking and drinking. Reportedly, his elementary-schoolteacher mother, involved constructively in liberal causes, permitted her free-spirited older boy and his friends to drink in the basement of their home, preferring, at least, to be able to keep a watchful eye over them.

Ben attended the University of Vermont for a semester, and next studied at Los Angeles's Occidental College for less than a year. By now a relationship with a high school sweetheart had fizzled. He returned to acting with roles in such films as *School Ties* (1992), *Dazed and Confused* (1993), and *Mallrats* (1995). By this point, brother Casey and Matt Damon were also in L.A., struggling for their breakthrough roles. Deciding to write their own showcase movie, Affleck and Damon devoted their free time over many months to refining their own screenplay. As the young stars and coauthors of their resultant film *Good Will Hunting*, they were launched into the big time by its instant success. Wanting to parlay his acting career while he was hot, Ben began making back-to-back movies.

Affleck was already dating actress Gwyneth Paltrow when they made *Shakespeare in Love* (1998). However, chain-smoking Ben was not ready to settle down and the couple split apart. He dated, among others, actresses Famke Janssen and Shoshanna Lonstein (Jerry Seinfeld's ex-girlfriend). He juggled a hectic filmmaking schedule that alternated between major studio productions (1998's *Armageddon*) and independent films (1999's *Dogma*). Affleck and Paltrow costarred in the romantic drama *Bounce* (2000), although each insisted they were no longer an item. In the movie Ben played a recovering alcoholic. He told the media that because of personal experiences with people suffering from alcoholism he was better able to understand his character.

By now, Affleck had a Spanish-style, 7,500-square-foot Hollywood Hills home (complete with a keg of Guinness always on tap), several motorcycles, two Cadillacs, and a fast lifestyle that included gambling forays to Las Vegas. He also had a loft apartment in New York City's Tribeca district for trips back east. (During one such visit in 1999, he was reportedly fined $135 for driving in Massachusetts with a suspended license.)

Unlike his good friend Matt Damon who seemed to handle fame better, success went to Affleck's head. As he acknowledged, "My life changed so quickly that I lost any sense of who I was." According to the star, "I made some poor choices in terms of the direction I took my life." He had also become a lavish gift giver, whether it was a pair of expensive diamond earrings to ex-galpal Paltrow or the keys to a vintage Mustang car he handed to Michele Parnelli-Venetis, assistant director on one of his pictures. He frequently sampled the L.A. bar scene with such actor pals as Vince Vaughn. When on location to make a film or on the road publicizing his latest picture, he was a night life habitué. In retrospect Ben said he tried "to embrace this [fast-lane] life people think I have . . . and I found myself even more miserable."

By spring 2001 Ben was in the news. Ben was the star of the year's upcoming blockbuster World War II combat entry *Pearl Harbor* and was about to start *The Sum of All Fears* (2002) taking over the Jack Ryan spy thriller franchise from Harrison Ford. As for Ben's dad, Tim, more than a decade earlier he had undertaken the rehab program at the ABC Recovery Center in Indio, California. Clean and sober since then, he had worked at the center as a substance abuse counselor for eight years before turning to still-life photography. Over the years he had remained in touch with both his actor sons.

It was not family however, but friends (Matt Damon was not present) who staged an intervention with Ben Affleck in late July 2001. They were concerned about his excessive drinking and, to a lesser extent, about his gambling habit. (Ben had been on a betting/partying spree in Las Vegas the weekend before, winning $800,000 playing blackjack at one casino and giving out nearly $150,000 in tips to dealers and waitresses in the high rollers' lounge.)

Affleck agreed voluntarily to enter a program at Promises, a Malibu-based facility, whose past celebrity clientele included Elizabeth Taylor, Tom Arnold, Melanie Griffith, Robert Downey Jr., and Charlie Sheen. It was the latter who drove Affleck to the detox retreat on July 29. At the time, stand-up comic Paula Poundstone was also a patient at the facility, which charged patients $33,850 a month. (Meanwhile, Samuel Adams Beer, made by the Boston Beer Company, dropped Affleck from their product commercials.)

During his treatment at the swanky Promises, Ben was not in lock-down and was spotted away from the facility, one day seeing a matinee of *Planet of the Apes*; another time shopping. He made a surprise appearance at the taping of the Teen Choice Awards, at which he won a Best Actor prize for *Pearl Harbor*. He told the audience, "I wasn't going to be here, but I felt it was important." Other Ben sightings outside of Promises included walking with his mom, Chris; another time strolling about Malibu with Paula Poundstone; attending a baseball game in Anaheim; and doing the rides at Six Flags Magic Mountain theme park with pal Matt Damon and others. Reportedly during this trying period Ben received emotional support from his dad.

After a month's stay at Promises, during which he celebrated his twenty-ninth birthday, Affleck left the rehab center. While on vacation in Georgia, he was driving back to Macon from Savannah on September 26. Others in the black Cadillac car were brother Casey and the latter's girlfriend. Ben was pulled over on Interstate 16 by a police officer for driving a clocked 114 mph in a seventy-mile zone. The celebrity posted a cash bond of $1,114 at the county jail and was released within twenty minutes. Ben was neither arrested nor would further action be taken. Ironically, Affleck's next movie—among several lined up for the coming years—was to be *Changing Lanes* (2002) in which he plays a young attorney involved with a businessman (Samuel L. Jackson) in a fender bender that escalates into road rage.

Roscoe "Fatty" Arbuckle

[Roscoe Conkling Arbuckle]
MARCH 24, 1887–JUNE 29, 1933

Even today, when one of Hollywood's famous is caught in disgraceful activity, the media is quick to remind the public of Tinseltown's first major scandal—one that occurred more than eighty years ago. That infamous event involved the lurid "facts" in the Roscoe "Fatty" Arbuckle case: of how this oversized (he usually weighed between 250 and 300 pounds), extremely popular screen comedian supposedly participated in debauchery at a San Francisco hotel during the Labor Day weekend of 1921 that led to the death of a sweet young starlet. This spin is what San Francisco District Attorney Mathew Brady put forth in his prosecution of the celebrated movie star. (The tabloids of the day embellished the story, suggesting that the victim had been raped with a champagne glass, a soda bottle, and so forth, and/or that she had suffered irreparable injuries from the weight of Arbuckle upon her.)

Midst the ongoing media frenzy over the incident, Arbuckle endured three courtroom trials—each time the jury refused to convict the celebrity of the lurid deeds attributed to him. Nevertheless, the movie industry utilized the situation to make Roscoe (his friends *never* called him Fatty) a scapegoat, a sacrificial lamb in the movie business's ongoing battle with nationwide morality groups who periodically insisted that Hollywood was a den of iniquity. Then too, the master comic's downfall allowed Arbuckle's studio boss, Adolph Zukor, to avenge himself on his high-priced star, whom he mightily disliked.

The future comedian was born in 1887 on a small farm near Smith Center, Kansas, to William Goodrich and Mary A. Arbuckle. At birth he weighed nearly sixteen (!) pounds. The next year the family relocated to Santa Ana, California, where the father opened a small hotel. Soon thereafter Mr. Arbuckle moved to Watsonville with his oldest boy (Arthur), leaving behind his wife and son Roscoe. In 1899, after

Roscoe "Fatty" Arbuckle relaxing on the studio soundstage in the late 1910s. (Courtesy of JC Archives)

his mother's death, Roscoe was sent to live with his dad, but his parent had departed before the youngster arrived. Taken in by townsfolk, the agile Roscoe learned to juggle in his spare time, and he was soon active in local amateur vaudeville. By 1902 the teenager was reunited with his father in Santa Clara, California, where his remarried dad operated a café. Roscoe worked for his father waiting tables, attended high school for a time, and gained his first professional vaudeville booking—singing illustrated songs, accompanied by the audience who could read the lyrics on screen. Within two years he was singing at two San Francisco establishments. His father opposed his son's show business aspirations and the two stopped communicating.

In 1908, while performing in summer theater in Long Beach, California, Roscoe met petite, seventeen-year-old dancer/singer Araminta (Minta) Durfee. Within weeks he and Minta were married. The next year, he was desperate enough for work to accept employment in the fledgling film industry. His first effort (*Ben's Kid*), a silent comedy short, was released in mid-1909. By 1913 Arbuckle had "resigned" himself to working in the flickers as a full-time career. Soon he was employed by Mack Sennett's Keystone studio and thereafter began directing his own pictures. Quickly, Arbuckle became a major star, signing a deal with Paramount Pictures that would bring him more than $1 million annually. Meanwhile, Minta had suffered her second miscarriage and the failing marriage led to a separation that was kept from the public. (The couple would not divorce until 1925.)

Roscoe engineered an even more lucrative pact with Paramount in 1921. (Studio head Adolph Zukor was furious that he had been forced into this costly new deal and quietly vowed payback.) By late August of that year, Arbuckle had completed three features without a break. To relax, the star drove to San Francisco for the Labor Day weekend, although Zukor had wanted him to remain in town for the opening of Roscoe's new movie. Arbuckle was joined on the trip by actor Lowell Sherman (whom the star had asked to join him) and by director Fred Fischbach (a lackey of Zukor—who had invited himself along).

On Monday, September 5, Fischbach (against Roscoe's wishes) asked three sleazy characters to join a Labor Day party in Arbuckle's twelfth-floor suite at the St. Francis Hotel. The trio included "actress" Virginia Rappe (actually a prostitute with a propensity for getting roaring drunk and for acquiring social diseases—she was in town to have an abortion); her manager, Al Semnacher (an unsavory character who was in the process of manipulating a divorce from his wife); and their acquaintance Bambina Maude Delmont (whose lengthy police record included bigamy, fraud, and extortion; she was to be a participant in Semnacher's divorce scheme). A local bootlegger, at Fischbach's request, soon stocked the premises for the festivities.

At the Arbuckle gathering, a drunken Virginia began running through the rooms tearing off her clothes in reckless abandon. A short time later she rushed into the bathroom of suite 1219 (Arbuckle's) unbeknownst to the star who found her there vomiting and in pain. He eventually moved her to his bed while he went in search of a bucket of ice. He applied pieces of ice against her stomach, hoping it would reduce her fever. He was also pressing a piece of ice against her thigh. (Roscoe had once been told by an actor friend that this was a sure test to determine if a woman was pretending to have fainted or to be having hysterics.) Maude Delmont was on hand when Virginia temporarily revived. Rappe screamed at Arbuckle "Stay away from me! I don't want you near me!" In her ramblings the ill woman said to Delmont "What did he do to me, Maudie?. . . Roscoe did this to me."

Later Virginia was moved to a room down the hall, a doctor was summoned, and by the next afternoon, being told that everything was under control, Arbuckle, along with Fischbach and Sherman, returned to Los Angeles. Three days later (September 9) Virginia died. An autopsy revealed she had been pregnant, was suffering from a venereal disease, and that she had died of peritonitis.

A shocked Arbuckle voluntarily returned to San Francisco where he was promptly arrested and charged with rape and murder. (District Attorney Brady hoped to use the case to promote his bid for governorship.) Meanwhile, Roscoe's current feature release (*Gasoline Gus*) was pulled from exhibition around the country, heeding the outcries of exhibitors and morality groups. The grand jury filed an indictment against the picture star for manslaughter on September 15. Between then and April 18, 1923, a befuddled Roscoe suffered through three legally bizarre trials in which the prosecution's witnesses were constantly discredited and each of which ended with the defendant being found not guilty. In fact, the last jury even issued a written statement of apology to the unfairly targeted movie star.

Despite his later proven innocence, the hue and cry over the notorious case led Paramount to immediately shelve Arbuckle's two unreleased movies and to cancel his filmmaking contract. Studio boss Zukor persuaded Will Hays, the head of the industry's self-censorship organization, to ban Roscoe from making any future movies at other studios. The fallen star, stunned by the unfathomable turn of events, had to sell his mansion and autos to pay his nearly $1 million legal fees.

Bewildered by his bad fortune and the cloud of scandal that continued to hang over his head, Roscoe turned to a vaudeville tour that met with much public rejection. In 1925 he wed actress Doris Deane. (They would have a short-lasting union and in 1932 he would marry Addie McPhail, nineteen years his junior.) In the later 1920s he directed a few films under the alias William B. Goodrich and then turned to unfulfilling scriptwriting assignments. Every bid Arbuckle made to return to screen acting would be shot down by the industry and/or still-enraged women's groups around the country. Finally in February 1932, eleven years after the unfortunate events, he was permitted to make a two-reel comedy short for Warner Bros. at their East Coast facility. It was well received and the studio signed the former star to make five more shorts and, perhaps, feature films.

On June 29, 1933, the day after he completed the last of these comedy two-reelers, forty-five-year-old Arbuckle died of a heart attack in his Manhattan hotel room. The man who had once made so many filmgoers laugh so hard was finally at rest. Yet even in death, this tainted Hollywood innocent remained (unfairly) a symbol of Tinseltown excess, a besmirched victim of alleged improprieties, fabricated misdeeds that had done in his career and eventually the man himself. This unfair image of the extraordinary comedian exists to the present time. It has been fostered by such fictionalized distortions of the "facts" of Arbuckle's lifestyle and downfall as the 1975 movie *The Wild Party* along with two subsequent musical adaptations. In addition, there was the mid-1997 San Francisco stage production of *The Fatty Arbuckle Spookhouse Revue*, a musical spoof that "reconstructed" the tragedy that befell Roscoe in the Golden Gate city back in 1922. In this song-and-dance presentation Roscoe was once again demonized for public consumption. Even in death, talented, fun-loving Arbuckle could not shake the legacy of scandal that has so long remained linked to his name.

Alec Baldwin

[Alexander Rae Baldwin III]

APRIL 3, 1958–

In the late 1980s handsome, cleft-chin Baldwin was on the cusp of major Hollywood stardom. The five-foot, eleven-inch actor had five releases in 1988 including *She's Having a Baby* (smarmy friend), *Beetlejuice* (benevolent ghost), and *Working Girl* (cheating boyfriend). In 1990 he was cast as Jack Ryan in the big-budgeted Cold War thriller *The Hunt for Red October*. Then Alec teamed with blond siren Kim Basinger for *The Marrying Man* (1991). The couple proved combustible *off* camera. On the other hand, making the comedy seemed to unleash the inner beast within Baldwin. The once polite and responsible actor frequently became a raging tiger on *The Marrying Man* soundstages. It was but a prelude of things to come.

Baldwin was born in Amityville, Long Island, New York, to high school teacher Alexander Rae Baldwin II and his wife Carol. The boy was the second of the couple's six children and the first of four boys (the other three—Daniel, Billy, and Stephen—would also become actors). The children were raised as Kennedy Democrats in Massapequa, Long Island. Despite acting in school plays, Alexander was headed for a political career. After high school graduation in 1976, he entered George Washington University in Washington, D.C. However, by 1979 he had become more intrigued with acting and transferred to New York University as a law and political science major, while taking acting classes at the Strasberg Institute.

In the summer of 1980 he won a recurring role on the NBC-TV daytime soap opera *The Doctors* (with his first name now shortened to Alec) and he abandoned college. When his soap opera chore ended in 1982, he moved to Hollywood. He was cast in the short-lasting teleseries *Cutter to Houston* (1983), and then spent 1984 to 1985 on the nighttime TV drama *Knots Landing* as a psychotic evangelist. During this Hollywood period Alec was engaged briefly to actress Janine Turner.

Worried that he would be caught in a rut of TV series, Baldwin returned to stage work (a 1986 revival of *Loot*) and played a cop in his first film feature, the low-budget *Forever Lulu* (1987).

In retrospect, it was in 1989 that Baldwin's career began to derail. He was supposed to star in *Henry & June* (1990) but bowed out of the sexually explicit narrative, claiming exhaustion. It was reported that he was set for the key role of Vincent Mancini in *The Godfather: Part III* (1990), but the assignment went to Andy Garcia. Even before its release, the buzz on Baldwin for *The Hunt for Red October* was excellent and revived his career, and the Disney Studio quickly hired him at $1.5 million to star in the Neil Simon–scripted *The Marrying Man*. Kim Basinger, still sizzling from playing Vicki Vale in *Batman* (1989), came aboard for $2.5 million. By the time filming began in May 1990, the two stars were enjoying a steamy romance with Baldwin frequently ensconced at the west San Fernando Valley home of divorcée Basinger. Their relationship carried over onto the set. Some of Kim's traits—self-involvement, tardiness, seemingly arbitrary decisions—apparently transferred to Alec. In turn, the increasingly infuriated Disney executives determined to keep the production on budget. (The $20 million movie ended by costing $26 million.) The studio's micromanagement infuriated Alec and Kim, and a battle of wills broke out, leading to reported temper tantrums and other childish behavior on the set. As suggested in a scathing *Premiere* magazine piece (February 1991), when the stars had a good night at home, the two coplayers grew embarrassingly amorous and indiscreet between scene set-ups. But, if the duo had had a bad prior evening, there was hell to pay on the soundstages: she pouting, difficult, being unavailable, and so on; he turning into a fury of anger who frequently smashed cell phones or openly blasted his Disney bosses.

If *The Marrying Man* had been a hit, all would have been forgiven, but the movie flopped. All that lingered was unflattering publicity for Alec and Kim. Thereafter Baldwin pursued Basinger to marry him. Meanwhile, his planned starring role in the big-screen version of *The Fugitive* went to Harrison Ford. Next, Baldwin turned down a more than $4 million paycheck to make the next Jack Ryan installment

(1992's *Patriot Games*) because he had committed to a Broadway revival of *A Streetcar Named Desire* (1992). Ford grabbed that movie sequel and its equally successful follow-up, *Clear and Present Danger* (1994).

As for Kim, she had recently lost a court case for failing to star in the movie *Boxing Helena* (1993). Rising to her defense, Alec wrote angry letters to national publications, putting himself further at odds with the Hollywood establishment. Later, when Basinger declared bankruptcy because she could not pay off the multimillion-dollar damages from the *Helena* case, Alec reputedly helped her out with his half of their $4 million paycheck from costarring in *The Getaway* (1994). A grateful Kim agreed to marry the three-years-younger Baldwin. They wed on the beaches of East Hampton, New York, in August 1993. The media found ways to photograph the private event, which further widened the gulf between Alec and the press.

While Baldwin's once-golden career fumbled with 1994's *The Shadow* and 1996's *The Juror*, Kim gave birth to their daughter Ireland Eliesse in October 1995. Three days later, on October 26, as Alec brought his wife and child home from the hospital, freelance photographer Alan Zanger filmed their arrival at their Woodland Hills home from his parked van. Reportedly, an angered Baldwin shouted to the man to stop and then reputedly began shaking the van. Alec then disappeared and returned to the van with a can of shaving cream that he squirted over the vehicle's windows to prevent further lensing. At that juncture Zanger emerged from the van, and according to some sources, he filmed the incensed actor with a still camera and a camcorder. A furious Baldwin allegedly punched him, breaking the photographer's nose and eyeglasses, and supposedly kicked the man when he bent down to retrieve his glasses. Thereafter, Zanger placed Baldwin under citizen's arrest.

Alec was booked for misdemeanor battery, but released on his own recognizance. On his part, Zanger filed a $1 million civil suit against Baldwin. In March 1996 Baldwin claimed in court that he thought the defendant might have been a stalker, a possibility that had badly upset him, and that he was thus acting in self-defense. The actor was acquitted of the battery charges. Baldwin insisted his victory proved that it was not open season on celebrities. The civil case filed by the paparazzo didn't reach a jury decision until July 1998. Alec was ordered to pay $6,000 in damages to the plaintiff; but since Zanger was determined to be 25 percent guilty the amount was reduced to $4,500.

As the 1990s progressed, Alec's career devolved to character roles (the bloated blue-collar father in 1999's *Outside Providence*) and to producing/costarring in the TV production *Nuremberg*. Having grown heftier in his middle age, matinee-idol leading roles were now eluding him. In contrast, Basinger won a Best Supporting Actress Oscar for *L.A. Confidential* (1997). The couple's marriage began to lose its spark: he wanted to live in their $5 million Amagansett, Long Island, mansion; she preferred the West Coast or globe-trotting. He had revived inter-

Chipper Alec Baldwin dealing with the media.
(Photo by Albert L. Ortega)

ests in a political career; she, suffering from bouts of agoraphobia, wished to remain part of the film business in which she could choose her public appearances. By the late 1990s there were sightings of the couple arguing in public and reputed periods of separation. The media dubbed them "the battling Baldwins." In mid-January 2001 she filed for divorce, remaining on the West Coast with their daughter, while he lived in their New York City apartment. There was talk of a reconciliation but the paparazzi—no friend to Alec—were only too happy to capture him in public shouting matches with his soon-to-be ex-wife.

Having begun to acknowledge the end of his relationship with Basinger and being "seen" with such dates as actress Kristin Davis (*Sex and the City*) apparently did not cool Alex's temper. In August 2001 the media reported an alleged incident of road rage as the star went "ballistic" on the traffic-choked Long Island Expressway when a car driven by a twenty-eight-year-old female cut into his lane.

John Barrymore

[John Sidney Blyth]

FEBRUARY 15, 1882–MAY 29, 1942

Handsome actor John Barrymore was nicknamed "The Great Pro-file." More importantly, he was an extraordinary acting talent—from a long pedigree of performers—who could be especially magnetic on stage. Barrymore's brilliant *Hamlet* was a rousing success on Broadway (1922) and the engagement could have continued far beyond its 101-performance run. However, Broadway's golden boy was self-indulgent and, at the moment, overcome by jealousy about his current (second) wife, the poet Michael Strange. She was then traveling abroad and as she was as independent and impulsive as he, he rightly feared the worst. But turning his back on his triumphant *Hamlet* was a minor whimsy in the long chronicle of the hedonistic stage/film star. This wastrel spent a lifetime combatting—but usually giving in to—his addiction to alcohol. Of more concern to John was his fear that he would die like his theater star father—a dissolute man who went mad from, and died of, syphilis.

John was born in Philadelphia in 1882, the third child of famed stage troupers Georgiana Drew and Maurice Blyth (who adopted the professional surname of Barrymore). His older siblings—Lionel (1878–1954) and Ethel (1879–1956)—would also enjoy extensive acting careers. When John was eleven his mother died of tuberculosis. A few months later, his father, without telling his offspring, married Mamie Floyd. Unlike the prior Mrs. Barrymore she was not illustrious, but she was young, fetching, and randy. When John was fifteen, his stepmother seduced him, introducing him to the arts of imaginative lovemaking. John was understandably guilt ridden at having betrayed his parent. The trauma established his distrust of pretty women, and left the teenager embarked on a lifelong battle with liquor.

Hoping to avoid the family tradition of acting, John—who devoutly refused to take anything in life too seriously—studied art abroad. Later he worked in New York City as a cartoonist and then as a newspaper illustrator. Dismissed from both posts, he fell back on the family profession, making his acting debut in Chicago in *Magda* (1903). Six years later this natural talent was a Broadway success with the comedy *The Fortune Hunter*. In 1910 at age twenty-seven, he impulsively wed Katharine Harris, a pretty socialite, who was just seventeen. It was a tempestuous marriage, with unfaithfulness on both sides. Seven years later they divorced.

Meanwhile, John continued his theater successes—at this point his carousing had not overwhelmed his extraordinary acting abilities— and performed sometimes in silent films, most famously in *Dr. Jekyll and Mr. Hyde* (1920). In 1920 the dissolute playboy married poet Blanche Oelrichs (who used the pen name of Michael Strange). She was eight years his junior and their daughter, Diana, was born in 1921. The turbulent union turned into years of separation, during which,

"The Great Profile" John Barrymore with Karen Morley in *Arsene Lupin* (1932). (Courtesy of JC Archives)

among many other romantic conquests, John seduced teenage actress Mary Astor (his costar of *Beau Brummell*, 1924, and *Don Juan*, 1926). The famed actor was at the peak of his screen popularity (where makeup and lighting could disguise the ravages of his lifestyle, and the requirements of the silent cinema did not demand he learn extensive dialogue). At this point he encountered nineteen-year-old blond actress Dolores Costello, herself from a notable show business pedigree. When her father objected to the May-October romance, cavalier John Barrymore retorted, "It is ridiculous to be prejudiced against a man because he is married. The divorce courts are made to take care of trivialities like that. As for the difference in our ages, an actor is no older than he admits." Six days after terminating his marriage to Strange in November 1928, Barrymore wed Dolores. They would have two children: Dolores Ethel Mae and John Jr.

When talkies arrived, the nearly fifty-year-old Barrymore, a legend in his own time, was still in great demand—for his rich voice and what was left of his great profile. He played opposite Greta Garbo in *Grand Hotel* (1932) and enjoyed comical character leads in *Topaze* (1933) and *Twentieth Century* (1934). In that year he and Dolores Costello (who could no longer endure his philandering) divorced, she winning custody of their children.

By the mid-1930s age and John's indulgences had taken their toll: his famed looks had grown flabby, he had tremendous difficulty remembering his lines on camera, and he suffered recurring bouts of near insanity. His last good screen roles were supporting assignments in *Romeo and Juliet* (1936), *Maytime* (1937), and *Marie Antoinette* (1938). By now, the once-great actor, again seeking distraction in youth, had come under the influence of nineteen-year-old Manhattan college student Elaine Jacobs (who soon used the stage name of Barrie). Ambitious and lovestruck, she fostered their absurd relationship. In typical fashion John's rash feelings for Elaine quickly veered from ardent lover to jealousy, boredom, and, in turn, to contrite reconciliations. His protégée pursued him from New York to Los Angeles with the media on their heels. On November 9, 1936, she and fifty-four-year-old Barrymore, a shell of his former self, eloped to Yuma, Arizona. Scarcely eight weeks later she filed for divorce, but they temporarily patched up their many differences.

On screen Barrymore had succumbed to playing pathetic caricatures of himself as in *Hold That Co-Ed* (1938). The once-great actor had not appeared on stage since the mid-1920s, but with his wife's persuasion he joined with her in *My Dear Children*. The feeble comedy played off the costars' offstage shenanigans and benefited from John's self-deprecating ad-libbing behind the footlights. Each performance sold out with most theatergoers eager to witness Barrymore's circus act. After an East Coast tour, John took ill. By the time the play reopened in St. Louis, John and Elaine were not speaking and she had been replaced in the cast. When the couple divorced in November 1940, the cynical but still glib star observed, "It's no particular distinction being called 'Mrs. Barrymore.' There have been so many of them. Now I'm free to resume my search for the perfect mate." True to his word, John retained his eye for pretty young girls, especially nubile lovelies in their midteens. However, he never remarried.

With his life in disarray, the ailing and debt-ridden Barrymore accepted any sort of buffoon screen parts. During this period, his twenty-year-old daughter Diana came to Hollywood to make her screen bow. Like her father, she already shared a love of drink, sexual adventures, and heavy partying. For a time she stayed with her sickly parent at his once elegant digs.

By May 1942 the fast-declining John was suffering from, among other ailments, cirrhosis of the liver. As he lay dying at Hollywood Presbyterian Hospital, a Roman Catholic pastor/family friend administered the last rites. By May 29 the end was near. Daughter Diana was told to come to the hospital at once. She begged off. "I can't possibly do it," she explained. "I have a very important appointment." Her caller retorted, "So has your father." A few hours later, after attending a preview of her movie *Eagle Squadron*, she rushed to her dad's bedside. But he had already passed away.

The screen's Great Lover—another nickname from his heyday—passed on the family legacy of alcoholism (a vice shared by his regal actress sister Ethel). Daughter Diana wasted her acting potential on drink and wild living. She died in 1960 of a possibly accidental mixture of liquor and sedatives. Regarding Barrymore's son John Jr., he made a promising screen bow in 1950's *The Sundowners*. But he ruined his career with substance abuse and bizarre antisocial behavior that included several misadventures with the law. By the end of the twentieth century he was rescued from his near-derelict existence by his actress daughter, Drew Barrymore.

As for Drew, at age seven she had been a sensation in the box-office bonanza *E.T.: The Extra-Terrestrial* (1982). She was, however, soon better known for her precocious partying than for her acting skills. To everyone's surprise, in the 1990s she overcame her addictions. Turning her untamed life around, she became a popular film star/producer (*Charlie's Angels*, 2000). Unlike her forebears, she seemingly conquered the curse of the Barrymores.

Warren Beatty

[Henry Warren Beaty]

MARCH 30, 1937–

During the 1959–60 TV season, he played handsome, snobbish Milton Armitage on episodes of *The Many Loves of Dobie Gillis*. At the time, few in the entertainment business would have guessed that newcomer Beatty would emerge as one of filmdom's most enduring screen stars or that he would become a multinominated Oscar contender and the winner of two Academy Awards (Best Director for 1981's *Reds* and the 2000 Irving G. Thalberg Memorial Award). Nor would many have anticipated that Warren would develop into a Tinseltown legend as the ultimate woman-chaser whose sexual conquests—both in quantity and quality—would (out)match any other contender in Hollywood's history. In short, in the early fall of 1959, six-foot, one-inch, sleepy-eyed Beatty was best known for being movie queen Shirley MacLaine's good-looking kid brother.

In retrospect, much of Beatty's life seemed an enviable mix of good fortune and careful strategy. Born in Richmond, Virginia, to schoolteacher parents in 1937, Henry Warren Beaty was three years younger than his sister Shirley. As a child "Little Henry" was shy, inclined to reading a lot and playing the piano. By the time he graduated from high school, he had burst forth as class president and gridiron champ. He enrolled at Northwestern University's School of Speech and Drama in the fall of 1956, but dropped out and moved to New York City where his stage-dancer sister Shirley had been discovered for the movies. Drama classes led Warren to small roles on TV and in stock shows. Already he was gaining amateur status as quite a ladies' man who had no use for monogamy. He eventually moved to Hollywood. A screen test led to his MGM contract and, while waiting for a picture to happen, he worked on TV.

Until he met British screen actress Joan Collins, most of Warren's many sexual conquests had been with unknowns—hit-and-run affairs. However, with the provocative English beauty as his lover, he suddenly gained status as a stud-about-town. Meanwhile, in the fall of

1959 he terminated his film studio contract to star in William Inge's new Broadway play *A Loss of Roses*. To much eyebrow-raising, Collins followed her companion to New York, a short-lasting trip since Beatty's play quickly folded.

Inge suggested Warren for a film he'd written (1961's *Splendor in the Grass*) and Beatty won the male lead (and gained a second "t" in his surname). Contrary to speculation then and later, Beatty did not have a romance with his year-younger vis-à-vis, movie star Natalie Wood. At the time her two-year-old storybook marriage to movie leading man Robert Wagner was starting to disintegrate, and the high-strung Wood was feeling extremely insecure. Her despair made her more neurotic and demanding than usual during the shoot, and some insist that she actively disliked the self-absorbed Beatty during the making of the picture.

Following *Splendor in the Grass*, Beatty flew to Europe to play the Italian gigolo in *The Roman Spring of Mrs. Stone* (1961). His live-in and possessive lover Collins soon arrived in London to watch over her boyfriend/fiancé, but when he went on to Rome for location work she remained behind to nurse her ill mother. While in the Eternal City, the always-on-the-girl-hunt Warren hooked up with actress Susan Strasberg and his reputation as a prodigious lover who didn't mind where he had sex gained further credence. (Susan spoke of his "tremendous need to please women as well as conquer them.")

By the time Warren and Joan returned to Hollywood, their romance was over (and her specially purchased wedding dress put in mothballs). Meanwhile, Natalie was at the emotional breaking point with her husband, Wagner, and was more than pleased when Beatty phoned her on the set of *West Side Story* (1961) asking his trademark line, "What's new, pussycat?" They began dating. Before long Natalie, separated from Wagner, had moved to digs in Bel Air and Warren was her permanent houseguest. When Warren went to Florida for location work on *All Fall Down* (1962), Natalie followed him; they continued their get-together in the Bahamas. Already Wood had discovered that Beatty, increasingly absorbed by his skyrocketing career and by his id, was not a man who could be pinned down to routines or fidelity. But she was hooked on the man in her time of great insecurity.

In the summer of 1962, Warren accompanied Natalie (who had filed for divorce) to France and then on to Rome. They were photographed everywhere by the eager paparazzi. Meanwhile, the British tabloids had snapped Joan Collins having a chummy dinner with Wagner in London. They speculated on a brewing (or in-progress) romance. Actually, Joan had already met actor Anthony Newley whom she'd wed in 1963.

One night in the Eternal City when Natalie and Warren dined out, they encountered Wagner having dinner with his old friend, actress Marion Marshall. Robert invited Wood and Beatty to his table for a drink. Later that evening Wagner tried for several hours to phone Natalie, but could never get through to her suite. It seemed Beatty, who

The meditative Warren Beatty.
(Courtesy of JC Archives)

had an obsession for talking endlessly on the phone to drum up business or sexual adventures, had been monopolizing the line. Robert had wanted to talk with Natalie about a possible reconciliation. The moment passed and he later wed (and then divorced) Marshall. Wood did not learn of Wagner's efforts to reach her for years thereafter.

Back in Los Angeles, Warren admitted confusion about marriage, an indicator that his on-again, off-again romance with Natalie was doomed. By the time she was in New York to shoot *Love with the Proper Stranger* (1963), the couple's high-profile relationship was ancient history. (One of the last straws for Natalie, supposedly, was the night Warren went out for dinner and didn't show up again for a week.)

If Natalie was out of Warren's life, the carefree swinger found many other replacements, ranging from singers Michelle Phillips and Joni

Mitchell to actresses Britt Eckland and Anjelica Huston (who became the live-in of Beatty's good friend and fellow skirt chaser Jack Nicholson). Even when Beatty "settled down" into a house-sharing relationship—as he did with Phillips—he still retained his legendary but unpretentious bachelor digs at the Beverly Wilshire Hotel for his extracurricular intimate entertaining and thinking.

Warren often dated current or future costars; some insisted it was an opportunistic fringe benefit of his innumerable love matches. One such leading lady was French-born Leslie Caron whom he began dating shortly after Wood left the scene. The charisma of charming Beatty led Leslie and British stage director Peter Hall to divorce. (In Hall's petition Warren was named as corespondent.) Beatty and Caron starred in the movie comedy *Promise Her Anything* (1966), but their union fizzled later and she wed another.

Over the decades many other of Beatty's costars were either involved in heavy romances with him or led the imaginative press to believe it was the case. The list included Goldie Hawn, Elizabeth Taylor, Diane Keaton, Julie Christie (who made three films with Warren over a seven-year period), and Madonna. The ex–Mrs. Sean Penn was nearly twenty-five years Warren's junior when she played opposite Beatty in *Dick Tracy* (1990). Their coupling was strange even by Hollywood standards. When the incongruous romance ended shortly after the film's release, many wondered what degree of the alliance had been prompted by mutual publicity opportunities.

Warren cast Annette Bening for his *Bugsy* (1991) production. During the making of that gangster yarn, the two fell in love. For a change, this time when Beatty's girlfriend got (accidentally) pregnant, there was no abortion. Annette gave birth to their baby girl in January 1992. Even more to everyone's surprise, Beatty and Bening were wed privately somewhere around the time of their child's birth. When the news of their nuptials was made known in March 1992, the Associated Press noted the "ending of an era for one of Hollywood's most prolific Lotharios." The Beattys would go on to have three other children.

John Belushi

[John Adam Belushi]

JANUARY 24, 1949–MARCH 5, 1982

In recent years whenever a Robert Downey Jr., a Paula Poundstone, or a Ben Affleck is the subject of public frenzy due to substance abuse issues, the media is certain to bring up the case of funny, off-the-wall, obsessive John Belushi. In the annals of Hollywood, he remains a benchmark of what excessive drugs can do to a once high-gear show business career.

A few days before his thirty-third birthday, the famed alumnus of TV's *Saturday Night Live* and the star of such features as *The Blues Brothers* (1980), told *Rolling Stone*: "In your twenties, you feel like you're indestructible, that nothing can kill you and you laugh at death. . . . [In] your thirties, you think, well, maybe I'll be around here a little longer, so I'm going to maybe take better care of myself." Less than two months later, the self-indulgent Belushi was dead of a massive drug overdose.

He was born in 1949 in Wheaton, Illinois, where his dad was in the restaurant business. Besides an older sister, there would be two other boys (one of whom, Jim, also became an actor). During his high school years, John played football, was the drummer for a rock 'n' roll band, and became captivated with acting. After being turned down for a football scholarship, he matriculated at the University of Wisconsin (at Whitewater), a school boasting an excellent drama department. He later switched to the College of DuPage in Glen Ellyn, Illinois. He spent summers doing dramatic roles in stock productions.

When rotund Belushi gravitated to the Second City Troupe, the Chicago-based revue group that specialized in outrageous improvisation, the world of comedy opened to him. He delighted in combining semislapstick with heavy satire and dramatic reality. Already the hyperactive performer was using liquor and a widening range of drugs (including sunshine acid and peyote) to bring him off his performance highs or to give him the vigor for his performance. Full of induced high energy, beefy John gained good reviews for his zany stage inven-

Kathryn Walker, John Belushi (center), and Dan Aykroyd in the comedy *Neighbors* (1981). (Courtesy of JC Archives)

tiveness. His meteoric rise led to his being cast in the off-Broadway production *National Lampoon's Lemmings* (1973)—for which he served as actor and writer.

Belushi's major career break was becoming a founding member of TV's cheeky, new *Saturday Night Live*. The NBC network offering bowed in October 1975 and soon was a major hit. Among the show's core stock company (which included Dan Aykroyd, Chevy Chase, and Gilda Radner), explosive and singular John became a favorite with viewers. His gallery of wacky characters included the leering Samurai warrior and being part of (along with Aykroyd) the singing, trouble-prone Blues Brothers.

Off camera the antiauthority Belushi gave new dimension to the expression "party animal." His thirst (and seeming stamina) for booze and hard drugs had already become legendary, and he was soon earmarking much of his more than $100,000 per year salary for illegal substances. This ongoing wild life made him more cantankerous and less disciplined. It caused him to be fired and then rehired several times during his *SNL* tenure. Physicians cautioned John that his ongoing consumption of cocaine, booze, and other drugs could easily kill him. He refused to accept such warnings seriously and continued to exist in a wired state. Meanwhile, in 1976 John wed his high school sweetheart, Judith Jacklin (a budding book illustrator/designer), with whom he had been living since his Second City days.

On the big screen Belushi scored in his first major picture—*National Lampoon's Animal House* (1978). In this box-office bonanza, five-foot, eight-inch John supplied a large portion of the coarse humor that so enthralled filmgoers. His success led him to quit *SNL* to devote himself to the more lucrative and less-pressured world of moviemaking. However, as a film favorite, Belushi—who looked nothing like Hollywood's typical leading man—grew increasingly insecure about his fluctuating weight (as he cascaded through food binges) and his capacity to keep friends. The more self-doubting he became, the more he relied on drugs to mask his emotional problems. This self-destructive cycle only added to his self-doubt and prompted him to stay away from friends. (One of John's chief rules was that he did not want his pals to see him when he was under the influence.) In Hollywood Belushi had close ties to Chevy Chase (who had quit *SNL* for the movies before John did), and Chase frequently tried to get John to abandon his drug regimen.

Somehow, Belushi did not have much luck in choosing his screen vehicles, leading to such misfires as *1941* (1979) and *Continental Divide* (1981). Several of these entries—like the bomb *Neighbors* (1981)—paired him with his pal Dan Aykroyd (who called John the "Black Rhino"). It also didn't help that often he was so drugged out during the shoot that he could hardly function enough to perform the script. Belushi may have been organized enough to have drug pals and suppliers in almost any city he might be in, but in the rest of his hectic life he was increasingly erratic and problematic.

Hoping to give himself a new screen image as a respected dramatic actor who could perform romantic leads, John wrote his own movie vehicle. However, Paramount Pictures rejected *Noble Rot* and wanted him instead to make *The Joy of Sex*. Furious over this latest career rebuff, John returned to Los Angeles alone, leaving his spouse back in New York City.

In a darker mood than usual, John began partying on the night of March 4, 1982. This banquet of drug taking (including a speedball injection of heroin and cocaine) was too much for his constitution and he died on March 5. He had been living on borrowed time for months. Back when he made *The Blues Brothers*, a doctor had been brought on the soundstage set to examine the star who was suffering from obvious drug abuse. The physician had begged John to mend his ways, but the outrageous comedian remained unresponsive to this medical S.O.S. At the time the medico predicted to others that the way the actor was headed, he wouldn't last much longer. Manic John certainly lived up to the prognosis.

Robert Blake

[Michael James Vijencio Gubitosi]
SEPTEMBER 18, 1933–

On May 4, 2001, forty-four-year-old Bonnie Lee (Bakley) Blake was murdered as she waited in her husband's parked car on a side street near an Italian restaurant in Studio City, California. That prior November, she had become Blake's second wife, climaxing their troubled relationship of well over a year. The reluctant nuptials had occurred only after a DNA test had proved that her child, born in mid-2000, was Robert's. (Earlier, she'd claimed that the baby girl was the result of her past association with Christian Brando, the ex-convict son of movie star Marlon Brando.) Media speculation included Blake as a possible candidate among those who had a motive for shooting her. However, officially, at the time, it remained just guesswork as the homicide investigation failed to resolve the case over subsequent months. Meanwhile, the notorious killing raked up the troubled life of the veteran actor who had begun as a child performer more than sixty years earlier.

A talented, but self-destructive star, Blake had long maintained a tremendous love-hate relationship with show business. He despised how the industry exploited talent and then turned away when the next hot person rolled onto the scene. His integrity was offended by the junk movies and production-line TV work he'd been forced to do in those long gaps between meaningful assignments like *In Cold Blood* (1967), *Tell Them Willie Boy Is Here* (1969), and *Electra Glide in Blue* (1973). He'd quit the business for years at a stretch only to drag himself back into the morass because of financial need and/or a burning urge to emote. On the other hand, he acknowledged, "If I hadn't gone in front of the camera I'm sure that I would have been a terrible criminal. At that, I was a criminal in my teenage years, but I would not have survived. My father wanted to be a movie star—and he was nuts. The only decent thing he ever did was kill himself back in the fifties. He wanted my brother to be a movie star. They hated the fact that I was successful and wanted to kill me for it. . . . I stayed in front of the camera in spite of my family, not because of them."

In different chapters of his life, Robert exploded with hatred—at himself or at others. The tormented Blake used crutches to survive: "I was taking sleeping pills every night so I could sleep fast. I'd get up with six cups of espresso in the morning and a ton of sugar. By the afternoon I was dragging ass and I was sipping brandy to get through it." To little avail loved ones and friends urged him to undergo treatment for his substance abuse.

Blake was born in 1933 in Nutley, New Jersey, the youngest of three children of a small-time song-and-dance man. The impoverished family lived on the edge of starvation. Mickey made his debut in their tattered act when he was two. Often Mr. Gubitosi would play guitar in local parks while the kids (called The Three Little Hillbillies) sang and danced for passersby as their father passed the hat. Mickey likened himself to an organ grinder's monkey on a collar and chain.

In 1937 the family moved to Southern California, settling in Venice. Two years later the youngster began appearing in the Our Gang comedy shorts at MGM, gaining notice as a cute performer with a winning, if somewhat sad, personality. By 1942—now known as Bobby Blake—he was appearing in feature films and in 1944 joined the Red Ryder Western series as Little Beaver, the young Native American. Years later, Blake described the horrors of his early childhood, claiming he'd been forced to eat from a bowl on the floor, been tied up and left under the porch for days at a time, and had been sexually assaulted. As a protection against his father's ongoing abuse (which his mother did not stop), the boy created a tough guy personality to keep people away.

When Blake reached the awkward teenage years, he was reduced to playing extras or doing stunt work. Unable to cope with his past or his present, he turned to drugs, including "pot and graduating to heroin." He bounced from high school to high school, constantly expelled because of his truancy or for being a persistent troublemaker. The nongraduate joined the military, asking for duty "where he didn't have to kill people." Based in Alaska, he was bored and started using and selling dope. He also fell in love with a sixteen-year-old girl. Her father wanted Blake prosecuted for statutory rape. Robert became frantic and he was eventually discharged from the military.

A tense moment for Robert Blake as the star of *Corky* (1972).
(Courtesy of JC Archives)

Now in his early twenties, five-foot, four-and-a-half-inch Blake returned to Hollywood where he gained increasingly important roles in such films as *Rumble on the Docks* (1956) and *Town Without Pity* (1961). None of his acting, however, got him major notice. Meanwhile, in 1964 he wed Sondra Kerry and they had two children over the next few years. Robert struggled to make ends meet for his family. Then came his memorable performance in the graphic drama *In Cold Blood* (1967). Delving into his characterization of the killer so affected Blake—along with not receiving the Oscar nomination he richly deserved—that he had an emotional breakdown. It was another two years before he worked again and by then he was flat broke.

In the 1970s he had a reputation as a perfectionist engulfed in personal problems that made him difficult on the set. He had a lucky break in early 1975 with the TV cops series *Baretta*. The show was a hit and he won an Emmy, but the pressure of starring in the weekly vehicle (which he hated for being pap) forced him to quit it in 1978.

By then his marriage was wrecked. He and Sondra separated for good in 1980 and were divorced a few years later.

Going through yet more emotional hell, he reemerged in 1985 with the TV movie/pilot *Hell Town*. He played an ex-con turned priest working in an L.A. ghetto, but the show lasted only four months. Blake claimed he walked away from the program when surfacing repressed memories of his childhood horrors became too hard to deal with. Having left the production, he went into a deep funk. After a self-imposed hiatus of seven years, he made a comeback in the tele-feature *Judgment Day: The John List Story* (1993), a dark account of a man who killed his entire family. Not only was the Blake of the 1990s well into middle age but also his face had changed drastically through plastic surgery. His last screen work to date was playing in David Lynch's *Lost Highway* (1997).

After his marriage to Bonnie in late 2000, the couple did not live together in his four-bedroom Studio City home. Rather, she and their daughter resided in a bungalow behind the main house. By then he'd learned that his spouse was a celebrity chaser with a checkered past. All this led to the spring night in 2001 when paramedics and police arrived on the scene to find his wife shot in the car while a near hysterical Blake paced up and down the street, vomiting, and then sitting dazed on the curb. He claimed she was shot while he had returned to the restaurant to retrieve a handgun he'd left there. The next week Robert conducted a short funeral service for Bonnie at Forest Lawn Memorial Park in Hollywood Hills. Her family avoided the ceremony, having their own memorial service two weeks later. Because his ranch home attracted so many gawkers, he put the house up for sale, hoping to find privacy elsewhere in which to raise his little girl, Rose.

Robert and baby Rose moved in with Blake's adult daughter Delinah (from his first marriage) at her secluded home in the San Fernando Valley. On April 18, 2002, the LAPD (after a lengthy investigation) arrested Robert on suspicion of murder in the first degree with special circumstances. (Blake's bodyguard/chauffeur was charged with one count of conspiracy to commit murder.) While Blake pleaded not guilty, if prosecuted and convicted of the charges, he could face life imprisonment without the possibility of parole.

Humphrey Bogart

[Humphrey DeForest Bogart]

DECEMBER 25, 1899–JANUARY 14, 1957

Humphrey Bogart ranks near the pinnacle of twentieth-century movie stars. He brought to the Hollywood screen a fascinating mixture of cynical aloofness and interior sensitivity, even when portraying a hard-boiled gumshoe (1941's *The Maltese Falcon*). On camera, the icon's mode ranged from thuggish as in 1936's *The Petrified Forest*, to upstanding as in 1938's *Crime School*, or to surprisingly romantic as in 1942's *Casablanca*. Sometimes his movie character was greedy as in 1948's *The Treasure of the Sierra Madre*, noble as in 1951's *The African Queen*, or lovesick as in 1954's *Sabrina*. Occasionally, Bogart played sarcastic funny as in 1942's *All Through the Night*.

Off screen, Humphrey was not so easy to categorize. A well-bred New Yorker, he loved booze (and sometimes made a spectacle of himself), sailing, and the latest industry gossip. Serious about his craft and his public image, he was vain enough to wear toupees and to use shoe lifts to make him seem taller than his actual five feet, eight inches. He chalked up four marriages—all to actresses—and while his last union (with Lauren Bacall) became part of pop culture history, it was his third mate (Mayo Methot) who led the screen celebrity into some of his most (in)famous bad-boy escapades. Bogart called this hard-drinking daughter of a sea captain "Sluggy" and their home "Sluggy Hollow." Reportedly their fighting perked up their lovemaking.

Humphrey DeForest Bogart was born in 1899 (some sources list January 23, but December 25 was the actual day) in New York City, the first of three children (there would be two sisters) of a successful physician and his magazine-illustrator wife. Humphrey attended private schools, but never graduated; instead, he enlisted in the U.S. Naval Reserve in May 1918. Most of his active duty was spent aboard a troop ship transporting American soldiers home from France during World War I. In 1920 the civilian tried show business as a production/stage manager. He made his Broadway acting debut in *Drifting* in 1922, the year he became engaged to stage star Helen

Menken. The two wed in 1926 but divorced a year later. In 1928 he married another Broadway talent, Mary Philips. By 1930 Bogart had made his feature film debut in *Up the River*. Over the next few years he appeared in several pictures, but it was not until he took on the brutish gangster role in *The Petrified Forest* on Broadway (1935) and in film (1936) that his acting career escalated. Meanwhile, in spring 1936, Mary, who had remained in New York for theater work, came westward to deal with rumors that Bogart was romancing a showy, fair-haired actress named Mayo Methot.

At the time, Methot, a former child stage performer, was playing supporting movie roles and was still hitched to her second husband. By the time the lovers worked together in late 1936 on the Bette Davis vehicle *Marked Woman*, Mayo was developing a blowsy look from her constant drinking. In 1937 she and Bogart each got divorced from their respective spouses.

It was on Humphrey and Mayo's wedding day in August 1938 that the combustible couple first established their reputation as the movie colony's "Battling Bogarts." The nuptials were held at his talent agent's Bel Air home. Soon after they said "I do," the newlyweds launched into a heated argument. It ended with Bogart and a pal driving to Tijuana, while the inebriated Methot fell into a drunken stupor at her hosts' home. The following day Humphrey and Mayo "reconciled."

In March 1939 the warring couple were part of a studio entourage headed by train to Kansas to promote a new movie. En route, an intoxicated Mayo became displeased with Humphrey's attention to two actresses in the contingent. Methot soon smashed a soda bottle against the wall. Closing in on her husband, she brandished the broken glass. Nearby photographers leapt to the rescue, one of them punching the attacking Mayo. Studio reps hushed up the colorful incident.

By 1940 Bogart's screen career was fast ascending, while Mayo's was in freefall. That year a Hollywood gossip columnist spotted the contentious duo outside a Sunset Strip restaurant. The agitated Methot was atop her incapacitated mate, hitting his head against the sidewalk. By the early 1940s Mrs. Bogart had been diagnosed not only as alcoholic, but also as suffering from paranoia and schizophrenia. How-

ever, she refused psychiatric treatment and the domestic wars continued. One night while entertaining
guests at their West Hollywood
home, the well-liquored hosts were
more combative than usual. When an
unsteady Mayo fell and became
wedged behind the living room sofa,
an enraged Bogart lashed out both
physically and verbally at her. His
snarling dialogue included "You
b****! You filthy b****!" Fortunately a studio publicist was present
to do damage control.

The above incidents paled next to
another night in the early 1940s
when actress Gloria Stuart (later to
make a comeback in 1997's *Titanic*)
and her husband were dinner guests
at the Bogarts'. Bogie announced
that the hostess had locked herself in

The contemplative Humphrey Bogart in his
superstardom years. (Courtesy of JC Archives)

the bedroom upstairs with a loaded gun. The concerned Stuart
insisted that the pickled actor must check on his wife's well-being. As
the guests stood outside the bedroom door inquiring how she was,
Mayo threatened to shoot a no-longer-amused Bogie, as well as the
others, through the door. On another occasion to gain attention from
Humphrey, Mayo tried to slash her wrists.

In 1943, the warring Bogarts were among the Hollywood talent
going abroad to entertain the Allied troops. Before embarking on their
overseas flight, the liquored twosome had a verbal, but not physical,
free-for-all in the airport lounge. During their ten-week trek, the duo
provided their own frontline combat with one another. Later, at a
Bogart Thanksgiving dinner back in Hollywood, when the turkey was
ready to be served, the inebriated Mayo and Humphrey argued as to
who would do the carving honors. An exasperated Methot solved the
question by tossing the turkey through the window.

With *Casablanca* confirming Bogart's movie stardom, the increasingly frustrated Mayo escalated her campaign of physical violence against her successful spouse (who sometimes acknowledged fear of his powerhouse wife). Typically, whenever she began humming the song "Embraceable You," everyone knew to race for cover, as it signaled the start of Methot's latest onslaught. By this juncture in their festering marriage, Bogart spent as many nights away from home as possible. Frequently he adjourned to the Finlandia Baths on Sunset Boulevard. There he could recoup from his drinking binges and have some peace and quiet. Ever-suspicious Mayo was convinced that Bogie's trips to the Finlandia were really a cover for visits to a whorehouse.

One evening when he returned from the Finlandia, he was greeted by a sauced-up Mayo who was already humming her battle anthem. She attacked him with a butcher knife, but he weaved out of harm's way. When he raced for the exit door, she stabbed him in the small of his back. The blade penetrated but, thankfully, not deeply. Warner Bros. police were summoned to contain Mayo while a circumspect physician arrived to sew up Bogart's wound. Once again, the Los Angeles Police Department was *not* alerted of the episode.

By 1944 Bogart had met nineteen-year-old Lauren Bacall, his costar of that year's *To Have and Have Not*. Their blossoming affair turned serious and after several contretemps between Bogie and Mayo, the latter agreed to a separation. The couple divorced in May 1945, the same month Bogie and Lauren wed. Mayo returned home to Portland, Oregon, where she died in 1951. Thus ended the many skirmishes of the Battling Bogarts.

Marlon Brando

[Marlon Brando Jr.]
APRIL 3, 1924 -

Unorthodox, rebellious, arrogant, eccentric, and exasperating. These are but a few of the negative adjectives that have been used to describe Brando as he evolved from a 1940s hunk to the mammoth-sized elderly man of the 2000s. As a screen star, the near-mythical talent won Best Actor Academy Awards for *On the Waterfront* (1954) and *The Godfather* (1972), was Oscar-nominated several other times, and turned in mesmerizing performances in such offerings as *A Streetcar Named Desire* (1951), *Viva Zapata!* (1952), *Julius Caesar* (1953), *Last Tango in Paris* (1972), and *Apocalypse Now* (1979).

Marlon the contrarian took joy in biting the industry hand that fed him. He labeled Hollywood "A cultural boneyard." As to his profession, he proclaimed: "Acting is just hustling. Some people are hustling money, some power. I don't put it down. But I resent people putting it up." The mercurial great one also went against the movie tradition of a star being accessible to the media and the world at large. Privacy freak Brando explained, "I'm not going to place myself at the feet of the American public and invite them into my soul. My soul is a private place." The iconoclastic man, who delighted in antisocial postures, also claimed that if he didn't wish to discuss his private self with the media, he certainly wasn't interested in what others said about him.

Despite his exalted status, this icon shared traits with more mortal men. One of them was a zest for chasing, charming, and bedding women. Like his voracious appetite for food, five-foot, ten-inch Brando had an insatiable sexual craving. (Actress Shelley Winters, once a Brando pal, explained this was an artist's way of filling the void caused by the demands of craft and life.) His preference was fiery Hispanic or exotic Asian women, and over the years his philandering around the world was legendary. He fathered possibly as many as thirteen children, although he did not admit paternity to some of them. As a major Lothario, self-absorbed Marlon said years back when he

Marlon Brando, the star and director of the western *One-Eyed Jacks* (1961), with costar Pina Pellicer. (Courtesy of JC Archives)

was still in his virile prime: "If you're rich and famous, getting laid a lot isn't difficult. I knew what I was doing but I didn't know why. I still don't have all the answers."

He was born in Omaha, Nebraska, in 1924, the third child (sister Jocelyn became an actress) and first son of Marlon and Dorothy Brando. His father manufactured chemical feeds and insecticides, while his mother was both a board-of-directors member and actress with the Omaha Community Playhouse. His dad was a cold-hearted philanderer with a taste for drinking; his odd mother was an alcoholic, her artistic abilities, good intentions, and propriety obscured by her drinking. While loathing one parent and pitying/despising the other, Marlon nevertheless hated being ignored by them. It created a raging anger within him. It also led him to insulate himself against life and people. The self-willed youth (known to many as "Bud") was a troubled and troublesome child, who preferred athletics to the classroom. He was eventually shipped to a military academy where he was expelled only weeks before graduation because of his many pranks.

After abandoning thoughts of becoming a Protestant minister, Brando, who had been rejected for World War II military service because of a bad knee (or, say some, by pretending to be psychotic), began studying acting at New York City's New School. He made his official Broadway debut in 1944's *I Remember Mama*, but it was as the slovenly, complex Stanley Kowalski in *A Streetcar Named Desire* (1947) that the "Method" actor was hailed as the new giant of the American stage. He made his screen debut in *The Men* (1950). After a streak of good movie assignments, he found himself caught in conventional or misguided fare: *Desirée* (1954), *Sayonara* (1957), *The Fugitive Kind* (1959). By then, he'd become difficult, inaccessible, and professionally inconsistent. A legend in his own time, he fled to his Tahitian island retreat of Tetiaroa whenever possible, returning to films only to replenish his coffers.

Brando the perpetual prankster had been a woman-chaser during his 1940s years in New York City, but many thought he was more fond of his pet raccoon, Russell, than he was of his conquests of the moment. He may have abhorred Tinseltown, but Marlon had great fun sampling wares in the candy factory. He dated Marilyn Monroe briefly, but he was far more drawn to Puerto Rican starlet Rita Moreno (who later won an Oscar for *West Side Story*). She had been seeing Geordie Hormel, son of the meat-packing entrepreneur and Marlon's former military school classmate. Brando met her at one of Geordie's parties and the two became tight. It began an intense but troubled twelve-year relationship that included her working with him on *The Night of the Following Day* (1968). His constant dallying with others frequently drove her frantic. In 1961, while staying at his place, she attempted suicide. Much later when the heat from their connection had evaporated, they became friends.

At the same time he was with Moreno, Brando was also seeing Mexican actress Katy Jurado, who had made a name in Hollywood films with *High Noon* (1952). Their fling was brief. She went on to wed character actor Ernest Borgnine, but she was among the cast of Brando's *One-Eyed Jacks* (1961), which he directed. Another Mexican actress that earlier drew the star's interest was Movita Castenada. She had played, among other films, in the Clark Gable vehicle *Mutiny on the Bounty* (1935). Marlon encountered her south of the border in 1951, and she next turned up as an extra on the set of *Viva Zapata!* She was eight or more years older than he, and far more experienced in life than the actor's prior girls. Their association was passionate but suffered from Brando's inability to be monogamous. Nevertheless, she remained a force in his life and, in June 1960, she became his second wife. Their son, Miko, was born in 1961 and their daughter, Rebecca, came in 1967. That same year the couple's marriage was annulled since her prior union to another had not been legally severed before she wed Marlon.

Back in 1954 while touring Europe, Brando had met nineteen-year-old Josanne Mariani-Berenger, whose stepfather was a fisherman in a little village on the French Riviera. Suddenly there were announcements that they were engaged. She came to New York, but their rapport fizzled. Later he would tell his first wife, Anna Kashfi, when she asked about Josanne, that the former girlfriend had "bad breath."

Kashfi was thirty when she came into Brando's life. To gain the role in her first film, *The Mountain* (1956) starring Spencer Tracy, she'd insisted she was from India; actually she was Joan O'Callaghan from Cardiff, Wales. She claimed she didn't know who Brando was when she came to Hollywood, but others suggest she'd already set her sights on him. Their wavering relationship led to an October 1957 marriage, and the following June their son, Christian, was born. They divorced in 1959 and she received a $500,000 property settlement. Thereafter the two battled furiously for years over custody of their son. She wrote the mean-spirited *Brando for Breakfast* (1979).

Among Marlon's many other relationships was his 1962 acquaintanceship with Philippine dancer Marie Cui. Her daughter, Maya, was born in February 1963 and she declared that Brando was the dad. Lab testing and a court decision said otherwise. Another entrant in Marlon's stable was Haitian Giselle Fermine. She was a Hollywood playgirl type with a strong interest in voodoo who'd intrigued Brando in the late 1960s. He had even rented her a Hollywood apartment, but their relationship soon broke off. By coincidence Fermine became friendly with Brando's ex-wife Kashfi in 1971. The two shared a bitter hatred of Marlon and concocted wild ploys to irritate their antagonist, including tossing a shoebox filled with symbolic items (dead mouse, and such) into Brando's yard, hoping to throw a curse on the star.

Then there was young Eurasian beauty France Nuyen who had made a name for herself on Broadway in *The World of Suzie Wong* (1958). Marlon was infatuated with her for a time—which happened to be during his union to Anna Kashfi. The two women became fierce rivals for Marlon's attention. Later, Kashfi insisted that Marlon had announced to her during their divorce mess that Christian was actually France's child! In contrast, there was Tarita Teriipaia, a former waitress turned actress whom Brando had cast in *Mutiny on the Bounty* (1962). He and his Tahitian mistress's offspring included a daughter, Tarita Cheyenne (who committed suicide in 1995), and a son, Tehotu. The ties between Marlon and Tarita endured over the decades.

And this is just a sampling of Brando's many women over the years.

Todd Bridges

[Todd A. Bridges]
May 27, 1965–

From 1978 to 1986 *Diff'rent Strokes* was a hit TV sitcom, making stars of its three young lead players. Sadly, none of the trio lived happily ever after. Dana Plato, who left the successful comedy in 1984 when she became pregnant (but was not married), spent the next years in emotional turmoil complicated by drug abuse and failed career comebacks. In May 1999 at age thirty-five she died of a drug overdose that was ruled a suicide. When the popular program expired, African American Gary Coleman was eighteen years old and only four feet, eight inches tall (due to a defective kidney). Thereafter, he made more news with court cases (suing his parents for his trust fund assets; being sued by a fan, and so forth) and strange jobs (owner of a video arcade; embarrassing TV commercials) than for any acting successes. And then there was the third member of the troupe—Bridges.

Bridges was born in San Francisco where his father was a theatrical agent and his mother taught dramatics. Like his older brother and sister, Todd began acting early. By age eight he had appeared in an episode of TV's *Barney Miller* and then became a regular on *Fish* (1977–78). He performed in the miniseries *Roots* (1977) and in segments of *Little House on the Prairie* and *The Waltons*. When Todd joined *Diff'rent Strokes*, the thirteen-year-old had to make a difficult adjustment—surrendering the center of attention to cute Coleman (as his younger brother Arnold) who quickly became the focus of the series. Over subsequent seasons the rivalry led to resentment. By December 1980 Bridges was describing to *TV Guide* his "adjustment" to the on-set competition with Gary: "Long time ago, when we first started, it made me mad. But now I don't care. I got used to it. It's like if somebody beats you every day, after a while you get used to that. You don't think of it as a beating no more."

Diff'rent Strokes was in its fifth season when eighteen-year-old Todd began having trouble with the law. In the summer of 1983 he was arrested on a misdemeanor charge of having a concealed weapon in his Porsche. He insisted that he had purchased the .45-caliber semi-automatic handgun as protection after twice being threatened physically by racists in his San Fernando Valley neighborhood. He paid the $240 fine. The next month while driving home, his car stalled and he had to push it back to his address. As he reached his house, he was stopped by police in several patrol cars. Accused of allegedly stealing the car, he was handcuffed and detained on the spot. Eventually released, he was given a citation for driving without a license, but that was dropped when he proved in court that he had the paperwork in his home. A year later he filed harassment charges against the police claiming "malice and ill will with the intent and purpose of oppressing plaintiff." The cops denied the allegations.

Some weeks after *Diff'rent Strokes* ended in the spring of 1986, Bridges was sentenced to one year in county jail for making a bomb threat over the phone to an auto mechanic because he'd taken too long to fix Todd's vehicle. Sentencing was delayed until January 1987 by which time if Todd remained out of trouble, met with a psychiatrist, and did three hundred hours of community service, the jail stretch would be lifted. Meanwhile, Todd paid a $2,500 fine and was barred from possessing any deadly weapons or explosives. (The jail term was lifted in November 1986 because of Bridges's exemplary probation.)

In January 1988 trouble-plagued Todd was arrested on suspicion of reckless driving. He pleaded guilty. Next came his detention for allegedly having taken his BMW car from a repair shop at gunpoint and for not paying the $500 repair bill. In mid-1988 he spent time at a drug rehabilitation center. By February 1989 the jobless one-time TV star was in police custody without bail for reputedly having shot several bullets at a man at a Los Angeles crack house (the same address where Todd had been arrested nine days earlier for possession of cocaine).

After pleading not guilty to the attempted first-degree murder charge (and noting that he had been in a drug haze at the time), Bridges spent several months in jail awaiting trial. In November 1989, he was acquitted on the attempted murder and attempted voluntary manslaughter charges, with the judge declaring a mistrial on the assault with a deadly weapon part of the case.

Despite this reprieve, the actor's misfortunes continued. In May 1990 he was arrested with a companion in North Hollywood on alleged possession of cocaine for sale. (The case was dropped later for insufficient evidence.) Meanwhile, the assault charge against Bridges from the 1989 crack house episode was refiled, but this time Todd was acquitted. Later in the year the actor's wife, Rebecca San Filipo with whom he'd been living since 1985 and to whom he had been wed in November 1989, filed for divorce. On the plus side Bridges started the Todd Bridges Foundation, a self-help group for young people in South Central Los Angeles. By late 1992, however, he had resigned his post, as he felt his recent arrest in Burbank, California, on charges of possession of drugs (methamphetamine) and a loaded weapon (a 9-millimeter Ruger gun) would discredit the foundation.

The year 1993 was no better for the beleaguered performer. In March he was arrested on suspicion of attempted murder in the stabbing of a friend/boarder at Bridges's modest Sun Valley, California, home. Law enforcers determined that the incident was a case of self-defense arising over a rent dispute, and Todd was released. Then, in July 1993 Bridges changed his March 1993 pleas of not guilty to guilty in the December 1992 drug and weapon possession case. That December he was ordered to a one-year live-in drug treatment program along with five years of probation. In 1994 he completed his recovery program and claimed that he'd conquered his drug habit.

A few years later Todd was again newsworthy. In January 1997 he was arrested on suspicion of assault with a deadly weapon. He had been playing video games with an acquaintance at a Marina del Rey, California, arcade when they got into a dispute. Thereafter he allegedly rammed his car twice into his friend's vehicle. Bridges was released on $20,000 bail, insisting the incident was an accident. Later, he was charged with vandalism, paid a fine, and did community service.

On a more upbeat note, in February 1997 while in Atlanta, Georgia, performing in a Christian play, Todd met Peach State–born Dori Smith. The couple wed later in the year. Their son, Spencer, was born in July 1998. By October 1999, Todd was telling *Jet* magazine: "I've been sober for seven years. I'm on a journey to do the Lord's work. I'm getting my career going." (In recent years he has appeared in such films as 1998's *The Waterfront*, 2000's *Dancing in September*, and 2002's *The Climb*.)

In April 2001, Bridges was back again in the news, this time hailed by the media as a hero. A fifty-year-old paraplegic woman was fishing at a lake in Encino, California. Her fishing line tangled in the controls of her electric wheelchair (in which she was buckled). The heavy chair lurched into the lake. Todd and his brother James, who were fishing nearby, rushed into the low-level water and saved the victim whose chair had tilted on its side and forced her head underwater.

Then in winter 2002 Bridges demonstrated his physical prowess when he beat Robert Van Winkle (formerly known as rapper Vanilla Ice) in a boxing match on an episode of *Celebrity Boxing* on the Fox network.

Lately, Bridges insisted, "The bottom line is I've made stupid choices. But I got my life together and now that's the difference. I'm not the same idiot I used to be."

Gary Busey

[Gary Busey]

June 29, 1944–

In 1978 this thirty-four-year-old Texan was Oscar-nominated for his outstanding performance as the rockin' lead in the musical biography *The Buddy Holly Story*. Although he didn't win the Academy Award, it seemed that intense Busey was destined for major film stardom. Over subsequent years, this hulking good ol' boy with buck teeth had several career ups and downs, many of them due to his wild personal life. Without doubt, this unorthodox personality has always marched to his own special drummer. For example, in 1987 he offered the following advice: "Only three things you need if you want to make it in Hollywood. Learn how to make your own salad. Learn how to fall in slow motion. And learn how to cry."

He was the first of three children born to construction worker Delmer Busey (Native American) and his wife, Ginny (Irish American). By the time Gary was five, the family had moved to Tulsa, Oklahoma. There his parents were cofounders of the Sheridan Avenue Christian Church. In school he was a jock (especially talented in football) and got involved in theater work. Out of the classroom, Gary, who suffered from attention deficit disorder, often worked on a ranch and rode bulls. He won a football scholarship to a junior college in Coffeyville, Kansas, but transferred to Oklahoma State University after an injury ended his gridiron career. Meanwhile, he became a drummer with his self-formed group, The Rubber Band. He quit college in the mid-1960s to make music his living.

In 1968 Gary married Judy Helkenberg (whom he knew from Coffeyville college days) and the couple moved to California with his band. Amazed by the hippie life in Los Angeles, Gary went overboard in adapting to the loose atmosphere. He continued with his group (now called Carp) while also taking acting classes. In 1970 Carp signed with Epic Records and made an album with Busey playing drums and doing vocals. Also that year, Gary got his first acting gig, in an episode of TV's *High Chaparral*, and the following year he made his movie debut in *Angels Hard as They Come*, a biker tale. His son, Jake (who would become an actor and musician), was born in 1971. Meanwhile, hard-living Gary moved his family back to Tulsa, Oklahoma, to do his own local TV show, playing his trademark alter ego, Teddy Jack Eddie. This act brought him to the attention of Willie Nelson and the two musicians became friends.

When his band broke up, Gary returned to Los Angeles and moviemaking, alternating between TV episodes (*Bonanza*, *Kung Fu*) and feature films (1973's *Hex*). The "instant" fame achieved as the grinning rock 'n' roller Buddy Holly went to Busey's head as did his cocaine habit. According to Busey "that's when I got trapped by the devil." He kept on working (1982's *Barbarosa*), but he was building a reputation as a Hollywood hellion on and off movie sets. By the mid-1980s his once high-voltage career was bottoming out with such movies as 1986's *Eye of the Tiger*.

Gary Busey in his Oscar-nominated performance as the star of *The Buddy Holly Story* (1978). (Courtesy of JC Archives)

One day in June 1985 Gary, who had been attending Cocaine Anonymous but who still hadn't conquered his addictions, looked in the mirror and "saw a dead man." He chose to become clean and sober. In the process the barrel-chested performer dropped from 230 to 180 pounds. His career rebounded with the role of arch-villain Mr. Joshua in *Lethal Weapon* (1987). It seemed he was back on track. Then came December 4, 1988. As an adult, hyperkinetic Gary found great release riding his motorcycle. That day he'd just picked up his Harley-Davidson at a repair shop. As he was riding (without a helmet—which he always refused to wear) along the Culver City road, he lost control of the cycle and swerved to avoid hitting an oncoming bus. He flew over the handlebars and smacked into the concrete road divider. The force of the impact left him with a hole in his head the size of a half-dollar. He was rushed to Cedars-Sinai Medical Center for emergency brain surgery. After the operation, he was initially without the ability to talk, walk, or even swallow and suffered from posttrauma amnesia.

As he gained mobility thereafter, Busey's inner rage grew so manic that he tried to break out of the facility. He was placed in a mental ward and later transferred to another hospital. During this arduous recovery, Busey remembered that he had a near-death experience as he lay on the road after the accident. He was visited by the Grim Reaper who told him: "Relax. It's not your time to go. You have been given gifts at birth that you are now ready to receive." The Reaper's sickle spun wildly and then the horrific vision was gone. (This was not Gary's first vision. During the making of 1978's *Big Wednesday* with Busey and Jan-Michael Vincent, costar Patti D'Arbanville said, "We partied all the time, and quite a few of us saw a UFO. During a cookout, a craft appeared, hovered for a few seconds, then disappeared at warp speed.") After several difficult weeks in the hospital, Gary was released to recoup further at home. Gaining a new perspective on life, he became a "seeker of truth." Meanwhile his career momentum had fallen apart and his floundering marriage ended in 1990. He turned back to drugs and liquor, furthering his reputation as a wild man.

In the early 1990s Gary had plenty of screen work but often in unworthy projects. He met aspiring actress Tiani Warden in 1994. She was twenty-six and recovering from a drinking problem. She soon moved into the Malibu home of fifty-year-old Busey. On the evening of May 4, 1995, Tiani found her boyfriend unconscious in the backyard of their home—passed out from a cocaine overdose. After four days in Santa Monica Hospital he was released. When the police responded to Tiani's 911 call, they had found drugs in Busey's home. He was later charged with felony drug possession and required to enter a drug treatment program for two years. The experience led to a spiritual awakening; he was convinced the overdose had been a message from God. In his new mode he became a member of Promise Keepers, a men's group devoted to Christ.

With renewed spirituality, Busey and Tiani married in September 1996 while he continued making such movies as 1997's *Livers Ain't Cheap*. In June 1997 a cancerous tumor (the size of a plum) was discovered in Gary's nasal cavity. It was one of five such known medical cases in the world. Three days after the surgery he was mobile. Meanwhile, there were growing problems in his marital relationship. In late January 1999 Busey was arrested after an alleged domestic dispute at his home in which he reputedly went berserk. But since the sheriff's deputies found no signs of trauma or injuries on the wife, the district attorney refused to press charges. After this episode, the couple, who had filed and withdrawn a divorce petition in 1998, parted ways in June 2000.

In 2000, after three years of plastic surgery operations initiated to rebuild his face following his nose cancer operation, the screen's recurrent celluloid villain was showing off his new self. Yet, whether this spare-time preacher had changed much from his rambunctious, renegade self was still an open question, especially after alleged events that took place on December 2, 2001. Gary was arrested at his Malibu home when his ex-wife Tiani accused him of attacking/bruising her some days earlier. He was later released on a $50,000 bond. However, later in the same month prosecutors declined to file charges because, as a district attorney office spokesperson explained, "We can't prove that a crime occurred. There are no independent witnesses. There is insufficient evidence for a prosecution."

On December 14, 2001, only a few weeks after the altercation with his ex-spouse Tiani, Gary got into another "situation." This time the other party was athletic, attractive actress Yancy Butler (who had costarred with Busey in the 1994 thriller *Drop Zone*). The supposed disagreement occurred in a parking lot in Malibu, where Busey reportedly grabbed the actress in what seemed to observers to be a heated discussion in which he may have "hit" her in the face. However, Gary insisted that was definitely not the case: "We were re-enacting our fight scenes from *Drop Zone*. Yancy and I are old friends and we hadn't seen each other for a while." Evidently, being a pal of Busey had its own occupational hazards.

Charlie Chaplin

[Charles Spencer Chaplin]

APRIL 16, 1889–DECEMBER 25, 1977

For many the British-born Chaplin is the screen's ultimate "King of Comedy." His persona of the Little Tramp remains a comic masterpiece. His beloved comic creation endured through silent shorts and features (1925's *The Circus*, 1928's *The Gold Rush*) as well as sound pictures like *Modern Times* (1936). Beyond his comic genius, the five-foot, four-and-one-half-inch Sir Charles remains legendary in another arena—that of a great lover. Boastful of being extremely well endowed and having tremendous sexual stamina, he had a strong penchant for bedding underage women. It was a proclivity that dragged the world's first international movie star into several scrapes.

Chaplin was the son of a vaudevillian and a music hall soubrette, she having had a previous marriage that produced a boy named Sydney. The father deserted the family a year after Charlie's birth in 1889 and died of alcoholism in 1897, while the mother was later confined repeatedly to an insane asylum. For a time, Syd and Charlie were shunted to a workhouse. Later Syd joined the Royal Navy while Charlie took to the streets. The youngster made his professional acting debut in early 1900 on the London stage. By 1906 Chaplin joined Fred Karno's music hall troupe, of which Syd was already a member. Working for the famed Karno, Charlie not only honed his comedic skills, but also noted his married employer's lascivious ways with chorines. It had a lasting effect on the comic genius.

When Charlie was nineteen he fell madly in love with a fifteen-year-old chorus girl named Hetty Green. After but one dinner date and a few later conversations, he proposed to her. Chaplin was crushed when she said she was too young to wed. He did not hear from her until she wrote him in 1918. By then she was married and living in London. Although the still entranced Charlie responded to her note almost immediately, he never heard back. Later he learned she had died that very year. Forever after, he sought a replacement for the idealized Hetty.

Charlie moved to Hollywood in December 1913, and by 1915, he had graduated from Mack Sennett screen comedies to being a well-paid star of his own silent shorts. That year he met blond Edna Purviance—an "older" woman of twenty—whom he made his leading lady and his lady love. However, the now worldly Chaplin had no notion of faithfulness, and maintained various dalliances with prostitutes or young Hollywood lovelies. Edna waited for him to settle down, and then, impulsively, had an affair with screen star Thomas Meighan. When Chaplin learned of this he broke off their romance, although he continued to work with her and, still later, after she retired, kept her on his payroll.

It was in 1916 that Charlie encountered fourteen-year-old movie actress Mildred Harris. He was immediately infatuated by the young lovely. Her wardrobe mistress–mother encouraged the unlikely relationship. In 1918 the parent informed Chaplin that Mildred was pregnant. Fearful of criminal prosecution, the screen star wed her on October 23. The pregnancy turned out to be false, but in 1919 she gave birth to a horribly deformed baby who died within days. By now Chaplin had returned to his pastime of entertaining (would-be) starlets in his studio dressing room. The death knell to the marriage occurred when ambitious Mildred went back to films billed as Mrs. Charlie Chaplin. The couple divorced in November 1920.

Having learned from the Harris fiasco, Chaplin focused on more mature women ranging from screen actresses Pola Negri and Claire Windsor to playgirl beauty Peggy Hopkins Joyce and sculptress Clare Sheridan. In the midst of his passionate association with Hungarian-born Negri, a young Mexican female dramatically entered Chaplin's life. Marina Varga had deserted her husband in Vera Cruz to sneak across the border, determined to meet her screen idol, Chaplin. One day Charlie's valet found the uninvited Varga ensconced in the comedian's bed, wearing a pair of the star's pajamas. The servant coaxed her to dress, and Chaplin spoke a few kind words to the disturbed soul. By the next day Marina realized her beloved idol was not to be hers. She purchased arsenic, supposedly took it, and then hurried to Chaplin's home where she lay down in the garden prepared to die. Discovered on the manicured grounds, she was examined by a doctor/neighbor who concluded she was merely suffering from hysteria. When Negri arrived at Chaplin's and found Marina there, the two jealous rivals got into a heated fight. According to legend, Charlie dowsed the two adversaries with a bucket of cold water.

In 1921 Chaplin had cast young Lita Grey in his classic *The Kid*. In 1924 he chose the nubile actress to costar in his upcoming feature, *The Circus*. Before long, randy Chaplin seduced her and when she told him she was pregnant, he suggested she have an abortion. Lita refused, and her grasping relatives threatened a paternity suit. As a result, an unhappy Chaplin wed her in November 1924. Charles Jr. was born in 1925 and Sydney in 1926. Meanwhile, the star/director recast the female lead in *The Circus*. By early 1927 the battling couple was near divorce and in a strategy ploy Lita's family had her lengthy divorce complaint published. It contained explicit details of the couple's sexual life, Charlie's sexual

Charlie Chaplin as his world-famous alter ego, "The Little Tramp."
(Courtesy of JC Archives)

preferences, and his several extramarital relationships (including a dalliance with movie star Marion Davies). A frantic Chaplin agreed to a $625,000 divorce settlement plus a $200,000 trust fund for their children.

In the 1930s Chaplin made a successful transition to sound movies and even married again, this time to beautiful and witty screen actress Paulette Goddard, with whom he costarred in *Modern Times*. His union to the twenty-two-year-younger actress ended in a 1942 divorce.

Meanwhile, Chaplin was introduced to Brooklyn-born Joan Barry in 1941. A would-be actress she was known as a "party girl." She was pert, persistent, and the fifty-one-year-old comedian put her under studio contract and into his bed. She got pregnant at least twice but had abortions. Soon Joan began drinking heavily and behaving increasingly erratic. Once, to gain Charlie's wandering attention, she cavorted naked on his stately front lawn darting through the spurting sprinklers. He gave her money to return to New York, but before long she showed up at his mansion waving a gun (which she claimed led to a passionate sexual reunion).

By now (1942) Chaplin was courting playwright Eugene O'Neill's seventeen-year-old daughter, Oona. Charlie wished to marry her and be rid of Barry. Joan retaliated by breaking into his house and jumping naked into his bed. As a result she was jailed but later released. When she learned she was pregnant, Chaplin insisted the child was not his. The FBI had Chaplin arrested for, allegedly, violating the Mann Act (which concerns interstate prostitution). With worldwide headlines, Charlie was booked and his mug shot taken. Eventually he was proven innocent of the charges; however, he agreed to pay Barry a weekly sum until her baby was born and blood tests could be taken. When the girl was born in October 1943, tests proved that Charlie was *not* the father. Nevertheless the media and the public had already convicted Chaplin. In court her lawyer told the jury: "There has been no one to stop Chaplin in his lecherous conduct all these years . . . except you." Despite the medical testimony to the contrary, Charlie lost the case and was forced to support Joan's daughter.

In 1952 after completing *Limelight* (1952), Chaplin and Oona and their four children sailed for England. When he was barred from later reentry to the United States because of his supposed Communist sympathies and his past record of immorality, the Chaplins settled in Switzerland. There the couple had four more children, the last born in 1963 when Charlie was seventy-four. In Oona, Chaplin had finally found a replacement for his long-lost young love, Hetty Green.

Montgomery Clift

[Edward Montgomery Clift]

OCTOBER 17, 1920–JULY 23, 1966

On Broadway in the 1940s and in his early feature films such as *Red River* (1948) and *The Heiress* (1949), this soft-spoken actor showed tremendous promise. A moody rebel against the norm, Clift set the standards for Marlon Brando and James Dean who modeled their nonconformist, trendsetting careers after him. Montgomery was extremely handsome, intensely serious about his craft, and should have prospered professionally even though he refused to play the Hollywood studio-system game (that is, long-term contracts, attending premieres, doing publicity). He was long plagued by emotional problems, however, including hatred of his controlling mother, confusion over his closeted homosexuality, and an inability to cope with massive insecurities about his talent.

Despite years of expensive psychiatric therapy, Clift's chief relief from the darkness of his existence came from anesthetizing himself against life through booze and drugs. His accelerating substance abuse made him more antisocial, more self-destructive, and more incoherently weird, as well as reckless in his choice of street-tough male sex partners. By the early 1960s Clift had gone so over the edge that at the premiere of *Judgment at Nuremberg* (1961—for which he would be Oscar-nominated), he arrived so drugged out and drunk that at one point in the screening he was on his hands and knees picking his way between the aisles and crazily shouting.

Clift, who feared/refused to deal with his gayness (in an era when such activity, if known, could have ended his career), always insisted he was attracted to females. Many women—including such celebrated talents and beauties as torch singer Libby Holman and actresses Elizabeth Taylor, Myrna Loy, Maria Schell, and Jennifer Jones—wanted to rescue and mother the tormented star. (Several of the opposite sex in his life during the more innocent 1940s and 1950s were unaware initially of Monty's conflicted sexual interests.) The great love of his life was bohemian Holman, fourteen years his senior. Eighteen-year-old Elizabeth Taylor first worked with Clift on *A Place in the Sun* (1951) and fell madly in love with him. Whether or not they ever had intimate relations, they became extremely close friends until his death. She remained loyal to Monty even as others, who could no longer deal with his self-destructive, anti-social ways, broke off contact.

Clift was born just after his twin sister, Roberta, in 1920 in Omaha, Nebraska. There was an older brother, Brooks. The father was a successful banker who would endure hard times during the Depression. The mother, Ethel "Sunny" (Fogg) Clift, had her own life's mission. As a child she had been adopted and only later learned that she came of southern aristocratic stock. Thereafter, she was devoted to "legitimatising" her family and spent much of her husband's money doing so. As the Clifts moved to Chicago in 1924 and then to New York in 1930, Sunny pampered her fantasies of a refined life. She often took her children abroad, but her spouse remained behind.

With Clift's good looks he was encouraged to become a model, but Monty insisted he wanted to be an actor. He made his Broadway debut in the comedy *Fly Away Home* (1935). By the time Monty appeared in *There Shall Be No Night* (1940) and *The Skin of Our Teeth* (1942) he had begun a series of clandestine gay romances, he and his various long-term partners usually never discussing their lifestyle. As to his bond with Libby Holman, she was as offbeat as Clift. There was later much speculation about their reportedly strange sex life together. Meanwhile, Clift was rejected for World War II military service due to chronic diarrhea, a result of the amoebic dysentery he contracted on an earlier vacation trip to Mexico with a mentor/special friend (music conductor Lehman Engel).

Filmmaker Howard Hawks had heard of Clift's Broadway success and hired him to play opposite John Wayne in the rugged sagebrush tale *Red River*. Made in 1946, it was not released until a few months after *The Search* (1948). (The latter film earned Monty the first of four Oscar nominations.) By the time of *The Heiress* (1949) with Olivia de Havilland, handsome Monty was earning $100,000 a picture and was Hollywood's major new find. He was already confounded by leading his double life: as a screen heartthrob and, on the side, as a homosexual man. The more famous he became and the more his private life was subject to media scrutiny, the more distraught he became. His drinking escalated and that, in turn, brought on frequent blackouts. (He also suffered from an underactive thyroid condition that exacerbated his disoriented behavior.)

Despite Clift's Tinseltown status, he kept Manhattan as his home base because there he could enjoy more privacy. Much of Monty's time in New York was spent with actor Kevin McCarthy and his actress wife, Augusta Dabney. The threesome was such a perennial sight around the city that observers speculated wildly about this close-knit trio. When on the West Coast, Monty traipsed around with Elizabeth Taylor as she paraded through marriages and divorces. When she was wed to British actor Michael Wilding in the 1950s, Clift became a fixture in their lives.

The turning point in his unlucky existence occurred on May 12, 1956. He had been working for more than a month on *Raintree County* (1957), a screen saga of the old South. That evening he had attended a dinner in Los Angeles hosted by Taylor and Wilding. After leaving their home and while driving down the winding road in the fog, Clift's car smashed into a power pole. (Even in the best of circumstances, Monty was often disoriented.) The accident left Clift's face a shattered mess requiring painful reconstructive surgery. Always vain about his looks (which he was convinced was the main reason for his fame), his self-confidence deteriorated further. He completed *Raintree County*, but on the big screen the postaccident star looked strange and haunted. Next, he was costarred with his rival Marlon Brando in *The*

Handsome screen star Montgomery Clift—before his near-fatal car accident in 1956 physically and emotionally disfigured him. (Courtesy of JC Archives)

Young Lions (1958), but in this World War II drama Clift seemed to be replaying his role from his superior *From Here to Eternity* (1953).

Ever loyal, Taylor insisted on Monty costarring with her in *Suddenly, Last Summer* (1959) but he could only bumble through the role, dragged down by his growing substance abuse. If he was bullied by director Joseph L. Mankiewicz on *Suddenly, Last Summer*, it was nothing compared to his humiliation on the set of *Freud* (1962). Directed by John Huston, a swaggering man's man, the filmmaker had just discovered that Clift was homosexual and he found that abhorrent along with Monty's mounting difficulties in getting through a scene. The disgusted director would have replaced him if he could have. Thereafter, the emotionally battered Clift did not work for another four years, and then it was in a Cold War spy flop *The Defector* (1966) in which he looked terribly pinched and old. By the time it was released Monty had died.

Officially the cause of the star's death was a heart attack, but it was his years of excessive booze and drugs that really did him in. Some refer to Clift's adult life as the lengthiest suicide in Hollywood's history.

Steve Cochran

[Robert Alexander Cochran]

MAY 25, 1917–JUNE 15, 1965

He may not have achieved the height of fame accorded movie gangsters Edward G. Robinson or Humphrey Bogart, but handsome, six-foot-tall Cochran was, nevertheless, charismatic as a big-screen tough guy (1949's *The Damned Don't Cry*). When the script required his character to slap around his leading lady (Virginia Mayo, Joan Crawford, or Doris Day), he was convincingly slimy. There was always something unsettling and a bit unsavory about good-looking Cochran. When this Tinseltown Romeo died under bizarre circumstances, Hollywood was not really surprised.

Although born in Eureka, California, in 1917, he grew up in Laramie, Wyoming. In high school he acted in plays but preferred basketball. After working as a cowpoke (among other jobs), he entered the University of Wyoming. There he was on the basketball squad until an episode of carousing around town led to his being benched from the team. To fill his free time, he joined the drama club and found he liked performing. In 1937 he abandoned college to try his luck in Hollywood.

In Tinseltown Cochran learned that he lacked the needed contacts; he returned home where he worked as a department store detective, carpenter, and such. In 1939 he made his summer stock debut and then moved on to the WPA Federal Theater in Detroit, followed by a stint with the Shakespeare Festival in Carmel, California.

He was turned down by the World War II draft board because of a heart murmur. Instead he directed and toured with shows for West Coast army camps. Later, moving to the East Coast, he did summer stock, was an extra in the film *Stage Door Canteen* (1943), and the next year was in two short-lasting Broadway productions. While in a road company of *Without Love* with Constance Bennett, he won a film contract shared by producer Samuel Goldwyn and Columbia Pictures. The latter put him into such celluloid trifles as *Boston Blackie Booked on Suspicion* (1945) while the former frequently teamed him with beautiful Virginia Mayo (1946's *The Best Years of Our Lives*).

When Steve's movie contracts expired in the late 1940s he headed back east. There Mae West hired the much younger Cochran to be her leading man in a revival of *Diamond Lil* (1949). The popular production led to Steve being signed to a Warner Bros. contract.

In the excellent gangster yarn *White Heat* (1949) he was James Cagney's underling who stupidly makes a play for the boss's moll (Virginia Mayo). His Warner Bros. pictures ranged from World War II yarns to musicals. When the studio did not renew his pact, he freelanced, even producing the wholesome family story *Come Next Spring* (1956). He dabbled in TV, tried filming abroad (1957's *Il Grido*), but was typecast playing villains (1958's *I, Mobster*). When the gangster genre waned, Steve's career nosedived. By now too much of the good life and advancing age had given him a dissipated and bloated look. Nevertheless he kept working (summer stock, TV, and so forth) and planned to produce movies in which he would star.

Always a dedicated ladies' man, Steve was married three times. The first Mrs. Cochran was artist Florence Lockwood with whom he had a daughter, Xandra. The couple divorced in 1946 and his daughter vanished out of his life. Spouse number two was actress Fay McKenzie whom he wed in 1946 and divorced in 1948. In 1961 the forty-four-year-old Cochran walked down the aisle in Las Vegas with Danish lass Heddy Jonna Jensen, nineteen. That match lasted three years. Among his other amours over the seasons were actresses Denise Darcel and Dorothy Hart, film mogul Darryl F. Zanuck's daughter (Susan), and belly dancer Nejia Ates. For a time he hung with freewheeling thespian and girl-about-town Barbara Payton. At one juncture Cochran was engaged to Gloria Howard, whose biggest claim to fame was being the key witness in a $250,000 jewel theft caper.

Steve was always rich media fodder. In 1952 he had an altercation with middleweight boxer Buddy Wright and bashed the man with a baseball bat. That New Year's Eve misadventure cost Cochran $16,500. The next year the actor was arrested for reckless driving and for evading arrest. (The police had to fire a gun to get Cochran to stop his vehicle.) There was also the time the law cited speed-happy Steve for reckless piloting in the air. In summer 1960, when his forty-foot schooner, *The Rogue*, strayed off course during a heavy fog and crashed into the Los Angeles breakwater, its preoccupied owner was below deck entertaining two lovelies. The Coast Guard came to the rescue as the vessel sank. While filming *Mozambique* (1966) in South Africa, a bit player in the cast dragged Steve into court for alienating his wife's affections. The suit was dismissed as was a 1964 California case in which young singer Ronnie Rae alleged that host Cochran had torn off her sweater and bound and gagged her.

In the winter of 1964 playboy Cochran advertised in the trade paper *Variety* for an all-woman crew to join him aboard *The Rogue* for a cruise in southern waters for a film project (*Captain O'Flynn*) he was supposedly producing. When they stopped in Ensenada, Mexico, on the Baja California peninsula, the women abandoned ship and Steve sailed on alone to Acapulco where he advertised for replacements, offering to pay seventy pesos (approximately $5.83) per day. Despite there being more than 180 applicants, he hired only three (all friends) because, according to the movie star, there were "no real lookers." The schooner left Acapulco on June 3, with its crew of three (ages twenty-one, nineteen, and fourteen). Off the coast of Oaxaca the boat ran into a hurricane and was badly damaged. Steve remained at the helm for two days and nights. Totally exhausted and now in severe pain, he collapsed. On June 15, 1965, he expired at age forty-eight.

The girls (none of whom spoke English) were not rescued by the Guatemalan Coast Guard for several days—by then the women were in total hysteria at being adrift (and sailing in circles off the port of Champerico) with a decomposing corpse aboard. The unofficial autopsy concluded that Steve died of acute infectious edema, an accumulation of liquid in the lung tissues. His body was shipped to California, where ex-wife number three, Jonna, petitioned to be named executor of his estate. She eventually shared the $25,000 balance with Cochran's daughter (some months before Cochran had transferred $100,000 of his assets to his aged mother). Mystery man Steve's last movie, *Tell Me in the Sunlight*, made in the early 1960s, received scant distribution in 1967.

Cochran's peculiar death generated several rumors. One theory had it that the victim aboard the boat was *not* Steve, but that Cochran had tremendous gambling debts and chose to disappear. Another hypothesis insisted that the autopsy—never authenticated as official by Guatemala—obscured the fact that the movie celebrity had expired of a deadly disease that might have scared away the tourist trade. Then there was the Los Angeles actress (Julie Gambol) who came forward to report that she had been one of those who sailed with Cochran to Ensenada, being coached in sailing (by Steve) and in Spanish (by a teacher) for her role in the upcoming *Captain O'Flynn*. Having gone ashore before Cochran went on to Acapulco alone, she was supposed to meet up with him in Costa Rica once he had hired the rest of the cast and crew. After the actor's death, the phantom film crew could never be located.

Bob Crane

[Robert Edward Crane]

JULY 13, 1928–JUNE 29, 1978

Because his murder was so brutal and the puzzling case *still* remains unsolved, the fact is often overlooked that the celebrity's death uncovered the shocking information that Crane—the beloved star of the classic sitcom *Hogan's Heroes* (1965–71)—was leading a bizarre double life. In the spotlight he had been the affable leading man of light-hearted fare. Away from the limelight, apparently he suffered from an escalating sexual addiction that led him to kinky sex with female pick-ups. Part of Crane's routine was to videotape and photograph these intense (often S & M sex) sessions, and also to show these "special" photo albums (or a screening of one of his X-rated videotapes) for family, friends, coworkers, and even his young son from his second marriage. In his last years Bob's addictive behavior had become so central to his existence that everything else suffered, including his once promising show business career.

Born in Waterbury, Connecticut, to Alfred and Rosemary Crane, he was the younger son in a middle-class, Catholic household. When the father's income improved—he was a furniture and floor-covering salesman—he relocated his family to adjacent, upscale Stamford. As a youngster, Bob displayed an affinity for drumming. His burgeoning musical talent superseded any academic interest in high school. By age sixteen Crane had quit school to become a percussionist with the Connecticut Symphony Orchestra, a job that lasted from 1944 to 1946. Later he toured the Northeast with several bands. By 1950, however, the era of big bands had passed and he had to find other work. A steady income was essential now because in 1949 he had wed his child-hood sweetheart, Anne Terzian. (During their twenty-one-year marriage the couple had three children: Robert David, Deborah Ann, and Karen Leslie.) Bob turned to being a disc jockey and radio host on local radio stations.

Crane developed such a strong reputation as a congenial, clowning radio host that he was hired to work on the airwaves in Los Angeles in 1956. There, on his celebrity interview show on KNX radio, he exhibited a sharp wit and a zany, entertaining brashness, which included impromptu percussion sessions and off-the-wall conversations with visiting celebrities. His accelerating popularity soon led to his more than $100,000 yearly salary. Not satisfied with this success, Crane dreamed of being an actor, someone in the mold of Jack Lemmon. He performed in local theater and soon was doing TV guest spots and occasional movie roles (1961's *Return to Peyton Place*). He also did a stint as a substitute host for Johnny Carson on *Who Do You Trust?*, a daytime TV quiz program.

It was a guest role on TV's *The Dick Van Dyke Show* in 1963 that paved the way for the handsome, five-foot, ten-inch Crane to be hired to be Dr. Dave Kelsey, the married next-door neighbor on *The Donna Reed Show* (1963–65). In turn, this TV exposure led to Bob being signed to portray the imaginative American colonel in *Hogan's Heroes*, which began airing in September 1965. Set in a Nazi prisoner-of-war camp, the program ran for six seasons.

Crane's show business success had changed him, and in the process he and his wife divorced in 1970. That same year he wed actress Patricia Olsen. (Using her professional name of Sigrid Valdis, Patricia had played Hilda, the young German woman, on several seasons of *Hogan's Heroes*.) The following year, the Cranes had a son, Robert Scott. After the TV series left the air in 1971, Bob guested on many TV programs and made telefeatures. He turned down several sitcom pilots—insisting he was still waiting for *the* right follow-up show.

In 1974 Bob declined an offer of $300,000 yearly to host an L.A. radio program four hours each weekday. Instead, he did *The Bob Crane Show*, an unimpressive TV sitcom that flopped in 1975, a career failure that embittered him. By 1977 he was reduced to being a guest star on TV's *Love Boat*, a definite indicator that his career had slipped. (Crane's last feature film had been a secondary role in the 1976 Disney comedy *Gus*.)

By 1978 Crane and his second wife had separated and she had filed for divorce. To keep busy, he was earning a healthy salary starring in featherweight comedies at dinner theaters across America. That June, the facile actor was headlining a sex farce, *Beginner's Luck*, at the Windmill Dinner Theater in Scottsdale, Arizona. During the engage-

ment, his second wife (Patricia) and
their boy came to Scottsdale, which
only led to arguments and their
departure back to the West Coast.

By this point in life Bob had a long-
standing habit on his out-of-town
treks of meeting up with John Carpenter, a Los Angeles–based video
equipment salesman. (The two first
became friendly when Bob had
initially wanted to tape his sexual
escapades and needed advice on what
video equipment to buy.) On their
nights out together, Bob and John
would go to a local bar, meet willing
young women, and take them back to
their rooms for fun and games with
their array of sex toys and such. At
some point prior to or during Bob's
fatal, final stay in Scottsdale, he was

Bob Crane (in drag) in a comedic moment
with Eddie Quillan from *The Wicked Dreams
of Paula Schultz* (1968). (Courtesy of JC Archives)

thinking of seriously dealing with his sexual addiction. Part of this decision was to cut back or cut off his association with Carpenter, a man
whose presence only brought out the worst in Bob.

On Wednesday, June 28, 1978, after the evening performance of
Beginner's Luck, Crane and Carpenter went to a Scottsdale bar where
their long discussion turned into an argument. (Supposedly, Crane had
told his pal that they needed to go their own ways.) Nevertheless, the
duo had drinks with two females there, and later the foursome went
to a coffee shop. Thereafter, John left the group to pack for his trip
back to Los Angeles the next morning. Later, from his hotel room,
Carpenter called Crane.

The next afternoon, a female cast member of *Beginner's Luck*
came by Crane's apartment when he failed to show up for a cast lunch
that day or to keep a later appointment to assist her with audition
tapes. She discovered Crane's corpse there, with one side of his face
so battered that, initially, she did not recognize him.

The police investigation made public Bob's dual life with his many female sex partners. Because of Crane's special penchants and habits, the law enforcers concluded there might well be many potential suspects, encompassing angered boyfriends/husbands of his bedmates or even jealous past female partners. While John Carpenter at one juncture was considered a key suspect, no formal charges were filed due to insufficient evidence.

Because of the continual reruns of *Hogan's Heroes*—and the unsolved murder case—Bob Crane's name kept popping up in the news for years. Finally, in May 1992 the homicide case was reopened in Arizona with John Carpenter named defendant. Because of charges (sexual misconduct with a minor) pending against Carpenter in California, it was not until September 1994 that the case actually went to trial. Despite the new prosecutor's best efforts, the case was stronger on theory than on hard evidence. Eventually Carpenter was acquitted of the charges. (Until his death in September 1998, John insisted he was innocent.)

Thus, the sensational death of this Jekyll-and-Hyde–like TV star, who led such a wild private life, remains an unsolved mystery in Hollywood history. (The notorious murder case was set to be reexamined yet again in 2002, but this time in a movie titled *Auto Focus* starring Greg Kinnear as the late star who led a double life.)

Bing Crosby

[Harry Lillis Crosby]
MAY 2, 1904–OCTOBER 14, 1977

Crosby, along with Frank Sinatra and Elvis Presley, was tremendously influential on twentieth-century music. Among Bing's many accomplishments as an entertainer, he made the most popular recording ever—"White Christmas." He had 396 charted records (an extraordinary achievement), with thirty-eight number one hits. (The crooner sold well more than 300 million records.) He was the foremost movie box-office attraction in the United States from 1944 to 1948, and was among the top ten film stars fifteen times between 1934 and 1954. (He was nominated for Best Actor Oscars three times, winning the Academy Award for 1944's *Going My Way*.) On radio Crosby was a major attraction from 1931 to 1962, a longer span than any other such contender, appearing on roughly four thousand broadcasts. His annual Christmas TV specials in the 1960s and 1970s were always well received.

In the years since Bing's death, most people still retain an idealized (movie studio–created) image of the pipe-smoking, mellow crooner with the big ears who starred in all those *Road* movies with Bob Hope and Dorothy Lamour. This image survives despite dramatic Crosby family events and startling new revelations about high-living Bing that prove he was anything but square. For example, several of the superstar's four sons by his first marriage (to actress Dixie Lee) were at one time or another heavily alcoholic; two of the quartet committed suicide (Lindsay in 1959; Dennis in 1961), allegedly the result of accumulated emotional scars from growing up with the famed crooner. A third son (Gary, who died of cancer in 1995) wrote a damning *Daddy Dearest*–type book (1983's *Going My Own Way*)—his account of living in the "house of terror" with his rigid, demanding, and punishing father. (On the other hand, Phillip, the one survivor of the original Crosby children, insisted as late as 1999: "My dad was not the monster my lying brother [Gary] said he was." Concerning his brother's memoir, Phillip argued, "He wrote it out of greed. He wanted to make money and knew that humiliating our father and blackening his name was the only way he could do it."

In recent years, FBI files have revealed that Crosby, like Frank Sinatra and many others in Tinseltown, not only had a fascination with gangsters, but often hung with them. In Bing's case this included playing golf with underworld affiliates such as Jack "Machine Gun" McGurn, and inviting one or more members of crime families on deer hunting excursions. (One of Bing's Los Angeles neighbors in the late 1930s was the notorious Bugsy Siegel, the underworld figure involved in dirty dealings within the film industry.) Then, too, Bing's passion for gambling sometimes led him into contact with mobsters whether while touring their (after hours) night spots or making payoffs for lost wagers.

Crosby was born in Tacoma, Washington (but grew up in Spokane), the middle of seven children of Harry Lowe and Kate (Harrigan) Crosby. The father was a bookkeeper and the mother was a strict disciplinarian in the heavily Roman Catholic, Irish-American household. As a youngster, Harry received the nickname "Bingo" (which became "Bing") after a favorite character in a newspaper comic strip. As a youngster he excelled in sports (particularly swimming, football, and baseball) and in high school did well in oratory and played drums in a dance combo. In 1925 he quit Gonzales College (a Jesuit institution where he was a senior—pre-law) because he could earn decent money singing. He and a local friend/musician (Al Rinker) relocated to Los Angeles. By July 1926 Bing and Al were singing with Paul Whiteman and his Orchestra and accompanied that popular group on its cross-country engagements. It was during this period that five-foot, seven-inch bachelor Crosby really sowed his wild oats, leading to drunken escapades and brushes with the law.

Actually Crosby's first experience behind bars occurred during the summer of 1922 when he visited his older brother Everett in Portland, Oregon. After eating at a local Chinese restaurant, Bing and a pal left without paying. They spent the night in jail. By the time he was in Los Angeles in the mid-1920s, the future star was a heavy drinker who frequented the Prohibition-era speakeasies, partying with fellow musicians and available women. He got smashed almost nightly, but hardly ever missed a performance (or a mass). Now teamed with Al Rinker and Harry Barris as Whiteman's "Rhythm Boys," Crosby was based for long stretches in New York City. He continued getting plastered nightly, often at Harlem clubs. One of the troubadour's good pals in those days was gravel-voiced singer/trumpeter Louis Armstrong; it was Satchmo who introduced the crooner to marijuana, but it never appealed to Bing the way booze did.

When not passed out under a speakeasy table, Bing, in the late 1920s, often dated chorine Ginger Meehan. Eventually the good life began taking a toll on Crosby and his hard-living cronies. Despite Whiteman's warnings, however, the wild group refused to reform.

In November 1929 Whiteman and his crew were in Los Angeles to make the big-budgeted picture *The King of Jazz* (1930). The bandleader earmarked Crosby for a special role in the picture; he was to be solo vocalist for an elaborate production number. One night after rehearsal, Bing and the others attended a studio-sponsored party. A well-liquored Bing drove one of the partygoers back to the Hotel Roosevelt in Hollywood. As they approached the hotel, Crosby's vehicle smacked into another car, causing him and his passenger to be propelled over the windshield, ending up on the pavement. Bing was unscathed while the woman was bloodied and unconscious (but declared OK by the hotel physician). Crosby and the other driver (also drunk) landed in jail. Crosby was bailed out the next morning. A week later Bing arrived for the court date wearing a jaunty golfing outfit and a sarcastic attitude. He was sentenced to sixty days behind bars. With much conniving, Whiteman and the studio had the defendant transferred to a more congenial local jailhouse, and Bing was allowed to work (under police escort) at the studio each day and then return to his cell nightly. While these negotiations were being

The mature crooner, Bing Crosby. (Courtesy of JC Archives)

finalized, Whiteman gave the big production number solo to actor John Boles.

When Crosby was courting movie actress Dixie Lee, he downplayed his high-living ways. But after the couple wed in September 1930, his teenage bride was soon apprised of the full picture. Six months into their union, Dixie announced plans to divorce Crosby because of his drunken and carousing ways. These bad habits, in tandem with his heavy work schedule, meant she rarely saw him. Bing soon negotiated a truce. He promised to cut way back on his hard-playing lifestyle, and he did (although he never gave up on imbibing to some degree). Ironically, in later years, Dixie, stuck at home with her brood and a husband always at work, became a heavy drinker. She died of ovarian cancer in 1952.

Long before his first wife's passing, Bing had been quietly dating others. In the 1940s he was linked, among others, with actresses Joan Caulfield and Rhonda Fleming. After Dixie was gone, he squired Mary Murphy and the more established film personality Mona Freeman. Later, he was one of the older men in the life of Grace Kelly (with whom he costarred in 1954's *The Country Girl* and 1956's *High Society*). However, Bing kept returning to Texas-born starlet Kathryn Grant and it was with this twenty-three-year-old actress that the thirty-years-older Crosby eloped to Las Vegas in 1957. The couple had three children. Crosby had learned from the past—he was a far more attentive, warm-hearted dad to his new set of offspring.

Russell Crowe

[Russell Ira Crowe]
APRIL 7, 1964–

He earned screen fame playing ferociously intense characters: the avenging cop in *L.A. Confidential* (1997), the tobacco industry whistle-blower in *The Insider* (1999—for which he was Oscar-nominated), a beleaguered Imperial Roman officer in *The Gladiator* (2000—for which he won an Academy Award), and the schizophrenic math prodigy in *A Beautiful Mind* (2001—for which he won another Academy Award nomination). Off camera the rugged New Zealander preferred to relax on his ranch in the bush country outside of Sydney, Australia, or do a gig with his rock band (30 Odd Foot of Grunts) rather than play the conventional Hollywood game. A staunch, outspoken individualist, the macho star pushed his way through life on his own terms—which included being temperamental, rambunctious, and headstrong. As a pub crawler and aggressive flirt he enjoyed a string of increasingly high-profile romances.

Russell Ira Crowe, one-sixteenth Maori, was born in Wellington, New Zealand, in 1964, the younger son of Alex and Jocelyn Crowe. His parents were film set caterers and the family moved around a good deal in Russell's earlier years. When he was four, the Crowes were based in Sydney, Australia. When he was six—and still painfully shy—he made his acting debut on the Australian TV Series *Spyforce*. In 1978 the Crowes moved back to New Zealand where the parents ran a pub. By this time Russell, who began smoking cigarettes at age ten and was renowned for bluntly speaking his mind, had become interested in music and put on rock concerts at school. When he was seventeen, the guitarist quit the classrooms. As a professional musician he adopted the name Russ Le Roq and began the group Roman Antix, garbed in retro outfits. His recordings (including "I Want to Be Like Marlon Brando") remained at the bottom of the charts, but that hardly dampened his self-confidence. In between odd jobs (waiter, fruit picker, and the like) he appeared in stage musicals, including *The Rocky Horror Picture Show* where he was Dr. Frank N. Furter for two years. He had a serious romance at the time, but hard-living Crowe was not about to settle down in marriage.

At age ten Russell had lost a tooth in a rugby match; he was twenty-five when he finally had it replaced. Suddenly he got film work, including *The Crossing* and *Prisoner of the Sun* (both 1990). Recognized for his burgeoning talent, he was cast in the violent skinhead picture *Romper Stomper* (1992) as a nihilistic neo-Nazi. In complete contrast he played a gay plumber in *The Sum of Us* (1994). He and his *Crossing* colead Danielle Spencer had developed a serious relationship, but his career ambitions demanded that he remain footloose and their four-year romance ended.

Movie star Sharon Stone had appreciated hunky Crowe in *Romper Stomper* and campaigned for him to join her western *The Quick and the Dead* (1995). The outspoken New Zealander did not see eye to eye with costars Gene Hackman and Leonardo Di Caprio, leading to much on-set tension, as well as speculation of a romance between Stone and Crowe. For the thriller *Virtuosity* (1995), Russell played a computer-generated villain and his nasty characterization gave the dreary picture some bite. Small movies like *Rough Magic* (1995) were followed by the high-profile *L.A. Confidential* in which his hard-living, edgy character accurately reflected the off-camera actor. (As for his on-set demeanor, *Confidential*'s director, Curtis Hanson, said of his driven star: "Russell was relentless in his pursuit of the essence of the character. If that made him a pain in the a** sometimes, you live with it.")

For his lead part in *The Insider* the nearly six-foot Crowe—a chameleon who changed his look from picture to picture—gained nearly forty pounds and dyed his hair white (then decided to shave it and use a wig). By now the American public had taken notice of Russell but couldn't figure out this tequila-drinking actor who'd rather motorcycle across New Zealand than mingle with the Hollywood establishment. Always unpredictable, he escorted Jodie Foster to the Golden Globe Awards in early 2000, causing a lot of speculation, but then he appeared weeks later at the Oscars with his niece in tow.

Crowe, the sometimes churlish perfectionist, had gained an industry reputation as being temperamental, difficult, and prone to tantrums. In his own defense he insisted he was intense and passionate. On *The Gladiator*, for which he had to learn the art of sword fighting, he was highly argumentative over the state of the script and how the film was being put together. It furthered his roguish reputation. In November 1999, he was at the Saloon Bar in Coffs Harbor, Australia, chatting up some of the female customers, which upset their boyfriends. A scuffle arose that the participants took out onto the street. Later, individuals got hold of the bar's surveillance videotape and attempted to blackmail Russell. He took the matter to the police and the suspected extortionists were apprehended.

A convivial Russell Crowe greeting his public. (Photo by Albert L. Ortega)

While filming the thriller *Proof of Life* (2000) on some dangerous South American turf, Crowe embarked on a high-profile relationship with three-years-older costar Meg Ryan, then still married to (but mostly living apart from) actor Dennis Quaid. Not since the Richard Burton–Elizabeth Taylor sexcapades during the making of *Cleopatra* (1963) had the worldwide media had such a field day with the daily status of a high-profile couple. By year's end the movie had opened to lackluster business and the dream romance had fizzled. Crowe said, "I'm not in my twenties—I just can't drop all the things that drive me as a man." For some fans, this statement meant that the burly New Zealander refused to trade in his 560-acre Down Under farm for Hollywood glitter. Others insisted that it was Ryan who had broken off the romance as Crowe was too intense about marriage.

Thereafter the media briefly linked Crowe (a man generally guarded about his personal life) with singer/actress Courtney Love and actress Peta Wilson (TV's *La Femme Nikita*) and suggested that Crowe and Australian actress Nicole Kidman (then in the midst of her divorce from superstar Tom Cruise) had kindled a romance Down Under.

Never out of the news for long, in 2001 the FBI confirmed their investigation of a $13 million kidnapping threat by gangsters against Crowe. As such the actor had a contingent of bodyguards and FBI operatives at hand when he attended the Golden Globe and later Oscar Awards, the latter with ex-girlfriend Danielle Spencer as his date. Later that year Russell was professionally the center of attention for his sterling performance in the screen drama *A Beautiful Mind* (2001). Earning great praise for his impressive performance in this drama, Crowe received accolades from the critics and awards from the film industry. As part of his speech in accepting the Best Actor trophy at the British Academy Film Awards in February 2002 in London, the star recited a poem ("Sanctity" by Irish bard Patrick Kavanagh). At the postevent dinner at the Grosvenor House Hotel he learned that his poetry recitation had been deleted from the tape just made for delayed BBC-TV broadcast in order to meet the demands of a fixed time slot. The actor grew incensed, and, reportedly, had two of his bodyguards lead the show's director, Malcolm Gerrie, into an empty storage room at the hotel. There the outraged star told Gerrie exactly what he thought of his poetry reading being excised from the tape. This encounter of an unpleasant kind was catnip for the media and made headlines around the world. A few days later, however, a contrite Russell apologized to Gerrie, the BBC network, and so forth. This led several journalists/pundits to headline their published resolution of the disturbing confrontation as "Russell Eats Crowe After All."

As for his future, Crowe, the complicated, often withdrawn risk taker, insisted, "If I ever feel I'm in danger of losing my perspective about the business of acting, I can always go home to the farm [in Australia]. . . . These animals are my friends, and I enjoy spending time with them because they open my mind up again when the small world of show business threatens to close it down."

As to his persistent tough guy reputation, Crowe has said, "Somebody tags you as a bad boy, man, and that stays. The reality is that it's other people's fantasies and other people's agendas and that's what gets put in the newspapers."

James Dean

[James Byron Dean]

FEBRUARY 8, 1931–SEPTEMBER 30, 1955

Few actors receive Academy Award nominations, let alone two posthumous ones (for 1955's *East of Eden* and 1956's *Giant*). But then there was *nothing* usual about James Dean, who, decades after his brief life and only three lead movie roles, remains in the pantheon of cinema legends. Over the years almost as much has been written about charismatic Dean as about Marilyn Monroe or Elvis Presley, with whom he shares a unique cult status even today.

No one disputes Jimmy's extraordinary screen presence or his much-imitated mumbling, T-shirt-and-jeans acting style (which owed much to the earlier Montgomery Clift and Marlon Brando). But even now much remains in dispute regarding his private life, including whether he was homosexual, bisexual, or just plain sexual, sharing moments with whomever appealed to him when the mood struck him. The subject is made more complex by "new" revelations popping up in the ongoing stream of memoirs that abound with claims to having known Dean up close and personal. Whatever Dean's actual sexual orientation, especially once he was no longer subject to the casting couch, he refused to play by anyone's rules. In his own distinctive way Dean was one of Hollywood's most self-indulgent provocateurs, who thrived on being shocking.

Although born in Marion, Indiana, James Byron Dean moved as a youngster with his parents to Southern California where his father got a better-paying job. When his mother died in July 1940, nine-year-old Dean was shipped to Fairmount, Indiana, to live on a farm with his aunt and uncle. By the time Jimmy was in high school he had explored his growing interest in acting and had come under the influence of Reverend James A. DeWeerd. The latter became the sensitive youth's mentor and the two shared intimate moments. (This included the strange experience of Dean placing his hand inside the shrapnel wound cavity that DeWeerd had acquired while becoming a World

War II hero.) Dean countered his relationship with DeWeerd by pursuing a young female physical education teacher at Fairmount High.

Soon after he graduated high school in 1949, he moved back to Los Angeles where he enrolled at Santa Monica City College to study drama. He stayed with his father and his stepmother, but the situation was strained. The next year he transferred to UCLA and moved out of his family's place. By January 1951 he had appeared in a TV commercial and quit college.

Since he was always fanciful about telling the truth or sticking to the same story, there remains much conjecture about Dean's personal life during this period. Women have come forth who insisted they slept with him, while rumors arose that to survive financially and to get ahead in show business, he became a male hustler. He did meet a gay TV director with whom he lived in Los Angeles with the latter arranging acting jobs for Jimmy (including a bit in a film, 1951's *Fixed Bayonets*). To some friends, iconoclastic Dean was alternatively resentful of prostituting himself and at times amused, tender, or ambiguous about his gay liaisons.

Moving to New York in October 1951 to study stage acting, he struck up a romance with Elizabeth "Dizzy" Sheridan (later famous as Jerry Seinfeld's TV mom). However, his relationship with the bicoastal TV director, now back in Manhattan, continued. Later the free-spirited Dean shared an apartment with Dizzy and Bill Bast, the latter a platonic pal from Los Angeles. By August 1952 Jimmy was studying at the Actors Studio, doing a lot of TV work, and as of February 1954, appearing off-Broadway in Jean Genet's *The Immoralist*, in which he was cast as a homosexual Arab procurer.

By now there was a revolving door of emotional and physical relationships in the actor's life. His actor friend Jonathan (later John) Gilmore insisted that the often moody Jimmy was actually multisexual. Also, by now Dean had developed a fascination with motorcycles and fast cars, enjoyed wearing leather, and was gaining a reputation for his affinity to S & M male sex, as well as winning, using, and dropping women at whim.

By the spring of 1954 Dean was on the professional fast track. He had been signed to star in *East of Eden* (1955) and by that June was on the Warner Bros. soundstages making the drama. Eccentric Jimmy hung out with a group of night crawlers, friends, and hangers-on who joined him in his nocturnal chasing around town to offbeat clubs and other venues. Sometimes he bunked out for the night on a studio soundstage, other times he found romance on an adjacent set.

Italian-born Pier Angeli was making a picture on the lot and Dean promptly fell in love with the twenty-two-year-old. She was moody, mother-dominated, and had a dark side. Jimmy focused on winning this young (seemingly puritanical) beauty. The couple had sex together (which is more than Pier's past fiancée, actor Kirk Douglas, had done). However, Pier's mother denounced the romance because he wasn't Catholic. He offered to convert and to become less the rebel. Meanwhile, his advisors suggested he postpone marriage plans until his movie career took off and both of them were on an equal industry footing. Reputedly, Pier thought she might be pregnant and he asked her to elope with him to New York, but Angeli refused to go against her mother's wishes. Once in New York for TV work, Dean learned she was to wed her former boyfriend, singer/actor Vic Damone. That November the couple wed. Dean was heartbroken, but often it was difficult to distinguish between his posturing and his real feelings. (In 1971 the twice-married Angeli committed suicide.)

Back in Hollywood to film *Rebel Without a Cause* (1955), the increasingly hedonistic Jimmy appeared in public with Eartha Kitt and Vampira (TV host of horror movies), although Dean was prone, like other actors of the time, to play the game of being seen publicly with interesting female dates. On the *Rebel* set he chased around with costar Natalie Wood and developed a bond with sixteen-year-old actor Sal Mineo. (The latter insisted that nothing happened between the two because Sal was too shy and in awe of Dean.) Meanwhile, the star was seen frequently with close friend and hanger-on Jack Simmons.

Because of his growing popularity, Warner Bros. coped with most of Dean's strange ways, but when he began squiring a hard-living woman (who happened to be one-legged) around Tinseltown, executives wondered about the effects of his bizarre behavior on his career. Before long, he had turned his attention to a nineteen-year-old Swede, Lili Kardell, an aspiring actress. By now Hollywood was truly baffled by the chameleon-like Dean who made a conscious effort to defy polite behavior. One minute he was acting shy and quiet with his current "girlfriend" and the next he was being loud and off-the-wall with her successor. Meanwhile, gossip kept insisting that Dean was frequenting the gay, leather bar scene in Hollywood where S & M activity flourished. (Supposedly, Jimmy was known as the "human ashtray" because of his penchant for having men snuff out their cigarettes on his body.)

By the time Jimmy returned from Texas location work on *Giant* (1956), he was seen about town with young Scandinavian actress Ursula Andress. However, she couldn't cope with his sulkiness and moved on to actor John Derek. The unruly actor with the unsettling behavior was considering doing *Hamlet* on Broadway when he was killed in a fatal car crash near Cholame, California. His untimely death sealed Dean's reputation as a Hollywood bad boy, an intriguing young personality whose exploits would be constantly recounted—and embellished upon—for later generations.

Johnny Depp

[John Christopher Depp III]
JUNE 9, 1963–

Renowned for being publicity shy, antimedia, and queasy watching himself on screen, Johnny Depp is very much his own man. His creed has been, "I don't want to answer to anybody. I don't have to explain myself to a single soul on Earth. That's my reality." He gained a reputation as a chain-smoking provocateur with notorious tattoos plus cuts on his arms that mark important events. ("My body is my journal. It's a journal of skin.") The five-foot, ten-inch actor hid his handsomeness with a grunge look, and in some periods avoided baths or shampooing of his greasy hair (perhaps inspiring his self-created nickname "Mr. Stench"). Over the years, he proposed marriage to several celebrity girlfriends (including actresses Sherilyn Fenn, Winona Ryder, and Jennifer Grey; and supermodel Kate Moss), but their relationships always ended before any walk down the aisle.

In addition, antistar Depp displayed scant interest in making mainstream movies, could be difficult on the film set, and was usually guarded with the media. As the world grew to know, the eccentric soul functioned best away from the establishment's dictates, such as in his L.A. hideaway boasting a nine-foot replica of a rooster in the driveway. Sometimes he could be spotted playing with his band (P) at Los Angeles's Viper Room (which he partly owned) or dealing with the Parisian restaurant in which he was partners with Sean Penn. Johnny's résumé also included: (1) an enormous acting talent, (2) a redeeming sense of humor, and (3) much-publicized tangles with the law.

Johnny was born in 1963 in Owensboro, Kentucky, the fourth and final child of John Christopher Depp II (a city engineer) and his part-Cherokee wife, Betty Sue (a waitress). The family went through some very lean years, including when they moved to Miramar, Florida, in 1971. Johnny was a strange youngster, a frequent loner who emitted peculiar noises, dug a tunnel in the backyard in tribute to the TV show *Hogan's Heroes*, and had a strong fear of clowns and singer

Johnny Depp with his significant other, Vanessa Paradis. (Photo by Albert L. Ortega)

John Davidson. He also suffered through recurrent nightmares of being chased by TV sitcom player Alan Hale Jr. outfitted in his *Gilligan's Island* costumes. Depp learned to love music when his preacher uncle introduced him to gospel songs. When he was twelve his mother bought him a used electric guitar and he became obsessed with learning to play it. School did not particularly intrigue him. He had been smoking cigarettes since he was ten, and as a rebellious young teen he experimented early with sex and a wide variety of substance abuses. He formed his own rock band when he was thirteen, and briefly got into a cycle of reported vandalism and shoplifting. By the time he was fifteen, his parents had divorced and he was part of the musical group Flame, playing electric guitar and sometimes doing vocals.

Depp quit high school in his junior year and made music his life, playing with several garage bands. As a member of the Kids, he was part of the opening act for such bigger attractions as the Talking Heads. When he was twenty he wed Lori Anne Allison, five years his senior. (She was a musician related to a band member.) By 1983 the band had relocated to Los Angeles, but they soon split apart. Two years later, Johnny's marriage also fell apart. He took to living in a car shared with a friend while working odd jobs (construction worker, busboy). It was through actor Nicolas Cage, whom Depp's estranged wife was dating, that he was introduced to a talent agent, which led to a small role in *A Nightmare on Elm Street* (1984). To Johnny's amazement he found he liked acting. He took lessons and then signed on for the puerile sex comedy *Private Resort* (1985). He had guest roles on TV series and a brief part in *Platoon* (1986). From that picture came his trademark outfit that he wore for years: torn jeans, combat boots, leather jacket, forehead band, and tarnished (sometimes multiple) earrings in both ears.

When his acting career suddenly dried up, he worked with the Rock City Angels band and began drinking a lot. Johnny lost out on the lead of the new TV series *21 Jump Street* to Jeff Yagher. However, after the pilot aired in April 1987, the series managers wanted Depp to take over the assignment. He signed the long-term contract believing the show would likely be cancelled after its initial thirteen-week run. However, as Officer Tom Hanson, the baby-faced undercover cop, he and the program were a big hit. He chafed at being America's latest heartthrob. To show his independence, he had a large heart tattooed on his left arm with his mother's name through it. This was followed later by the head of an Indian chief on his right arm, honoring part of his heritage. In the late 1980s Depp and his then fiancée, actress Sherilyn Fenn, split and his new romance was with eighteen-year-old Winona Ryder, leading to his next arm tattoo— "Winona Forever."

His TV series filmed in Vancouver, British Columbia. In March 1989 Depp, who once had an argument with a law enforcer over a jaywalking ticket, made headlines when he was arrested on an assault charge against a security guard at a hotel where friends were lodged.

When the guard had refused him entrance and touched him, Depp allegedly wrestled the man to the floor and then reportedly spit in his face. Six months later when the case was heard in court, the actor was acquitted.

By the start of the fourth season of 21 *Jump Street* in September 1989, Depp, despite a $45,000 per episode paycheck, wanted his freedom. He was phased out of the series, and it was cancelled in May 1990. By now twenty-seven-year-old Johnny had two rented homes: one in the Hollywood Hills and another in Malibu.

Wanting to bury his sex symbol TV series image, Depp starred in *Cry-Baby* (1990), a parody of 1950s musicals. He and the picture were a hit. He next teamed with director Tim Burton for *Edward Scissorhands* (1990). Following this, *Arizona Dream* (1993) with Jerry Lewis was shot in the Grand Canyon state in 1991. That October Johnny was stopped by the police who clocked him driving 95 mph. The actor was "super courteous" to the police, and the case soon dropped out of the news. Carefully crafted performances in such unusual fare as *Benny & Joon* (1991), *What's Eating Gilbert Grape* (1993), and *Ed Wood* (1994) enhanced Johnny's Hollywood reputation.

After Depp and Winona Ryder broke up in the early 1990s, hard-partying Johnny adjusted his "Winona Forever" tattoo to read "Wino Forever." He became a twosome with celebrated skinny model Kate Moss who also became his fiancée. In mid-September of 1994—only days after he was in a fight at a London club—Depp was arrested (and spent a few hours in jail) for allegedly having trashed his posh suite at the East Side Manhattan hotel The Mark. Charged with two counts of fourth-degree criminal mischief, he later agreed to pay the $9,767.12 damages and the charges were dropped. Although there were suggestions that he may have been intoxicated at the time, his explanation for the much-hyped episode ranged from his chasing and throwing things at a "big cockroach" in the room to his pursuing a "huge rat" in the suite. (Rumors insisted that prior to the hotel room mayhem, a riled Kate Moss had been overheard to comment on her beau's "shortcoming.") Depp and Moss finally broke up in 1997.

In the later 1990s the still boyish-looking Depp began alternating between arty pictures (1998's *Fear and Loathing in Las Vegas*, 2001's

Blow) and mainstream entries (1999's *The Ninth Gate*, 2001's *From Hell*, 2002's *Once upon a Time in Mexico*). On the personal front, in June 1998 in Paris, Johnny met ten-years-younger French actress/singer Vanessa Paradis. They quickly became an item. Their first child, Lily-Rose, was born in May 1999. In April 2002, the couple's second child, Jack, was born. While still maintaining a house in Los Angeles, the reformed Depp, who battled his inner demons for years, lived quietly with Vanessa and their growing family in France. The family shared an apartment in Paris and had a farmhouse some forty minutes away from Saint-Tropez on the French Riviera.

Andy Dick

[Andy Dick]
DECEMBER 21, 1965–

The term *Hollywood bad boy* typically connotes a self-indulgent show business personality who is hunky, macho, and charming in a very masculine, if roguish, way. Not so with wispy Dick, a skinny stand-up, wild man comic filled with odd charms and sagging shoulders. This bespectacled entertainer looked more like a nerdy Woody Allen type than such lady killers as Don Johnson, Ben Affleck, or Russell Crowe. Andy's many idiosyncrasies included an inordinate preoccupation with vitamins, a dislike of eating apples with bare hands, a predilection for discussing in public his penis size (reputed to be large), a frequent desire to be naked while performing stand-up comedy, and a penchant for verbalizing in public forums his (past) bisexuality and his perpetual dilemma in choosing between the current women in his life. What he does share with generations of Tinseltown bad boys is a troubled past, including bouts of reputed substance abuse (including dropping acid, cocaine, and heroin), run-ins with the law, guest status at rehab clinics, and complex domestic relationships.

Dick was born in Charleston, South Carolina, in 1965, to an unwed mother who was pressured by her father to give up the child. Andy was adopted by Allen Dick (a navy submarine officer) and his wife, Sue. The family, which also included another adopted boy, was frequently on the move because of the father's constant reposting. As a result, military brat Andy lived part of his childhood in Connecticut, Pennsylvania, New York, Virginia, Georgia, and Yugoslavia. Most of his high school years were spent in Joliet, Illinois. As the skinny geek newcomer in a succession of classrooms, shy Andy (who's surname made him the butt of jokes) learned to be the class clown. At home both his parents were emotionally restrained; his father was both overly reserved and highly disciplined. It led a repressed, frightened Andy (who wet his bed until he was twelve) to harbor dreams of becoming the absolute opposite of his parents. (One rebellious burst of independence for this self-admitted "freaky loner" was a penchant for streaking through his neighborhood.) During his difficult maturation, Andy was sexually molested by a family friend. The traumatic experience "tweaked my brain and erased boundaries. . . ." His tough childhood impelled him to start smoking pot and drinking (tequila becoming his favorite beverage). These crutches helped him to be more outgoing.

After a few stabs at college (including Illinois Wesleyan University), he attempted improvisational comedy at Chicago's Second City where he had earlier taken classes. He became friendly with one of the cast regulars there, oversized comic Chris Farley. In 1986 Andy married a woman named Ivone and two years later their son, Lucas, was born. He supported his family mostly with odd jobs (waiter, food delivery). By then the Dicks were living in Los Angeles where he did stand-up comedy and bits in movies (1991's *For the Boys*). A friendship with Ben Stiller resulted in Andy becoming a regular on the TV sketch comedy series *The Ben Stiller Show* (1992–93). Although Andy and Ivone divorced in 1990, they continued to live together for a time for the sake of their child. By the mid-1990s he was living in the top half of a West Hollywood duplex with his new companion, Lina Sved (with whom he had two children: Jacob and Meg); downstairs Ivone and Lucas resided.

While Dick had roles in several movies (1994's *Reality Bites*, 1996's *The Cable Guy*), it was his TV series work that made him known to the public. A month after the short-lived new edition of *Get Smart*

The comedic Andy Dick of today.
(Photo by Albert L. Ortega)

died in February 1995, Andy returned as a cast regular on the sitcom *NewsRadio*. Seen as inept reporter Matthew Brock, his twittery character was a vital part of the ensemble comedy.

If transcendental meditation had helped substance-abusing Dick keep his bizarre life in relative check (a comparative term in show business where out-of-control is often the norm), things spiraled downward in late 1997. The death of his good pal Chris Farley from a drug overdose in December of that year left him stunned. In the midst of this chaos, Dick's relationship with Lina Sved was evaporating. The increasingly unpredictable Andy (a loose cannon who once bounced around *The Rosie O'Donnell Show* in his underwear proclaiming he was a Calvin Klein underwear model) phoned into *The Howard Stern Show* in 1998, rambling erratically about his bisexuality. Shortly thereafter, Lina, reportedly, convinced Andy he had to deal with his off-the-wall behavior. He entered Promises, a Malibu-based rehab center, where he spent weeks in treatment.

In May 1998 Andy had to cope with another shock. His *NewsRadio* castmate Phil Hartman was shot to death by his wife who then committed suicide. The tragedy left the future of the sitcom in peril. Dick was one of those who thought the show should be terminated; instead Jon Lovitz was hired to replace Hartman and a deeply distressed Dick was forced contractually to continue onward for another season.

After about five months of sobriety, a very distraught Dick returned to substance abuse and heavy partying (often at L.A.–area strip clubs). In March 1999 Andy accompanied his sitcom-actor pal David Strickland (*Suddenly Susan*) to Las Vegas. After a night of binge drinking as they made the rounds of (lap dance) clubs, the two separated in the pre-dawn hours. Strickland returned to his motel room and hanged himself. Andy was devastated by David's suicide. A few months later, in May 1999, NBC-TV announced that it was finally canceling *NewsRadio*. In the early A.M. of May 15, Andy, who was feeling no pain after a night of reported cocaine overindulgence, smashed his car into a utility pole (or tree) in Hollywood and then tried to flee on foot before being apprehended. He ended up in jail, a whimpering mess. He was released on $10,000 bail. Later, after pleading no contest in court to several charges that included drug possession, he was remanded for substance abuse treatment and placed on three years' probation. He returned to Promises and completed his program in June 1999. Once freed, the wacky comic returned to the world of show business by making an off-the-wall guest appearance on David Letterman's late night TV talk show.

Since then, with his focus on psychotherapy, special health diets, sober living, and chasing women, Andy pushed out of his professional rut to guest bits in feature films (2000's *Road Trip*) and animated sitcoms (2000's *Sammy*), entertaining on televised award programs, and touring the United States with his one-man show, a tribute in format to his idol, the late Andy Kaufman. He was showcased on MTV's sketch comedy program *The Andy Dick Show*, an intentionally demented weekly series that began in February 2001 and on which he was chief writer, director, and star. He also found time to perform with his band, The Bitches of the Century, as well as to make new movies (including 2001's *Zoolander* and 2002's *You'll Never Wiez in This Town Again*).

Kirk Douglas

[Issur Danielovitch Demsky]

DECEMBER 9, 1916–

With his cleft-chin, trademarked smirk, and distinctive timbre, this intense actor bucked life's odds for decades. He rose from abject poverty to movie superstardom, being three-time Oscar-nominated (1949's *Champion*, 1952's *The Bad and the Beautiful*, and 1956's *Lust for Life*) and winning an honorary Academy Award in 1996 for being a longtime creative/moral force in the movie industry. A recipient of the American Film Institute's Lifetime Achievement Award, this forceful personality who had authored several books (autobiographies, fiction, and children's literature) proved himself anew in the 1990s. In that decade he survived a near-fatal helicopter crash, got Bar Mitzvahed, endured a major stroke, and made a big-screen comeback in *Diamonds* (1999). For such a gutsy, driven man, it seemed that no obstacle was too big. However, over the years this twice-wed celebrity—who for a time was one of Hollywood's greatest playboys— just couldn't win out in the love game with most of the women in his life.

Douglas was born in 1916 in central New York, in Amsterdam. He was the middle of seven children and the only son of Russian Jewish immigrants Herschel (Harry) and Bryna (Sanglel) Danielovitch. The father was a peddler who, before deserting the family, changed their name to Demsky. Living a hand-to-mouth existence, the future star not only graduated from high school, but went on to college thanks to a scholarship and odd jobs. On campus he became adept at wrestling and developed a liking for the theater. In 1939 he won a scholarship to the American Academy of Dramatic Arts (AADA) in New York. One of his classmates was Betty Persky (later Lauren Bacall). She was a nice Jewish girl but, despite her crush on him and vice versa, their relationship was never consummated. After graduating from the academy, Douglas made his Broadway bow in 1941 (by which time he was renamed Kirk Douglas). In 1943 he joined the World War II navy. After being injured in seaboard duty, he was honorably discharged in 1944. Meanwhile, in November 1943 he wed

Diana Dill, a fellow AADA student. Their first child, Michael, was born in 1944 and their second son, Joel, came in 1947.

The handsome, muscular, and edgy Douglas soon turned to the movies. His first was *The Strange Loves of Martha Ivers* (1946). By the time of *Champion* (1949) and *Young Man with a Horn* (1950), he was a certified star. Already his marriage had fallen apart and his wife and two sons were now living back in Manhattan. As a bachelor about Tinseltown, Kirk was much in demand even before he and Diana finally divorced in 1951. Joan Crawford bedded him, but she was too overpowering for this new man about town. He was Rita Hayworth's mate briefly, but he found her sad and lonely. He explored romance with actress Patricia Neal, but that rising talent was bewitched by married Gary Cooper. Douglas became infatuated with movie star Evelyn Keyes (then divorcing filmmaker John Huston) but later claimed his entanglement with Keyes came undone when her studio boss, Columbia Pictures mogul Harry Cohn (who supposedly had his eye on Evelyn), barred Kirk from the lot.

Beautiful Gene Tierney, the star with the sexy overbite, found Douglas quite appealing, but the day he mentioned he had no plans to get married again, their affair fizzled. Douglas enjoyed a brief fling with worldly, older Marlene Dietrich, but she had more notches on her sex-escapade belt than Kirk did. For a time Douglas dated (and then lived with) the daughter of a wealthy Oklahoma oilman. She had emotional problems, however, not the least of which was her controlling, bigoted dad. Douglas, ambivalent about marrying her, resolved the stalemate when he caught her in bed with another man. While making a western, Kirk was introduced to S & M sex by one of his costars, but the short-lasting liaison left him emotionally numb. It seemed that Douglas, so insistent and focused on his acting career, just couldn't get beyond bedroom games in the swinging Hollywood of the early 1950s.

When Kirk made *The Story of Three Loves* (1953) at MGM, his costar in the multiepisode movie was Italian actress Pier Angeli, then under studio contract. Douglas was thirty-five (and now divorced), Angeli was nineteen, beautiful, and ambitious. When she left for filmmaking in Europe, Douglas found pictures he could make abroad. The excited suitor arrived in Rome, thrilled that he was about to reunite

Kirk Douglas (left) pointing out the facts to Ray Teal in *The Big Carnival* (aka *Ace in the Hole*; 1951). (Courtesy of JC Archives)

with his lady love, who would soon become his fiancée. He discovered that she, despite knowing that he was arriving, had gone off to Venice with her domineering mother to join other relatives. Douglas determinedly pursued her to the romantic city of canals, but once there he hardly had a moment alone with her as her family always seemed to be on hand.

While filming *The Juggler* (1953) in Israel, Kirk may have been dreaming about Pier who was somewhere on the Continent, but he managed to cement good international relationships with an eighteen-year-old local named Leah. They had a lark, but she was serving in the Israeli army and soon had to report back to duty.

Douglas returned to Rome with side trips to Paris as he began preparations to star in *Act of Love* (1954) in France and *Ulysses* (1954)

HOLLYWOOD BAD BOYS

in Italy. Ethereal Angeli proved as elusive as ever, blaming everything on the demands of MGM and her ever-present mama. Lovesick Kirk accepted the excuses, but he covered his bets by playing the field European-style. He encountered pretty Belgium-born Anne Buydens, who did public relations in the film business. Divorced but still emotionally attached to her ex-husband, she rejected Douglas's offer to do publicity for a picture he was starring in and producing. A romantic relationship developed, however, even though her former spouse appeared again in her life, and Kirk was still bemused over his invisible fiancée, Pier. Finally, on New Year's Eve 1953, Douglas and Angeli were set to rendezvous in Paris. To his surprise she actually showed up, but now Kirk, long the pursuer, suddenly realized he had lost interest in this frustrating romance. He called off the engagement, which caught Angeli off guard. Later, back in Hollywood, she tried to revive the relationship, to little avail.

In May 1954 Kirk wed Anne Buydens in Las Vegas. (They would have two sons: Peter in 1955 and Eric in 1958.) Douglas finally settled down to a steady family life.

As for Pier, she married singer-actor Vic Damone in November 1954. He had not been her first choice, as she had preferred Jimmy Dean whom she had encountered at Warner Bros., but her mother insisted she wed a Catholic. So eventually she accepted wedding Damone with whom she had had an affair before Dean arrived on the scene. Angeli and Damone had a son in 1955, but by 1958 she had filed for divorce, and in 1971 she committed suicide.

Robert Downey Jr.

[Robert John Downey Jr.]
APRIL 4, 1965–

One of Hollywood's most talented younger actors, he was Oscar-nominated for his sterling performance in *Chaplin* (1992). Sadly, Downey's promising screen career became overshadowed by his enormous drug and booze addictions, which caused him to be jailed repeatedly for failure to clean up his act. Until the mid-1990s Robert, who was more recently diagnosed with bipolar disorder, generally masked his drug habits by his acting proficiency on screen and by his facile charm off camera. That is not to say that Hollywood movers and shakers were unaware of his problems, but in their eyes his addictions were outweighed by his great talent. Nevertheless, this extremely able actor seemed emblematic, if at an extreme, of the drug problems affecting so many of his generation of Hollywood stars (such as Charlie Sheen, Christian Slater, and many others).

For compulsive, chain-smoking Downey, acting, even in superior vehicles like *True Believer* (1989), *Natural Born Killers* (1994), *Restoration* (1995), and *Wonder Boys* (2000), came second to his substance abuse. These dependencies shielded him against his nature, a temperament that made it difficult for him to deal with life's mundane aspects. Over years of accelerating drug usage, Downey evolved what he termed his "lizard brain," a state in which his mental and physical capacities became slaves to his overwhelming need to find the means of getting away from whatever he was then doing, score drugs, get himself high, and return to the previous activity—all within forty-five minutes.

He was born in Greenwich Village in New York City, the younger of two children (the other was sister Allison) of underground filmmaker Robert Downey Sr. and his actress wife, Elsie. In his chaotic early life he moved with the family frequently: within the city; to Woodstock, New York; to London (where Robert studied ballet); and back to Manhattan. Robert made his film debut at age five in his dad's offbeat movie *Pound* (1970). The boy played a puppy. The maverick father was part of the flower child generation and smoked pot. He and his wife agreed that there was nothing wrong with letting their kids do so also—after all, it was cute to see them toking away. (Explained Robert Jr.: "When my dad and I would do drugs together, it was like him trying to express his love for me in the only way he knew how.")

By 1977 the Downeys' marriage had collapsed. The teenager lived with his mother for a time, then moved to Southern California to be with his dad. He attended Santa Monica High School where he became pals with the likes of Ramon Estevez, the son of actor Martin Sheen. A precocious young man with little regard for conventional matters, Robert was bored by high school except for music and drama classes. Thus, he skipped school a lot. Eventually, with his father's approval, he quit his education in the eleventh grade and moved back to New York City.

To sustain himself while auditioning for parts in regional theater, he worked as a busboy, shoe salesman, and such. In the spring of 1983 he was cast in an off-Broadway play and that year made the screen drama *Firstborn* (1984). Also featured in the cast was actress Sarah Jessica Parker and they began a seven-year relationship. Along with actor pal Anthony Michael Hall, Downey auditioned for and became part of the cast of TV's *Saturday Night Live* (1985–86). By now he was not only hooked on alcohol and marijuana, but while making the TV miniseries *Mussolini: The Untold Story* (1985), he had experimented with cocaine as well. In *Less than Zero* (1987) twenty-one-year-old Robert played a wealthy, nihilistic Los Angeles drug addict. It was a case of art imitating reality. In 1988 his then agent confronted him about his addiction problems and Downey went into rehab. But after a few years, the actor was back to his old bad ways.

By the time of *Air America* (1990) with Mel Gibson, the talented Downey was caught in the dilemma of whether to continue with high-paying trash or hold out for artistic projects. He acknowledged, "I'm in a very precarious position now of having made a lot of money and not knowing its value. It's going to be very uncomfortable for me to stick to what I believe." Taking the high road he invested great research and energy into his performance as "The Little Tramp" in

1992's *Chaplin*. Next, he cowrote and was featured in *The Last Party* (1993), a quasi documentary about the Democratic and Republican national conventions. Buoyed by his recent work, Downey made additional quality movies (1993's *Short Cuts*) and fewer junk offerings (1994's *Hail Caesar*).

Robert also continued to battle substance abuse. While in a rehab program he met actress Deborah Falconer and six weeks thereafter, in May 1992, they married. Their son, Indio, was born in 1993. While his new family grounded him to a degree, Downey's addictive behavior still ruled him. On one occasion he was detained by the police when they found him naked in his car and flinging imaginary rodents out the car window. When he had bad cocaine seizures in spring 1995, he checked into rehab for the third time. Meanwhile, on screen he was seen that year in *Restoration*, *Richard III*, and *Home for the Holidays*.

By 1996 Downey was an exploding volcano. In June he was charged with driving under the influence in Malibu. Los Angeles County Sheriffs found heroin, cocaine, and an unloaded .357 magnum gun (with bullets in the glove compartment). While awaiting trial, in mid-July the actor wandered into his Malibu neighbors' unlocked home and was found zonked out on the empty bed belonging to the owners' eleven-year-old boy. (The family declined to press charges against Robert.) Recovering in the U.S.C. Medical Center's prisoner ward, the bizarre event made Downey a national joke. On July 18, L.A. County Municipal Court Judge Lawrence Mira ordered the actor (now down to 138 pounds from his normal 170-pound weight) into a full-time, supervised drug rehab program. Two days later Downey escaped from the facility through a window. Recaptured at a friend's house, he was placed in county jail for nine days and then sent to another lockdown rehab center. In September he pleaded no contest to both the felony drug possession charges and the misdemeanor charges of driving under the influence and possessing a concealed weapon. That November the defendant was sentenced to six additional months at a live-in treatment center, along with three years' probation and periodic drug tests. Twice during the next months he received temporary releases to host *Saturday Night Live* and to do a TV interview.

In 1997 Downey made, among other films, *Hugo Pool* with his father. Robert and his wife separated with Deborah gaining custody of their boy. When the actor missed mandatory drug testing, Judge Mira ordered that he now serve 180 days in the Los Angeles County jail. Five weeks later, Robert was permitted out to make the film *U.S. Marshals* (1998). Upon returning to county jail, in February 1998, the actor got into a disagreement with three other inmates and received a gash for his efforts. For protection, he was placed in solitary confinement. After a few days of furlough to finish the screen thriller *In Dreams* (1998), he was released from jail on March 31, 1998, and put into a four-month treatment program.

During 1999, in which he had three movie releases including *Bowfinger*, Downey acknowledged in court that June to having ignored in recent months his scheduled/required drug

A contemplative Robert Downey Jr. meeting the media. (Photo by Albert L. Ortega)

testing. Judge Mira sent the handcuffed celebrity to a tightly monitored rehab program. In August, at his sentencing, despite Robert's pleas not to be shipped to state prison, an unmoved Mira ordered the defendant to three years of incarceration. Receiving credit for 201 days already served, Downey was taken to North Kern State Prison in Delano, California. The press noted that with good behavior the prisoner might be released as early as November 2000.

Later in August 1999, Robert was transferred to the California Substance Abuse Treatment Facility and State Prison at Corcoran. He became inmate number P50522 and lived in Building F-1 with several cellmates. While incarcerated in this facility he was interviewed by several major publications, acknowledging that after the shock of being in prison, he had time to reassess his priorities. He also admitted that "The threat of prison has been eliminated for me. I know I can do time now." Thanks to his lawyers' appeal he was released from confinement in late summer 2000.

Not only was Downey now a free man, but he had the opportunity to see his son away from the prison setting. In addition, he'd been hired for several episodes of the TV series *Ally McBeal*. In his role as an attorney who comes to Boston and falls in love with the show's heroine, Robert's presence gave the show a big ratings boost and his performance was praised. (He later won a Golden Globe and was Emmy-nominated for the recurring part.)

Then on Thanksgiving weekend 2000 everything fell apart—again. Reportedly depressed about his estranged wife's divorce proceedings, he embarked on an alleged binge in Palm Springs that included visits to girlie bars, followed by the supposed use of drugs in his expensive hotel room. He was arrested on suspicion of possessing cocaine and methamphetamine, for being under the influence, and for committing a felony while out on bail. (The anonymous phone tip to police included a claim that Downey also had guns on the premises, but none were found.) The celebrity was released on bail the next morning, with a court date set for a month thereafter.

While awaiting the new hearing, Judge Mira ruled that Robert had served enough time for probation violations on his past drug convictions. When arraigned in Indio on the separate (Thanksgiving weekend) charges, the actor pleaded not guilty. While awaiting the court proceedings in 2001, Downey returned to his *Ally McBeal* chores. The quiet period broke when he was arrested again in April 2001, this time in Culver City on suspicion of being under the influence of a controlled substance. (Robert claimed to the police that he was on antidepressants and Valium to deal with the ongoing custody battle over his seven-year-old son.) Meanwhile, the actor and the TV series parted company. The court concluded that the Culver City brush with the law did not demand further jail time, especially since the defendant was already in a detox center where he was to spend six months.

In May 2001 the well-groomed, beleaguered star appeared in an Indio courtroom where, after the prosecution reduced their charges, he still pleaded not guilty. By that July he changed his pleas to no contest. This allowed him to take advantage of a new state proposition that mandated treatment *instead of* prison for many types of drug offenders. As such, Downey was sentenced to a year of live-in drug rehab and three years' probation. As part of his treatment at Malibu's Wavelengths rehab facility and of his probation, he was permitted to work in his profession if under supervision. His first such job was filming a music video in Los Angeles for the song "I Want Love," a single from Elton John's new CD. The tune could also be an anthem for the talented but troubled movie star who had spent decades searching for inner peace.

Chris Farley

[Christopher Crosby Farley]

FEBRUARY 15, 1964–DECEMBER 18, 1997

The twentieth century produced several successful rotund movie/TV comedians, ranging from Bud Abbott's partner Lou Costello to "The Great One," better known as Jackie Gleason. Many of these heavy-set comics had more in common than their girth. They often suffered tragedies, sometimes a quirk of bad health as in the relatively early death of comedic favorite John Candy, or in the instance of funster Roscoe "Fatty" Arbuckle, a lurid sex/death case that smashed his major Hollywood career in 1921, which led to his fatal heart attack in 1933. Still other oversized funny men cut short their show business success through deadly substance abuse. One classic example was hefty John Belushi who succumbed to a drug overdose in 1982. Another such instance was Farley, whose liquor, drug, and eating addictions abruptly ended his well-paid film and TV career in 1997.

Chris was born in 1964 in Madison, Wisconsin, the child of Thomas (a thriving businessman) and Mary Anne Farley. The youngster was the third of five offspring in this Catholic household. (Farley's younger brother Kevin would also become a comedian, costarring in the MTV series 2Gether, 2000, and featured in such films as 2001's Joe Dirt.) As a child Chris already had a weight problem (as did his father, who would eventually reach six hundred pounds). Typically taunted by classmates, Farley learned quickly the knack of making his peers laugh before they could insult him.

On the other hand, Farley's comedic posture did not sit well with the nuns at the Edgewood grade school he attended. When he moved on to Edgewood High School in 1978, he used his bulk to become a lineman on the Crusaders, the school's football team. As an upper-classman he was a party animal who craved the center of attention. Despite his seemingly lighthearted approach to life, his grade average was good enough for him to be accepted by Marquette University in Milwaukee. He majored in theater and communications at this Jesuit school. While he may have seemed a typical good-natured lout to some on the campus, Chris could be thoughtful and religious at times. He also had developed a strong interest in the performing arts.

After graduating from college in 1986, the next year he moved to Chicago where he joined the ImprovOlympic, the training ground for the famed Second City Troupe. Many of his role models (John Belushi and Bill Murray) had worked there and Farley wished to follow their success. By the fall of 1988 Chris was part of the Second City group, but not only was he impatient for quick recognition, his compulsive need to be always partying also had become more dominant.

Chris was recruited from the Second City Troupe by TV's *Saturday Night Live* and, in the fall of 1990, the five-foot, eight-inch talent joined the ensemble along with Adam Sandler and David Spade. Wasting no time, Farley made himself well-known that first season. He constructed a range of vulgar, perspiring characters that appeared on the show. (One of his trademark bits was dropping his trousers at the slightest provocation.) Matching his professional appetites were his personal cravings. Now having the cash to throw around—he was earning a six-figure salary—he began pursuing prostitutes as well as accelerating his substance abuse. His bad habits began intruding on his work and before long *SNL* producer and creator Lorne Michaels insisted that the out-of-control comic start drug rehab—or face the professional consequences. After three months in recovery, Farley returned to the TV show. Meanwhile the self-destructive twenty-something laugh maker displayed another side of himself by attending mass faithfully at St. Malachy's Church and working in their volunteer program for older individuals.

Before too long Chris's erratic behavior resurfaced, confirming to others that he was back to his excessive substance abuse. His unprofessional actions were becoming a liability to the mainstream TV show. Desperate for a remedy, the show asked comedian Tom Arnold, one of Chris's pals, to head an intervention. As a result Chris entered the Exodus Recovery Center in Los Angeles. By the time he finished his program there, the jokester seemed to have dealt with his drug abuse problem. However, his compulsive nature was still in overdrive regarding food and hookers. At the time he blamed a lot of his addictive behavior on the pressures of trying to be constantly funny on live TV.

Farley made his big-screen movie debut in 1992, playing a security guard in the hit picture *Wayne's World*. This led to *Coneheads* and *Wayne's World 2* (both 1993) and *Airheads* (1994). To many it seemed that Chris was now channeling all of his excess energy and needs into his professional life, but not doing much to balance out his private side with a healthy social life.

Like many before him on *Saturday Night Live* who had used the weekly show as a springboard for movie projects and greater fame, Farley felt he had outgrown the TV series. At the end of the 1994–95 season, the thirty-one-year-old left *SNL*. In *Tommy Boy* (1995), a crude comedic outing, the oversized Chris was paired with wispy comedian David Spade. Farley was paid $2 million for the lowbrow movie project, which grossed $32 million at the box office.

Now in Los Angeles to concentrate on his mushrooming screen career, Chris felt adrift in the sprawling city. To compensate for the voids in his life, he relied on drugs and alcohol, as well as his food and sex sprees. (Thanks to his binges his weight, at times, jumped to 350 pounds.) Cautioned by friends and fellow workers to get his life under control somehow, he, on the surface, refused to take their warnings seriously. Privately, he was seeking counsel from Father Michael Rocha at St. Monica's Church in Santa Monica, believing that prayers would bolster him during this torturous period.

While his life and health were falling apart, Farley reteamed with Spade for *Black Sheep* (1996), and then he was on his own—for a $6 million paycheck—in *Beverly Hills Ninja* (1997). With everything spinning out of control, he made stabs at recovery at an Atlanta, Georgia, rehab facility. After finishing *Almost Heroes* (1998) with Matthew Perry (who was also having substance abuse problems at the time), Farley flew to New York in late October 1997 to host an episode at his alma mater, *SNL*. Reportedly, the star was so frequently high on drink and such that an oxygen tank was kept just off camera in case Chris had an urgent need for medical assistance.

Upon leaving Manhattan, Chris entered a drug treatment center in Chicago, but before the end of October 1997 he had quit the facility and was back to his addictive ways. He devoted much of November in the Windy City to a menu of food, alcohol, drugs, and prostitutes—all in staggering quantities. He understood that he badly needed to drop some weight and get sober because of a pending film commitment. However, the huge-sized Farley couldn't curb his stupendous appetites.

Between making his customary rounds of Windy City venues, he would return to his skyscraper apartment to snort cocaine and so forth. In retrospect the account of his last days and nights seemed pathetic as the famous comic sought to hide his loneliness with strippers, party devotees, and an exotic dancer. The latter was with Chris during his last hours. Even she left him on the morning of the eighteenth, exhausted by their treks around town. When she left his apartment, he was crashed out on the floor; she assumed he was sleeping off his overindulgences. When his brother John stopped by the apartment that afternoon, however, he found Chris dead.

Farley's passing was an illustration of the dangers of living life too plentifully.

W. C. Fields

[William Claude Dukenfield]
JANUARY 29, 1880–DECEMBER 25, 1946

On camera this bulbous-nosed, raspy-voiced comedian played a rancorous tippler who had no use for the law, children, animals, or most people—he did make an exception for comely females. He was wonderful at physical comedy, doing exaggerated double takes whenever astounded by mankind's follies. Off camera, the cantankerous show business veteran was self-centered and greatly suspicious of his fellow man. He was a lifelong imbiber of liquor who kept a huge private stash of his favorite booze, ever fearful that Prohibition might return. So strong was his devotion to his libations that he refused to deal with his chronic alcoholism, the disease that eventually ended his career and his life.

An extremely private man, Fields kept many facts concerning his life—especially his youth—to himself. (He preferred to exaggerate and to create an Oliver Twist–like childhood.) He was born in 1880 in Philadelphia. His supposedly bad-tempered, liquor-guzzling father, James Lyden Dukenfield, was a Britisher who managed a pub and was later a fruit peddler. His mother, Kate (Felton) Dukenfield, would have four other children after William Claude. Rebelling against his conformist childhood, the boy was away from home for much of his young teens. As "Whitey, the Boy Wonder" he demonstrated his juggling ability and made his stage debut at age fourteen. Four years later he was successfully performing vaudeville in New York City.

In 1900 the comedian took his juggling act (in which he played a mute tramp) to London. Also that year he wed chorine Harriet Hughes. Their son, William Claude Jr., was born in 1904. Diametrically opposed on most everything in life, the mismatched couple separated months later. Despite his later reputation as a miser, the show business figure sent his family money. (The Catholic Hattie never would divorce her unreligious husband; but it did not stop him from several romantic liaisons over the years, the last being with supporting actress Carlotta Monti.)

W.C. was on Broadway in the *Ziegfeld Follies of 1915* and that year made his screen bow in the one-reel silent comedy *Pool Sharks*. After participating in several *Follies*, he later starred in the stage musical *Poppy* (1923) as irascible Prof. Eustace McGargle, a classic role he repeated on camera in *Sally of the Sawdust* (1925). It was the best of his silent films. His talkie debut was the short subject *The Golf Specialist* (1931), and then he turned to feature filmmaking at Paramount, typically cast as the curmudgeon (*If I Had a Million*, 1932; *International House*, 1934; *Poppy*, 1936) and often scripting his own pictures—under aliases (such as Charles Bogle). This inimitable talent became a big hit with the filmgoing public.

In 1936 tuberculosis and pneumonia forced Fields to spend nearly a year of recuperation away from the soundstages. Once again his physicians ordered him to stop drinking, but he, as always, refused. By the late 1930s the new Paramount studio regime determined that Fields's box-office value was outweighed by his constant drinking on the set, his excessive ad-libbing on camera, and his increasingly unpredictable behavior.

If Paramount had no further use for this alcoholic eccentric, the fifty-eight-year-old found a new venue of success on radio as the foil of ventriloquist Edgar Bergen and his dummy Charley McCarthy. Soon, at $150,000 a picture, Fields began an association with Universal Pictures in 1939's *You Can't Cheat an Honest Man* as the irascible (what else?) operator of a trouble-prone circus. The next year W.C. teamed with another dethroned movie legend, Mae West, in the comedic western *My Little Chickadee*. A teetotaler, West was badly upset by Fields's imbibing during production—not to mention his scene-stealing ways. The

The many faces of W. C. Fields.
(Courtesy of JC Archives)

movie was a hit so the studio forgave his drunkenness and misan-thropic behavior.

The great funster turned down a return to Broadway in the early 1940s because of increasingly poor health—he was now suffering the cumulative results of decades of heavy drinking. His last movies (including 1944's *Song of the Open Road*) were inconsequential and afforded him scant screen time because he was too ill to make extended on-camera appearances. By late December 1946, W.C. was a terminal patient at the chic Las Encinas Sanitarium in Pasadena, California. Because of his long-term substance abuse, there was little that could be done for the dying, persnickety movie star. One day when asked why he was suddenly reading the Bible, the screen giant snapped, "Looking for loopholes." But actually Fields did not believe in an afterlife. (It was W.C. who said once, "Most people have a feeling they're coming back to this life someway, somehow. But me, I know I'm only going through once.")

In death, the parsimonious Fields (who left an $800,000 estate) was eulogized by friends as a great artist. In fact, his pals placed an ad in the trade paper *Variety* lionizing him as "the most authentic humorist since Mark Twain." But W.C., despite his many foibles and self-absorption, knew that he had dissipated his rich talent and ill-spent much of his life in pursuit of booze. Thus, once, when asked how he would restructure his life if he could relive it, he had admitted, "I'd like to see how I would have made out without liquor."

Errol Flynn

[Errol Leslie Thomson Flynn]
JUNE 20, 1909–OCTOBER 14, 1959

At six feet, two inches, the 175-pound Flynn was the epitome of male magnificence. He was a superb cinema swashbuckler who was totally adept at screen romancing. Away from the soundstages, the hard-living star had an insatiable sexual drive that favored spicy young women but reportedly also included handsome young men (ranging from movie star Tyrone Power to male hustlers in Mexico).

In retrospect, devil-may-care Errol intuitively knew he would not reach old age. Thus he crowded so much carousing and drinking into his daily life that, when he expired at fifty, the coroner observed that he had the body of an elderly man. By then Flynn had experienced such an amazing array of adventures—including alleged spying for the Nazis in World War II—that in the retelling it *seems* fantasy.

Errol Leslie Thomson Flynn was born in 1909 in Hobart, the seaport capital of Tasmania. His randy dad was a marine biologist and his self-centered mother was preoccupied entertaining male friends. (Later, a bitter Flynn would say, "I have nothing good to say about her, so why expound on it?") When Errol was eleven, his sister Rosemary was born and the family relocated to the more cosmopolitan Sydney, Australia. (Eventually, Mrs. Flynn left her husband, departing for France to find romance elsewhere.) By seventeen, Errol had a reputation as a ladies' man and was known for being an exhibitionist. He'd also been tossed out of school. In New Guinea he failed as a civil servant. Later, Errol oversaw a copra plantation and prospected for gold. He and a pal bought a small schooner. They took a client, Dr. Herman Erben, through the waters of New Guinea on an expedition to film a travelogue. (It proved to be an undercover intelligence operation on behalf of Germany. It would be Nazi Erben who allegedly recruited Errol's help for the Third Reich during World War II.) Thereafter, while a slave trafficker, Errol got into a skirmish with natives and killed one, which necessitated a court hearing. The young man claimed self-defense and was acquitted.

Handsome Flynn had been filmed as part of the Erben expedition, and that led to his being cast in the Australian-made *In the Wake of the Bounty* (1933). This experience was followed by Errol's wanderings in Manila, Hong Kong, Ceylon, India, Marseilles, and on to England. At every port he enjoyed hair-raising adventures, romantic liaisons with exotic partners in and out of whorehouses, and heavy drinking bouts. Now broke, he found repertory work in Northampton, did a few plays on London's West End, and won a role in *Murder at Monte Carlo* (1935), a potboiler turned out by Warner Bros. at their British facilities. This resulted in the studio shipping him to Hollywood. During the crossing he met French-born actress Lily Damita who was returning to California to make movies. She was eight years his senior and proved helpful in introducing him to the right Tinseltown crowd. The mismatched duo wed in 1935, which did not curb his womanizing, including a fling with Hollywood-based Mexican actress Lupe Velez. Soon Flynn starred in *Captain Blood* (1935) and that paved the way for more romantic, swashbuckling roles. Meanwhile, Dr. Erben arrived in Hollywood, expounding his Third Reich propaganda that intrigued elitist Flynn.

With such hit features as *The Adventures of Robin Hood* (1938) Errol was a big success. Although married, he was still bedding a long list of women. Flynn felt more at ease in Mexico away from industry scrutiny. There he indulged his bisexual interests as well as his voyeurism. In the year Errol starred in *The Private Lives of Elizabeth and Essex* (1939) he purportedly had a clandestine romance with his soon-to-be screen-genre rival Tyrone Power, also then wed to a French actress.

Errol and his wife had one child, Sean, born in May 1941. By the next year he and Lily Damita had divorced. Because of health problems, Flynn, now a naturalized American citizen, was classified 4-F during World War II. This meant he was available to star in a variety of movies including 1942's *Gentleman Jim*. At his mansion on Mulholland Drive he hosted his buddies and his sexual conquests. One of the latter, aspiring actress Peggy LaRue Saterlee, he entertained on his yacht while docked at Catalina Island. She told her mother that he had seduced her. Since she was fifteen (albeit a mature-looking young woman), the parent contacted the Los Angeles district attorney. Flynn's lawyer blocked the charge, but cautioned Errol to be especially discreet henceforth.

However, the irrepressible Flynn lacked self-control. At a Bel Air party in 1942 he came to the aid of inebriated Betty Hansen. This led to their making love. She told her sister who informed the district attorney about the movie star and the seventeen-year-old "victim." The DA now prosecuted both rape charges. Rarely had such a case garnered such widespread attention—and this at the height of a global war. Thanks to the public's admiration for the playboy star and to legal craftiness, the credibility of both women was undermined. The jury found Flynn innocent. (If he had lost the case, Errol was ready to flee

Hollywood's premier swashbuckler, Errol Flynn. (Courtesy of JC Archives)

the United States by plane.) The courtroom testimony had revealed much about Errol's seduction scenario and led to the popularization of the expression "in like Flynn."

The trial also brought Errol his next wife, Nora Eddington, the eighteen-year-old daughter of a Los Angeles sheriff. (During the case she'd been working at the cigar counter in the L.A. County Hall of Justice.) They wed in summer 1943 and had two daughters, Deidre (1945) and Rory (1947). During the couple's rocky relationship he continued his philandering, including a romance with Argentina's Eva Peron, plus assorted trysts in Acapulco, Panama, and Jamaica (where he had purchased an estate). Nora and Errol finally split in 1949.

By 1950 Errol's hard-paced lifestyle had prematurely aged him, but he kept making pictures. On the western *Rocky Mountain* (1950) he met twenty-four-year-old blond actress Patrice Wymore and they soon married. (At the wedding reception abroad he was served with an arrest warrant for alleged recent intercourse with a sixteen-year-old, but the case was dismissed later.) In 1953 the couple had a child, Arnella. One of Errol's last solid movie roles was in *Too Much, Too Soon* (1958) playing his old friend, actor John Barrymore. While making that picture Flynn romanced fifteen-year-old Beverly Aadland although he was still a married man.

With Beverly, Errol made the tacky *Cuban Rebel Girls* (1959). A month after his fiftieth birthday he had a heart attack and was told he had a year to live. He turned to Beverly for comfort, but weeks later he died of another heart attack in Vancouver, British Columbia. Later, Aadland's mother sued Flynn's estate for $5 million, alleging he had debauched her daughter with his "perverted philosophy for wringing every pleasure out of life. . . ." The case was dismissed. But even if it had not, the profligate Flynn had been nearly broke when he died. Like his physical constitution, everything had been used up.

Mark Frechette

[Mark Frechette]

DECEMBER 4, 1947–SEPTEMBER 27, 1975

As part of the late 1960s counterculture many young Americans rebelled and dropped out of normal society, becoming pot-smoking hippies. One of the movement's many enthusiasts—and victims—was Frechette, a handsome twenty-year-old whom fate decreed to be in the right place at the wrong time one day in 1968. That event transformed the Adonis-like Mark into an overnight international movie "star." Tragically, it also led to his death in prison a few years later.

Of French-Canadian heritage, Mark grew up in upwardly mobile Fairfield, Connecticut. In his Roman Catholic household, he was one of four children. Once a good student, he grew restless during his junior high school years, and thereafter became disaffected with the establishment (especially after the assassination of President Kennedy). He quit school in his senior year, preferring to booze it up and get into difficulties. He met a girl named Betsy whom he wed after she became pregnant. They had a son, but the couple fought a lot and separated and then reunited. Betsy became pregnant again with a second son. However, there were constant battles about Mark's lack of a steady job and the couple was twice in trouble with the law for marijuana smoking. Finally she left with their two boys.

At loose ends, Mark was in the Boston area searching for some meaning in the mid-1960s. He happened across an article by Melvin Lyman, a self-proclaimed prophet, who had a small commune (the Fort Hill Community) in Roxbury, Massachusetts. Drawn to the strangely charismatic Lyman and his family of followers, Frechette became an enthusiastic disciple. Thereafter, Mark's biggest frustration was to find a proper way to thank Melvin. Then fate intervened.

While standing near a bus stop in downtown Boston where he often panhandled, he became absorbed watching a sailor and his combative date argue. Unexpectedly, a woman from a fourth-floor apartment above threw a flowerpot in the sailor's direction. This infuriated Frechette who raised his hand in anger at the lady, and shouted, "You motherf*****!"

Suddenly, Mark felt a hand on his shoulder. As he whipped around—expecting it to be a police officer—a stranger asked, "How old are you?" Mark said, "Twenty." "Ah," said the newcomer, "Twenty and angry." Soon the bewildered Frechette was being whisked off in a limousine. The man and his pretty young female companion told Mark they were representatives of Italian filmmaker Michelangelo Antonioni and had been scouring the United States for the right candidate to play the college revolutionary lead in the director's first American-made movie. The nearly six-foot-tall Mark was soon cast in *Zabriskie Point*. Blasé about the much-publicized opportunity, the novice's greatest joys in making the picture included the nearly $60,000 salary he earned (which he earmarked for Lyman's commune) and meeting costar Daria Halprin, a pretty teenage college dropout.

When *Zabriskie Point* was released in 1970 it was a box-office bust but Frechette had registered well on camera. Mark was indifferent to the movie's failure for he was now involved with Daria and had convinced her to join him at Lyman's Roxbury commune. When Frechette was offered a key role in *Uomini contro* [*Many Wars Ago*] (1970), he was reluctant to leave Daria and go on location to Yugoslavia. But the picture paid a $50,000 salary and he accepted, again turning his movie salary over to Lyman. Soon after Mark returned, a disaffected Daria left Mark and the commune. (She returned briefly to moviemaking and would be wed to actor Dennis Hopper in the mid-1970s.)

With no further movie offers, Mark remained with Lyman's group, doing menial tasks to earn his keep. One afternoon in late August 1973 while he and others of the family were watching the televised Watergate hearings, something snapped within Frechette. Suddenly he realized that it was time to change his life and that according to Lyman's doctrines such a transition could involve "physical violence on the lowest level." Eager to make a political statement, he set off with two other equally enraged men from the community. Their intention was to hold up a federally insured bank as a way of robbing President Nixon but not hurting others. Without a real plan—not even thinking to wear masks or to have an escape route—they marched into a local bank. They brandished half-loaded guns obtained from the commune. In the process of their botched attempt, one of the trio was shot dead by the police. For his criminal activity, Mark was sentenced to six-to-fifteen years at the medium-security Massachusetts Correctional Institution at Norfolk (about twenty-five miles southwest of Boston).

At MCI–Norfolk, the one-time movie star joined six hundred other prisoners. His "bible" in the tough new environment was Lyman's 1971 book *Mirror at the End of the Road*. To make time pass, he recruited for the commune among the inmates and undertook a weight-lifting regimen. Time passed behind bars. As he told a reporter in 1975, "The days are OK. It's just that they're so short. The nights are what get to you." It was in the dark of night that he had especially to protect himself against the deadly in-fighting among rival convict groups and to cope with being a constant target for homosexual rape. (According to a former inmate there, Frechette was molested many times.)

Early on the morning of September 27, 1975, Mark was found dead in the prison rec room/gym. A 160-pound weight bar lay across his throat. The official autopsy and investigation concluded that Frechette had apparently been lifting weights alone (which is unusual when one bench presses) and that the weight bar must have slipped out of his grasp and killed him. Friends of Frechette stated that Mark had been in a funk lately and had lost weight. They reasoned that perhaps, in a weakened moment, the equipment had slipped out of his grasp. Others, including his lawyer, suggested that Frechette's misadventure might have been a deliberate "reckless" deed. (Earlier, a court psychiatrist had warned that incarceration could trigger a deep depression in the defendant.) Still others argued that the handsome ex-actor might have been a victim of an angered prisoner whose sexual advances had been rebuffed by Frechette.

What was certain was that being discovered for the movies had done Mark Frechette no favor.

Clark Gable

[William Clark Gable]

FEBRUARY 1, 1901–NOVEMBER 16, 1960

Charisma and an oversized public image can compensate for much that is lacking in a screen lover's real-life attributes. Take, for example, Clark Gable, the six-foot, one-inch brash movie star. The legendary he-man had big ears, rotted teeth (when his badly capped ivories were replaced by dentures he still emitted a bad mouth odor), and smaller-than-usual sexual equipment. To make matters worse, Clark was of the no-nonsense sex school that usually didn't linger with his bed partner once the deed was done. Thus in his choice of sex mates, he much preferred prostitutes because "they go away and keep their mouths shut. The others stay around, want a bit of romance, movie lovemaking. I do not want to be the world's greatest lover."

So what made this Hollywood king so sexy off screen to so many notable beauties? As celluloid queen Joan Crawford—Gable's recurrent lover over two decades—described, "He wasn't a satisfying lover, I often tried to distract him from the bedroom. But he had more magnetism than any man on earth."

Clark was born in 1901 in Cadiz, Ohio. His mother died ten months after he was born. His gruff, tough father, Will, was a wildcatter, who chased from one oil site to another, leaving his baby son with relatives until he remarried in 1903 and settled in Hopedale, Ohio. The Kid, as the youngster was nicknamed, quit school at sixteen and worked in an Akron tire factory. Later, he was a tire salesman, a lumberjack, a telephone lineman, and (to please his father) an oil field worker. Meanwhile, between jobs he gained theatrical experience (at first as a handyman) in stock companies, for he had come to love acting (which his father thought was sissy work). He gravitated to a stock company in Astoria, Washington, where he met his first great love, a young actress named Franz Dorfler. But he traded her in for a Portland, Oregon, acting coach, Josephine Dillon, thirteen years his senior. When helpful Dillon relocated to Hollywood, Gable soon followed and they married in 1924.

Clark's first movie roles were walk-ons (1924's *White Man*). It was during this period that ambitious Gable reputedly had sexual relations with the homosexual William Haines, an MGM movie star. If so, it helped the newcomer's career. Switching to stage work, Clark generally courted the production's leading lady—usually years older than he. One such was forty-four-year-old Pauline Fredericks, who even paid to have his teeth recapped. Gable's possessive and interfering wife refused to let go of him until her wandering spouse became a Broadway success. This led to his starring in the West Coast production of *The Last Mile*. The part was engineered by wealthy Texas socialite Ria Langham, seventeen years Gable's senior. Following his divorce from Dillon, Gable wed his new mentor in mid-1931.

Gable was soon signed to an MGM contract at $650 a week. Among his several 1931 releases was *Dance, Fools, Dance*, the first of eight features with Joan Crawford with whom he began an affair, despite each of them being married. However, studio boss Louis B. Mayer, worrying about his two stars' reputations, forced the duo apart (at least for a time). When Clark overtly took up with Joan again, the MGM mogul shipped his misbehaving leading man off to Columbia Pictures to make *It Happened One Night* (1934). To everyone's amazement, the screwball comedy won several Oscars including one for Gable.

Over the years, when Clark had drunk driving accidents, the studio kept it from public scrutiny. The damage control was more difficult, however, when he went on location to Mount Baker, Washington, to make *Call of the Wild* (1935). Gable became so giddily in love with costar Loretta Young that the production suffered expensive delays as he wooed her. Later, a pregnant Young created an elaborate ruse so that when their baby (Judy) was born, she could pretend she had adopted an orphaned girl. (Young did not publicly acknowledge the truth about her daughter's parentage until near the end of her own life in 2000.) Meanwhile Gable earned another Oscar bid for *Mutiny on the Bounty* (1935).

His drinking/hunting cronies remained firm friends, but women tumbled rapidly in and out of Clark's life (ranging from movie star Merle Oberon to rising actress Virginia Grey). Gable had worked with

Jack Oakie (left) observes a romantic moment between Clark Gable and Loretta Young in *Call of the Wild* (1935). (Courtesy of JC Archives)

self-willed actress Carole Lombard in *No Man of Her Own* (1932). She was then married and found Gable's flirtations humorous—even purchasing a ham that she labeled with Clark's name, telling friends, "I'm one costar he did not seduce." However, by 1933 Carole was divorced, and Clark and Ria separated in 1935. The two movie stars constantly ran into each other at Hollywood events and were an item by 1936. Lombard was drawn by Clark's unaffected manliness and he was intrigued by her good-humored unpretentiousness and her indulgence of his love of fishing and hunting. Days after Clark's divorce from Ria in 1939, he and Lombard wed. It was also the year he reached his career apex in *Gone with the Wind* (1939).

Although Gable adored Lombard tremendously, he was too self-indulgent to abandon his flings with minor actresses, prostitutes, and available socialites. In 1942, with America in World War II, he sent his wife on a bond-selling tour that he was supposed to attend. En route home, she was killed in a plane crash and Gable (who had been out philandering that tragic night) went into mourning, seeking comfort from Joan Crawford and from his young new studio costar Lana Turner. He joined the U.S. Army Air Corps, and, still full of guilt over Carole's passing, embarked on death-defying missions.

His war experiences aged Gable, but once back in Hollywood he was still the restless flirt romancing former model Anita Colby, socialite Dolly O'Brien, heiress Millicent Rogers, and starlet Nancy Davis (the future Mrs. Ronald Reagan). He toyed with movie goddess Paulette Goddard, reveled in earthy Ava Gardner, and while on a drunken binge in December 1949, wed Lady Sylvia Ashley, the widow of swashbuckling star Douglas Fairbanks Sr. The nuptials devastated actress Virginia Grey who everyone thought would become the next Mrs. Gable. When Gable's titled spouse divorced him (for a healthy settlement) in mid-1951, he was already again cavorting with Ava Gardner.

By the time Clark went to Africa to make *Mogambo* (1953) with Ava, she was unhappily wed to Frank Sinatra. On location he turned to the film's third star, twenty-four-year-old Grace Kelly, a soon-to-be Oscar winner with a penchant for older movie icons. They read poetry together and made love in the bush. The romance continued back in Hollywood, but he refused to be tamed.

As of the mid-1950s Gable had left MGM to freelance in more tough-guy roles. After a fling with Susan Hayward, his *Soldier of Fortune* (1955) colead, he married Kay Williams Spreckels, a one-time MGM contractee and a Carole Lombard look-alike. Three months after their marriage she suffered a miscarriage. Days after finishing *The Misfits* (1961), Gable suffered a fatal heart attack. Four months later Kay gave birth to their son, John Clark, who later dabbled in screen acting and race car driving. But there never was another legend like Clark Gable.

John Gilbert

[John Cecil Pringle]

JULY 10, 1895–JANUARY 9, 1936

In Hollywood there is nothing sadder than to witness a box-office magnet whose career is damaged by changing times. And when that movie star had once been a major movie matinee idol, the downfall is all the more poignant. Such was the fate of Gilbert, whose decline was attributed to (1) the coming of sound movies and his "weak" speaking voice, (2) the hatred of MGM studio boss Louis B. Mayer for his once-prized contractee, and (3) the declining star's escalating alcoholism and accompanying temperamental behavior on the sound-stages during the 1930s. All three were contributing factors, but the most crushing blow was that the once jaunty star had lost his appealing self-confidence and rakishness.

Born John Cecil Pringle in Logan, Utah, in 1895 (some sources list 1897), he was the son of a touring stock-company performer (Ida Adair), but never knew his father. As a baby, he was sometimes utilized in his mother's stage offerings. When he was fourteen, his uncaring mother passed away. By then he was long used to being on his own, often surviving on the streets by eating refuse from garbage cans.

With his wretched youth in the past, Gilbert followed his aspiration to be in Hollywood films. He began working at Triangle Pictures, initially in walk-on parts. He was noticeable in William S. Hart's sagebrush entry *Hell's Hinges* (1916), and by the next year—using the screen name of Jack Gilbert—he was the lead actor of *The Princess of the Dark* (1917). Let go by Triangle in 1918, he worked for lower-echelon lots. That same year, in August, he wed movie extra Olivia Burwell.

Gilbert pushed on in the industry, especially drawn to scriptwriting and directing. Next, he negotiated a deal to helm features on the East Coast, with Hope Hampton to star. When the first entry (1921's *Love's Penalty*) failed, he hastened back to Hollywood where he accepted a three-year (1921–24) acting pact at Fox Films. By the time of *Cameo Kirby* (1923) he was billed as John Gilbert and had become popular with filmgoers.

The rising actor and his wife (Olivia) had been living apart for some time when they divorced in 1921. That same year he married screen actress Leatrice Joy. Their union was tempestuous (due mostly to her career doing better than his) and in August 1924 she filed for divorce, noting his foul temper and drinking. (Gilbert had begun imbibing seriously in 1915, an escapist habit that remained with him till death.) The Gilberts' daughter (Leatrice Joy) was born weeks later. The couple's split was finalized in mid-1926.

At the newly created Metro-Goldwyn Mayer, Gilbert was the profligate prince in *The Merry Widow* (1925) and had a great success with the World War I saga *The Big Parade* (1925). He was a major star by the time of *Flesh and the Devil* (1927), the first of his pictures with Swedish import Greta Garbo. While many sources question the depth of Gilbert's off-screen relationship with Garbo, the media coverage of their "love" ignited their box-office appeal. John was now Tinseltown's highest-paid star, earning $10,000 weekly. But he was not that big that he couldn't be locked up in the newly constructed Beverly Hills jail. One night in April 1927 he had marched into the station and demanded that the police arrest a particular person (although he was too inebriated to state just who). When the officers balked, he brandished a revolver. The cops told him to go home. He insisted he "go to jail." He was sentenced to ten days for disturbing the peace, but was released after twenty-three hours behind bars.

In 1929 John made his talkie-film bow in *The Hollywood Revue of 1929*. He and Norma Shearer burlesqued the balcony scene from *Romeo and Juliet*. Gilbert's movements were stilted and he displayed a weak timbre to his voice. *His Glorious Night* (1929) and *Redemption* (1930) were the death knell for his career. While his professional life was shattering, he wed stage star Ina Claire in May 1929. Long before the pair divorced in August 1931, the union had soured. In the meantime, Gilbert was involved in another high-profile "incident." Writer Jim Tully had penned a vitriolic magazine piece disparaging

John Gilbert with his bride-to-be, actress Virginia Bruce, by the swimming pool at his Beverly Hills mansion in 1932. (Courtesy of JC Archives)

Gilbert's screen acumen. In February 1930 the two men happened to be at the Hollywood Brown Derby at the same time. A fistfight erupted, and Gilbert was knocked unconscious.

Before his screen career had begun fizzling, Gilbert had won a new MGM agreement at $250,000 a picture. Now the studio sought, unsuccessfully, to buy out his pact. Contrary to legend, he had not entirely lost his touch and was more than up to playing the villainous chauffeur in the little-seen *Downstairs* (1932), based on an old script of his. His costar was beautiful, twenty-one-year-old MGM actress Virginia Bruce whom he wed in 1932. Their daughter (Susan Ann) was born the next year, but by 1934 the mismatched couple had divorced.

Greta Garbo insisted that Gilbert play opposite her in *Queen Christina* (1933), despite his MGM contract having expired. He looked tired and ill at ease and once the costume film was completed he left the lot forever. Columbia Pictures hired John—at cut rates—for a secondary role as a disenchanted, drunk writer in *The Captain Hates the Sea* (1934). When the petulant star proved to be a bother on the set, Gilbert was washed up in Hollywood.

Gilbert's final years reflected the cruelty of the film business. By now screen siren Marlene Dietrich was trying to save the ex-matinee idol. For several months he had complained of chest pains and had even collapsed while swimming in his pool. Six weeks thereafter—on January 8, 1936—he fell ill. The next day he had a major heart attack and could not be revived. (Some sources insist that Dietrich was in bed with Gilbert at the time he died but that she left hurriedly before the media arrived on the scene.)

Such was the rise and fall of a once great movie star.

Kelsey Grammer

[Allen Kelsey Grammer]

FEBRUARY 21, 1955–

On television, he led a charmed life as psychiatrist Dr. Frasier Crane, first playing the pompous fussbudget on *Cheers* (1984–93) and then on his own equally popular sitcom, *Frasier* (1993–   ). In fall 2001 Grammer signed a new two-year contract providing him a whopping $1.6 million per *Frasier* episode, making him television's highest-paid star (and that did not include income from episodes already in syndication, or from other creative ventures). Lucky guy . . . or was he? In his private life, Kelsey endured more real-life tragedy and drama than any soap opera could concoct for one of its characters.

He was born in 1955 on St. Thomas (one of the American Virgin Islands), the first of two children of Allen Grammer (a part-time music teacher, coffee shop owner, and, later, bar and grill proprietor) and Sally (Cranmer) Grammer. When the future star was two years old his parents divorced, resulting in Sally moving with her son and daughter (Karen) to her parents' home in Colonia, New Jersey. The boy became very attached to his grandfather Gordon. In 1966 the now-retired Gordon relocated his clan to Pompano Beach, Florida. Soon thereafter he died, an event that greatly affected the youngster. As a result, the emotionally burdened Grammer felt an overwhelming responsibility to be a caregiver for the three generations of women in the household. The summer after Gordon's death, Grammer and his sister visited their dad on St. Thomas—their first reunion in about six years. Two years later Allen Grammer was shot to death outside of his home by a crazed assailant.

If these two tragedies were not enough, in July 1975 Kelsey's sister, Karen, then living in Colorado Springs, Colorado, was abducted, raped, and murdered by three teenage boys. Grammer became guilt ridden, blaming himself that he had not somehow protected her from this horror. Adding to the cumulative calamities, in 1980 two of Grammer's half-brothers (from his dad's second marriage) died while scuba diving in the waters off St. Thomas.

During high school Grammer had found it emotionally rewarding to be in class plays and that set his career path. He was accepted into the prestigious Juilliard School in New York City. While his scholarship paid for his tuition, finding odd jobs to cover room and board was tough. In the classroom Grammer, much the loner, proved contentious and was asked to leave the school. Later he was hired to join the Old Globe Theater Company in San Diego, California. He remained there for nearly three years. His best friend at the time was his dog, Goose—given to him by a girlfriend who later committed suicide when the couple broke up—and his favorite hobby was riding his motorcycle. Later, back on the East Coast, six-foot, two-inch Kelsey Grammer (his chosen stage name) joined a production of *Othello*, eventually playing the role of Cassio on Broadway in 1982. Also in May of that year, he wed Broadway dancer Doreen Alderman. Their daughter was born in 1983. Almost from the start, the union was stormy, and finally they divorced in 1990.

When Kelsey auditioned for *Cheers* (then about to start its third TV season in fall 1984), the producers planned to use the character of erudite, self-focused Dr. Frasier Crane for only seven episodes. However, Grammer proved so successful as the pretentious but affable therapist, that he became a program regular. Meanwhile, in December 1984 Grammer and his wife, Alderman, split. Now living in Venice Beach, California, the actor began actively dating—usually troubled relationships—and badly abusing alcohol and drugs. In July 1987 he was arrested in Los Angeles for driving under the influence of alcohol. As a first-time offender, he was given probation, required to do ten days of community service, and ordered into rehab. After ten days in the program, however, he quit the recovery regimen. In April 1988 he was arrested for possession of one-quarter gram of cocaine. The popular actor was again ordered into rehab, and when he failed to comply or to keep assorted court appearances, he was eventually sentenced to a month behind bars in 1990, but was released early because of the jail's overcrowding. (Also during 1988 his beloved Goose disappeared, along with his then girlfriend, and the pet never returned.)

In September 1992 thirty-seven-year-old Kelsey wed former exotic dancer Leigh-Anne Cshuany, fourteen years his junior. The ill-fated match, full of alleged tremendous abuse on her part as well as self-acknowledged obsessive behavior by Grammer, finally ended in divorce in June 1993. That fall *Frasier* debuted to acclaim (leading to the first of several Emmys for the star). Riding a professional crest (which included such other projects as the telefeature *The Innocent*, 1994), Kelsey was in a constant heavy partying mode. He was still engulfed in difficult romantic relationships, including the situation of having a love child in 1992 by one girlfriend while he was living with another woman.

In 1994 his current live-in companion was twenty-eight-year-old blond model Tammi Alexander. Reportedly, at her urging, he'd dieted to control his ballooning weight, tried to control his substance abuse, and thought of converting to Catholicism so they could someday wed in the Catholic Church. In spring 1994 he proposed to Tammi in front of a studio audience at a *Frasier* taping and she said yes. Belatedly, he learned that the shapely Tammi had a colorful past, but the lovestruck Kelsey "forgave" her.

As 1994 progressed, Grammer made headlines again, this time on allegations that in the summer of 1993 he supposedly had had sexual relations with a fifteen-year-old babysitter (for his nine-year-old daughter, Spencer) while he was on vacation in New Jersey. The plaintiff's parents claimed they had discovered the affair when they listened to supposedly X-rated phone messages he had left for their teenager. Law enforcers in New Jersey and Arizona (where other incidents of wrongdoing between Grammer and the teen purportedly occurred) investigated, all accompanied by much tabloid hype. Eventually the Arizona authorities deferred to whatever disposition their New Jersey counterparts made in the high-profile proceedings. In a closed hearing in February 1995 the Somerset County grand jury chose not to indict the defendant on criminal charges.

Also in 1995, Grammer wrote his cathartic autobiography, *So Far*, telling of his chaotic life and disappointing relationships but insisting that he still considered himself "to be one of the luckiest men alive," thanks to his relationship with Tammi Alexander. However, by November 1995 Kelsey and Tammi had broken up, reportedly because he announced to her that he felt that marriage would restrict his freedom to have fun.

The unending "good times" for Kelsey stopped in 1996 on September 21. While driving near his Agoura Hills, California, home, he lost control of his red Dodge Viper and the $60,000 vehicle flipped over. Bruised and cut but not seriously injured, the celebrity was charged by the police with the misdemeanor of driving with an expired license. (There was insufficient evidence to charge him with driving while under the influence.) A few days after the accident, thanks to friends' intervention, the actor checked into the Betty Ford Center in Rancho Mirage, California. Later in the fall, having completed a one-month program at the celebrity facility, Kelsey returned to his show and was the subject of a Friars Roast that November.

Back to work, Grammer continued dating blond Camille Donatacci, a former *Playboy* model, who had been one of those to urge him to deal with his substance abuse. On August 2, 1996, Grammer wed the fourteen-years-younger Camille. (Later she gained recognition crusading for IBS—irritable bowel syndrome—of which she was a sufferer. Because of her ailment the couple turned to having a child through a surrogate mother. Born on October 24, 2001, the baby girl was named Mason Olivia Grammer.)

Apparently having turned over a new leaf after decades of wild partying and chasing his personal demons, Grammer claims to be "an eternal optimist. Along with personal tragedies, I've had success. I don't regret any of the sadness."

Hugh Grant

[Hugh John Mungo Grant]

SEPTEMBER 9, 1960–

On screen this British charmer gained international recognition in *Four Weddings and a Funeral* (1994) playing the slightly flustered, cheeky Englishman who had difficulty with long-term romantic relationships. Midst his five 1995 features, versatile Grant was the cruel stage director in *An Awfully Big Adventure*, one of the ensemble in Jane Austen's *Sense and Sensibility*, and the hem-hawing mapmaker in *The Englishman Who Went Up a Hill but Came Down a Mountain*. That same year London's *Empire* magazine named the handsome six-foot, one-inch actor one of the "100 Sexiest Stars in Film History."

If on camera Hugh was typed as the clean-cut Brit with the fluttering eyes and the boyish mop of hair, his image changed dramatically in the early A.M. of June 27, 1995.

Hugh John Mungo Grant was born in London, England, the second son of James Grant (carpet salesman; artist) and his wife Fynvola (a primary-school teacher), and grew up in the suburb of Chiswick. He attended London's Latymer School. While there, his interest in an acting career flourished. At Oxford University Grant focused on English literature, but he remained fascinated with the stage. He began modestly in repertory theater, then branched out with a satirical comedy sketch group (The Jockeys of Norfolk). In 1982 he made his screen debut in *Privileged* and thereafter alternated between TV work (such as the 1986 series *Ladies in Charge*) and movies (1987's *Maurice*). While playing Lord Byron in the Spanish-made *Remando al viento* (1987), he met actress/dancer Elizabeth Hurley. Hugh and the five-years-younger beauty fell in love, a romance that endured career separations but somehow never led to marriage.

Hugh's first American-made movie was *Nine Months* (1995) in which he costarred with Julianne Moore and scene-stealing Tom Arnold (who became his partying buddy). The comedy was scheduled to open July 12, 1995. In June he arrived in Los Angeles to undertake the publicity chores required of a star making more than $4 million per picture.

On Monday evening, June 26, 1995, having had the day much to himself, Hugh dined with *Nine Months* film director Chris Columbus. After a jovial dinner at the Matsuhisa restaurant, the two parted around 12:30 A.M. About a half hour later, Hugh was driving his new white BMW 325i car along Sunset Boulevard near Courtney Avenue, a tenderloin district favored by street prostitutes. As the vehicle cruised slowly down the street, it was spotted by two LAPD undercover vice officers who saw its driver motioning to an African American woman on the street who then got into the passenger's seat. The auto drove off and soon was parked on a Hollywood side street (Hawthorne Avenue).

As the cops approached the stationary BMW—one on each side of the vehicle—they shined their flashlights inside. According to their report a "lewd act" was in progress at 1:30 A.M. in the front seat in which the man had his trouser pants unzipped and was seated with his thighs spread apart. The alleged oral sex situation interrupted, the police ordered the two out of the car. The male reputedly admitted to having paid $60 for services to be rendered by the female (Divine Brown—born in Texas in 1969 as Estelle Marie Thompson). Before the handcuffed offenders reached the Hollywood precinct, the police officers had become aware that the male was English actor Grant, although Divine claimed not to have known his identity—he supposedly told her his name was "Larry." The two were booked for a misdemeanor lewd act and on suspicion that Brown was a prostitute. When their mug shots (which would soon appear everywhere) were taken, Grant wore a sheepish, grim look, while Divine, her arms crossed over her bare midriff, bore an almost defiant appearance. Before Grant was released on his own recognizance without having to post the $250 bail, he phoned girlfriend Hurley to explain the embarrassing situation.

By Wednesday, June 28, the scandal was news worldwide and so was Grant's public apology: "Last night I did something completely insane. I have hurt people I love and embarrassed people I work with. For both things I am more sorry than I can say." Aghast at his now tarnished image, Hugh went into retreat at his brother James's New York apartment, while Hurley—then in London to launch her post as Estée Lauder's new fragrance spokesmodel—found herself besieged by the press. Later she issued a statement: "I am still bewildered and saddened by recent events and have not been in a fit state to make any decision about the future. For years I have turned to Hugh for help in difficult times and so now, even though my family and friends have been very kind, I am very much alone." (The *New York Daily News* tagged their June 30, 1995, article on Hurley's ticklish situation as "It's Hugh-miliating.")

While Hugh was retaining celebrity attorney Howard Weitzman, Divine Brown was informing the British tabloid *News of the World* that the entire situation could have been avoided had her celebrity customer paid $40 more to secure a motel room. Meanwhile, in Hollywood, Twentieth Century-Fox speculated about what effect this unexpected incident would have on *Nine Months*.

In the following days a badly shaken Grant jetted between England, New York, and Los Angeles, trying to restore his badly dented relationship with Hurley, console and be consoled by his family, and cope with the media onslaught. Deciding to face the public, Hugh arrived at the NBC-TV studios in Burbank, California, on Monday July 10, 1995, to appear on *Late Night with Jay Leno*. When the guest was ushered onto the stage, the host employed meticulous timing when he paused before asking his timorous guest: "What the hell were you thinking of?" It broke the ice. A stammering Grant confided, "I think you know in life pretty much what's a good thing to do and what's a bad thing and I did a bad thing. There you have it."

After facing the music on other national TV shows, Hugh appeared in court on July 11, 1995. On behalf of his client, his lawyer pleaded no contest to the charges. Grant was ordered to pay court costs and a fine totaling $1,180, to accept two years of unsupervised probation, and to undergo a course in AIDS counseling. Unfortunately, Divine Brown was not as lucky because she had two prior convictions in 1993 on prostitution charges. Having thus violated her probation, this young mother did herself little good in changing her earlier not-guilty plea to one of no contest. She received a six-month jail sentence, a $1,350 fine, five days of community service, and a requirement to complete an AIDS counseling course.

As for Hugh's future, *Nine Months* debuted on schedule in mid-July 1995. Grant attended the Hollywood premiere with the strikingly beautiful Elizabeth Hurley at his side. The comedy received middling reviews, but grossed a respectable $69.7 million in domestic box office. After starring in the thriller *Extreme Measures* (1996—produced by Hurley), Grant was not in another movie until 1999's *Notting Hill*. Fortunately for him that picture costarred box-office magnet Julia Roberts and was a huge hit. Now redeemed in the movie business, Grant was again considered box office–worthy. On the other hand, in 2000 he and Hurley ended their on-again, off-again relationship. While life did go on, the tawdry 1995 escapade remained part of Grant's public dossier forever and a day.

Rodney Harvey

[Rodney Michael Harvey]

July 31, 1967–April 11, 1998

During Hollywood's heyday, potential movie stars were sometimes discovered in soda shops. More recently—in the mid-1980s—Rodney Harvey was spotted by an underground filmmaker in Manhattan's then tawdry Times Square. At the time the teenager with the knock-out looks was arguing with a vendor over the purchase of a knife. Before long, the striking, five-foot, six-inch South Philadelphian had launched an acting career, soon becoming the new darling of the print ad media. All this led to Rodney costarring in a TV series and to making several feature films.

During his fast-times Hollywood years, Rodney had several high-profile friends, including Drew Barrymore, David Arquette, and Uma Thurman. With such good fortune, the charismatic toughie had everything to look forward to; but instead his life became a roller-coaster ride of drugs, prison, and broken promises. By age thirty Rodney's corpse lay on tray table 108 at the Los Angeles County Coroner's office. The deceased was the appealing individual Drew Barrymore once characterized as "one of the biggest life-grabbers. I don't know many people that beautiful and fun and exciting and sensitive and strong and anxious about life."

Rodney was the second son of Lois and Edward Harvey. When he was two months old his father moved out, but kept in contact with his boys for the next decade. Meanwhile, his mother remarried and had a son by her new spouse, Sam Fusco. As a youngster, shy Rodney was easily moved to tears. Taunted by his peers for being short and pretty, he took up boxing to even the odds. To make quick money, he learned to play cards and throw dice. Expelled from junior high for being an audacious troublemaker, he spent nine months at reform school in northeastern Pennsylvania. He was released to visit his dying grandfather. Three years later, a favorite uncle committed suicide. Such situations left Harvey feeling abandoned and insecure.

Once Rodney was discovered by moviemaker Paul Morrissey (Andy Warhol's protégé) in the mid-1980s, it wasn't long before the teen was cast in *Mixed Blood* (1985) as a young Hispanic caught in a lower Manhattan turf war. The movie newcomer impressed Allan Mindel, head of a modeling agency/film production company. Mindel became Rodney's avid mentor. Between movie assignments (including 1987's *Five Corners*) Harvey did photo shoots and began a volatile relationship with model Lisa Marie. He was cast in the teleseries *The Outsiders* (1990) and found a new family among his cast mates. However, when the show came and vanished quickly, it broke his professional heart. By now, he was partying hard, acting the punk, and was deep into substance abuse. After breaking up with Lisa Marie, he had a string of heterosexual romances, but men also chased after him. By 1991 Harvey had been in and out of drug-related trouble with the law, including burglaries committed to finance his growing habit.

Along with River Phoenix and Keanu Reeves, Rodney played a male hustler in *My Own Private Idaho* (1991) and joined Drew Barrymore in *Guncrazy* (1992). Unbeknownst to the twenty-five-year-old, it was his acting swan song. His drug dependency and bad behavior had made him too unreliable on movie and TV sets. In 1995 he spent four months in substance abuse treatment, but left the facility after breaking the rules. In February 1996 he was sentenced to the Delano Community Correctional Facility. While incarcerated the high school dropout earned his GED. He was released that November.

For a period the "new" Harvey worked a low-responsibility job refurbishing houses for HUD and followed his substance abuse program. He even regained the confidence of benefactor Allan Mindel, who gave him work and let him stay at his upscale apartment. Mindel arranged for him to be considered for a role in *Good Will Hunting* (1997). But that career break vanished when, two weeks later, it surfaced that Rodney was using drugs again. Thereafter, he was back on the streets begging acquaintances for help. Now on parole violation, he sought refuge back in Philadelphia, but stole from his relatives. His uncle finally had to call the California authorities to have Rodney shipped back to the West Coast. He was incarcerated in the Los Angeles County Jail through the rest of 1997 until spring 1998. Harvey seemed to respond maturely to his imprisonment, even planning more realistically for the future. But some past friends with whom he had gotten back in touch suspected he was still on drugs.

Released on April 9, 1998, Rodney made his way to a former friend's Los Angeles house, arriving unannounced. A half hour later he made a mysterious phone call and then left, claiming he must visit his parole office. Instead he went to a deteriorating section of downtown Los Angeles and spent the afternoon getting high on rock cocaine and heroin in a vacant lot with several other junkies. At one point he passed out and nearly expired, but was revived by one of the group. Later he checked into the nearby rundown Hotel Barbizon. He devoted the next day (Good Friday) to getting really high at the hotel and partying with local prostitutes. That evening he had a cumulative bad reaction to all the drugs he had taken. Building residents helped him back to his room.

The next morning the hotel's cleaning woman unlocked the door to Room 222 and found Harvey slumped over from a sitting position on his bed. An empty syringe stuck out of his left arm; the floor was littered with drug paraphernalia. Rigor mortis had already set in.

To appreciate the toll that drugs and the wild life took on once beautiful Rodney Harvey, one need only examine his various LAPD mug shots taken between 1987 and 1996. The shocking progression of photos reveals graphically how the hope and soul drained out of this once-promising screen personality, leaving a broken wreck.

Pee-wee Herman

[Paul Reubenfeld]

AUGUST 27, 1952–

On his Saturday morning TV show, *Pee-wee's Playhouse* (1986–91), geeky, nasal-voiced Herman—he of the body-hugging gray suit, bow-tie, white patent-leather loafers, and brush-cut hairstyle—ended each episode by riding off on his scooter. Kids loved the goofiness of the program and adults appreciated its hipness. At the time the merchandizing of Pee-wee toys, books, magazines, and so forth, was big business. Then in the space of a few minutes on July 26, 1991, his comedic reign and his career came crashing to a halt, all because he went to a movie in Sarasota, Florida. Granted it was a triple-X porno theater, but even so . . .

He was born Paul Reubenfeld in Peekskill, New York, the eldest of three children. As a youngster he was obsessed with watching TV and was especially devoted to *I Love Lucy* and *Howdy Doody*. In 1961 his parents (who ran a retail lamp store) relocated the family to Sarasota, Florida. The move was fine by Paul, especially when he realized the city was the winter headquarters of the Ringling Bros. and Barnum & Bailey Circus—the boy loved clowns. As a teenager he participated in local theater groups. After graduating high school he went to Boston University to be a theater major. During this time he was arrested on a marijuana possession charge and was placed on a two-year probation.

Paul moved westward, enrolling at the California Institute of the Arts to study acting. Before long he switched his focus from drama to comedy. By the mid-1970s he was based in Los Angeles, had changed his surname to Reubens, and was doing odd jobs (pizza maker, door-to-door salesman) while waiting to get his show business career break. (In this period he made four winning appearances on the TV game program *The Gong Show*.) A few years later he joined an improvisational group, the Groundlings, and focused on its comedy workshop. He developed a roster of characters and began doing a weekend midnight outing at the Groundlings. It was a kiddie show for adults and was quite risqué. One of the other participants in the ongoing production was Phil Hartman.

In 1983 Reubens was visiting his family in Sarasota. One evening he headed to a local adult entertainment center seeking late night entertainment. At 3:15 A.M. he was arrested for reportedly loitering in the theater parking lot. Later the charges were dropped and the case records sealed.

By the mid-1980s he'd appeared successfully in concert at Carnegie Hall. Although he failed to be hired as a cast regular on TV's *Saturday Night Live*, he scored well as the star of the big-screen comedy *Pee-wee's Big Adventure* (1985). Next came his hit TV series, more movies, and greater fame. For the public—and even friends—it was increasingly harder to distinguish between the on-camera, androgynous Pee-wee Herman and the offstage Paul Reubens. (In fact, when he received his star on the Hollywood Walk of Fame it was for Pee-wee Herman, *not* Paul Reubens.)

In the fall of 1990, having taped back-to-back episodes of his TV show (which would last for another season), he felt burned out and took time off to travel and regroup. In the summer of 1991, thirty-nine-year-old Paul, still single, turned up in Sarasota, Florida, to visit his parents (Milton and Judy). Meanwhile, the local sheriff's office was on a campaign to "clean up" the morality of this area on behalf of the conservative citizenry. For example, arrests were made of individuals wearing flimsy bathing suits on the public beach, and a neighborhood record store employee was taken into custody for having sold a rap record to a minor.

On the evening of July 26, 1991, four men from the Special Investigation Bureau of the Sarasota County Sheriff's Office were dispatched to the South Trail Triple X Theater on Route 41 in Sarasota. When the detectives arrived it was just getting dark outside and the cinema was nearly empty. During the showing of the triple bill, which included *Nancy Nurse Turns Up the Heat* and *Catalina Five-O: Tiger Shark*, four patrons, including Reubens, were arrested for indecent exposure. Paul was taken into custody in the lobby as he left the men's room.

According to the police report, Paul had been observed masturbating once, and then again, some twenty minutes later. While he tried to talk himself out of the situation, he was nevertheless taken into custody and booked under the name Paul Reubens. It was not until later that a crime beat reporter from the *Sarasota Herald-Tribune* realized that the suspect was Pee-wee Herman. The story made headlines around the world, with Paul's police mug shot (in which his hair was long and greasy and he wore a goatee) exhibited everywhere.

Once Reubens was released on $219 bail, he disappeared from public sight until the day of his court hearing. (He spent a month of this time hiding out at Doris Duke's New Jersey estate.) The repercussions from his predicament became immediately apparent. Toys R Us yanked their Pee-wee dolls and other Pee-wee products from the shelves. CBS-TV at once cancelled his TV show (which was due to go off the air in fall 1991), while the Disney Studio discontinued using a promotional video about their studio tour that had featured Herman.

In short order Reubens became the butt of smutty jokes on TV talk shows, and it seemed much of America had turned against him. But a few celebrities (including comedian Bill Cosby and singer Cyndi Lauper) stood behind him, and there were pro–Pee-wee rallies held in several U.S. cities. Even in Sarasota, Florida, some locals were questioning why so much of so many law enforcers' time was being devoted to staking out a porno theater.

Herman was scheduled to appear before the judge on November 7, 1991, for having allegedly exposed his sex organ in public. (If found guilty, he faced a $500 fine and up to sixty days behind bars.) There was talk that a video surveillance tape of the theater's lobby would exonerate Pee-wee by proving he was not in the cinema's screening area at the time of the police round-up, but such a tape never materialized. At the proceedings before Judge Judy Goldman, the defendant's lawyer had his client plead no contest. Reubens was ordered to pay a $50 fine and $85.75 in court costs and to perform seventy-five hours of community service (he chose to make and pay for an anti-drug TV spot for the Drug-Free America campaign). As part of the case settlement, all legal papers involved in the arrest were sealed and Reubens emerged with no criminal record. Through it all, he still maintained his innocence.

In disgrace for his bad-boy behavior, his climb back up the career ladder was slow. He had small roles in films like *Batman Returns* (1992) and *Dunston Checks In* (1995). From 1995 to 1997 he had a recurring part as a snide, untrustworthy TV network executive on the sitcom *Murphy Brown*, and by June 2001 he was hosting the TV game show *You Don't Know Jack*, as well as appearing in new movies (2001's *Blow*).

In November 2001, the Los Angeles Police Department, under a warrant it had obtained, searched Reubens's Hollywood Hills home. In the process, and with the cooperation of the actor, who was not present at the time, the law enforcers reportedly removed several items for further study, including the performer's photo and vintage erotic art collections. At the time the police had no comment on the situation while a spokesperson for Reubens told a media outlet that the allegations involved may have been "financially motivated."

There was another result of the Notorious Scandal That Really Wasn't. After appearing as his prancing alter ego Pee-wee Herman on the autumn 1991 MTV Music Video Awards, the devastated Reubens retired his alias identity from the public arena, insisting the character would never reemerge. Lately, he's been having a change of heart on the subject. Said Reubens about a possible new project, "It's kind of *Valley of the Dolls*. Pee-wee becomes a famous pop singer, goes to Hollywood, and turns into a monster."

Howard Hughes

[Howard Robard Hughes Jr.]

DECEMBER 24, 1905–APRIL 5, 1976

Today, with inflation soaring and high-tech fortunes being amassed in short order, being a billionaire is not quite what it used to be. Nevertheless, Hughes, who inherited a large family estate in the 1920s and built upon it (despite years of lavish expenditures), remains one of the most colorful eccentrics in the history of the world's upper class. Long before advancing age, increasing paranoia, and health problems turned him into a crazed recluse, the Texas-born Howard had been a dapper man about Tinseltown. As a mover and shaker in Hollywood from the 1920s to the 1950s, he commanded respect and the community was willing (or forced) to overlook his egocentric ways. (He also attained glamour status for the many aviation records he set, the plane crashes he miraculously survived, and his ability to turn TWA into a major airline.) Being one of Los Angeles's bigger-than-life prodigious playboys, Hughes pursued a wide variety of screen leading ladies. He often treated his love objects like prey to be stalked, caught, and isolated—caged for his own use at a given whim. This hunter-after-big-game routine escalated in the 1940s. Many tales about Hughes are still legend in Hollywood.

Born in Humble, Texas, in 1905, Hughes was an only child and excessively overindulged by his mother, who died when he was sixteen. In his youth, besides demonstrating a great affinity for aviation and exhibiting superior mechanical skills, Howard developed quirks about his eating habits (such as the thickness of a proper tomato slice, the size and number of green peas on his dinner plate), about cleanliness (his hand-washing ritual would have put Lady Macbeth to shame), and so on. When his now-widowed father (who owned a profitable tool company) began chasing Hollywood young lovelies (Howard and his father had moved to Hollywood in mid-1922), the teenager witnessed how money could buy a lonely man the attention of exciting silver-screen beauties.

Howard studied at the California Institute of Technology and then at Rice Institute. In early 1924 his father dropped dead and the young man inherited great wealth. Thereafter Hughes indulged his growing interest in filmmaking and the glamour that surrounded the entertainment industry. The only problem was his loveless marriage in 1925 to the two-year-older Ella Rice, the offspring of a wealthy Houston entrepreneur. (The couple had little in common. She hated the glitzy Hollywood life and was rightfully wary of Howard's wandering eyes. By 1929 the sterile union ended.)

Tall (six feet, three inches), dapper, and charming, Hughes could have easily been a big-screen leading man himself. Instead he chose to be a producer, starting with such silent entries as *Swell Hogan* (1926). His first big crush/love among the movie set was major film actress Eleanor Boardman. He courted her, but she found him to be too shy and aloof. (These characteristics were partly caused by Howard's embarrassment over his growing deafness and his unwillingness to acknowledge that he could not hear much of what was going on around him.) Despite Hughes's wealth and attention, Boardman rejected him as a suitor and, instead, wed film director King Vidor. Then Hughes became enamored with beautiful movie leading lady Billie Dove who was at the peak of her popularity. Unfortunately, she had already married film director Irvin Willat in 1923. But with money and his newfound power in the film business, obsessed Howard was unperturbed by any obstacle to wooing his new love object. Extravagant in romantic gestures, he was prone to following her by plane as she took rides in the countryside, scattering rose petals on her from on high. By 1930 persistent Howard had "arranged" for Billie to divorce by offering her then spouse $325,000 to step out of the way. With the chase over, however, Howard lost interest, while she realized that he could not be a one-woman man. In 1932 she married a millionaire rancher.

In the early 1930s Hughes gained prestige within the film community for his successful films *Hell's Angels* (1930) and *Scarface: The Shame of the Nation* (1932). After that the multifaceted moviemaker abandoned the industry until the early 1940s. He became preoccupied with the world of aviation, smashing flight records, surviving plane (and car) crashes, and disappearing somewhere around the world to carry out his whims. When earthbound and in Los Angeles, the increasingly quirky blueblood dated a bevy of Hollywood lovelies ranging from Jean Harlow to Katharine Hepburn (with whom he seriously contemplated marriage), from Joan Fontaine and Olivia de Havilland (Fontaine's sister) to Ginger Rogers (this screen partner of the great Fred Astaire considered the dapper Howard an excellent dancer). With the petulant Bette Davis, Hughes courted near disaster. She claimed that in bed she helped him to overcome his bout of impotence (brought on by growing self-consciousness over his aging looks and poor health), but that her then husband (bandleader Ham Nelson) bugged the house and threatened to blackmail Hughes over the liaison. The entrepreneur supposedly swore he would have underworld connections liquidate Nelson. After the police were alerted of the threat, Howard reputedly paid off Davis's spouse. In turn, Bette purportedly arranged a loan and reimbursed Hughes for the $75,000. It ended their alleged affair.

Howard was in his mid-thirties when he discovered and nurtured busty Jane Russell, turning her into a screen sensation in *The Outlaw* (1943), a flaccid western that broke many of the film industry's morality strictures. When not promoting Russell as a movie star, Hughes was designing a newfangled bra that would give his screen goddess a magnificent chest lift and create a titillating cleavage. But Russell was not Howard's big amour; he much preferred discovering beautiful young women (such as Jane Greer and Faith Domergue) and bringing them to Hollywood to be (1) his private showcase and (2) possibly film actresses. While feisty, clever Greer created her own screen career, starlets such as Domergue would claim that their mentor stymied their professional lives irreparably. To make amends to Faith, Howard starred her in 1950's *Vendetta*, which ended up a $1 million fiasco. Other less fortunate young women hired by Hughes *never* got on camera. Unaware of their rivals, they remained stashed away in Hughes's many Los Angeles hideouts, kept busy with acting and vocal lessons while being spied upon by their hugely possessive boss. Most of them eventually left town without having made any mark on show business. (Especially after his near fatal plane crash in

Beverly Hills in the mid-1940s, the physically ailing Hughes preferred to control rather than to have intimate relations with most of "his" women.)

One of the more famous of Hughes's amours was earthy Ava Gardner. They met in 1943 soon after she divorced screen star Mickey Rooney. Like Howard, she was born on Christmas Eve. Their on-and-off sparring lasted a decade as the independent-minded Ava constantly foiled the jealous, possessive Hughes. The apex of their much-gossiped-about romance came in late 1944 when Hughes visited Gardner just as a bullfighter date was leaving her place. Enraged by her insubordination and rebellious attitude, Howard smacked her across the face, dislocating her jaw. The equally aroused Ava picked up a nearby brass object and threw it—he went down for the count and had to be carted back home by his ever-present bodyguards.

In the late 1940s shapely starlet Terry Moore claimed to have secretly wed Hughes on the high waters, a relationship that supposedly lasted until shortly before he wed movie actress Jean Peters—an old flame—in early 1957. By then Hughes had lost interest in Hollywood and the RKO film studio he had owned since the 1940s. Instead, he focused on his Las Vegas interests, becoming a mysterious recluse. Gradually, the once dapper Tinseltown playboy was overwhelmed by phobias, drug addiction, and intrigues within his corporate empire, as well as his increasingly poor physical and mental health. He spent his time on several continents, usually hidden away in a darkened room where the Old Man (as his retainers called him) sat naked, engrossed in minutiae. The recluse died in 1976, alienated from a world he once tried to control.

Don Johnson

[Donnie Wayne Johnson]

December 15, 1949–

Like a cat, he always seemed to land on his feet. Whenever his acting career nosedived, a hit TV series like *Miami Vice* (1984–89) or *Nash Bridges* (1996–2001) came along to resurrect it. He was twice married to screen actress Melanie Griffith and had an assortment of high-profile romances that included two big-name singers: Tanya Tucker and Barbra Streisand.

In his earlier career he was labeled a Hollywood cute boy. However, dimple-faced, five-foot, eleven-inch Johnson disagreed: "I resented that part of it—looking pretty—when I had these strong emotions inside of me that weren't matching what was in my face. . . ." Over the years he also had an enormous substance abuse problem. As he once told *Playboy* magazine, "I know that when I was drinking and using, I built my day around it. . . . Nobody got higher than I did for longer than I did. I look back now and say, 'What the f*** was I doing?'—waking up in a joint with a bunch of people lying around with needles in their arms. First you want to know how you got there—then why the f*** you're still there."

Donnie Wayne Johnson was born in 1949 in Galena, Missouri. He was the eldest of four children of Wayne Fred Johnson (a farmer) and his sixteen-year-old bride, Nell (later a beautician). Both parents were of Cherokee heritage. The family moved to Wichita when Don was five and he was persuaded to sing in the church choir by his fundamentalist preacher grandfather. At age eleven, Johnson's battling parents divorced and he lived with his mother in Kansas. The next year the young charmer had his first relationship—with a seventeen-year-old babysitter. He was also rambunctious and was arrested for car theft. He spent two weeks in a juvenile detention center, then was released into the custody of his dad (now living in Missouri) and his stepmother. When the fighting at his father's home got too much to endure, Don moved back to Wichita to continue high school.

He supported himself with a part-time job at a meat-packing plant and cohabited with a twenty-something cocktail waitress. Exhausted by his strenuous after-school life, he was about to flunk out of high school. A guidance counselor suggested he try dramatics. Within a day he had the lead in the school's production of *West Side Story*. He finally felt he belonged. After graduation he earned a drama scholarship to the University of Kansas. During the next two years he became absorbed in theater and lived with his twenty-nine-year-old female drama professor. Through her, he auditioned for San Francisco's American Conservatory Theater (ACT) and was accepted.

While working at ACT he had a two-month-long marriage to a dancer in a road company cabaret group. He also met movie actor Sal Mineo who hired him to costar in the Los Angeles production of *Fortune and Men's Eyes*, a play about gays in prison. This showcase led to Johnson's film debut in *The Magic Garden of Stanley Sweetheart* (1970). When that picture flopped he thought his acting fling was over. He took whatever assignments he could find in TV. In 1973 he wed again, a well-to-do woman, but, a few days later, they annulled their union. That year he made *The Harrad Experiment*, starring Tippi Hedren. Her fourteen-year-old-daughter, Melanie Griffith, was an extra in the picture and was strongly drawn to Don. She pursued him but he was torn between her and the older Pamela Des Barres (later the author of *I'm with the Band: Confessions of a Groupie*). He eventually gave in to determined Melanie, not realizing the consequences of being involved with a minor. They lived together, but there were several breakups as both dealt with substance abuse. Meanwhile, with his huge sexual appetite, he was still playing the field. In spring 1976 a long phone conversation with Melanie led the two to elope to Las Vegas. Later he admitted this was a last-ditch effort to save their faltering relationship. They divorced in 1977. (During their legalized union they posed nude for a couples pictorial for *Playboy* that the magazine published years later.)

As a journeyman actor, Don went from one TV guest spot to the next, as well as a string of telefeatures, TV pilots, and failed series. When not on the town and high, he also found satisfaction writing music for the Allman Brothers. In 1980 he was in another short-lived

TV series (*From Here to Eternity*). To play the drug-dependent, obese Elvis Presley in the TV movie *Elvis and the Beauty Queen* (1981) he gained forty pounds. While he was being seen on the big screen in the lackluster *Soggy Bottom U.S.A.* (1982), his new off-camera companion was actress Patti D'Arbanville. They had renewed a past acquaintanceship one night in early 1982 at an L.A. club. He abandoned his date, Tanya Tucker, and he and Patti went to bed for seven nights and eight days. Their son, Jesse Wayne, was born in December 1982, but they did not wed. (Their relationship ended in 1986, although they remained friends.)

Don Johnson (left) with Ava Gardner and Jason Robards on the set of the two-part telefeature *The Long Hot Summer* (1985). (Courtesy of Doug McClelland)

In September 1983 Don entered a forty-five-day detox program and emerged clean, if shaky. Johnson vowed never to use drugs or alcohol again. That November he tested for yet another TV series, this one called *MTV Cops*. The show, retitled *Miami Vice*, debuted on September 15, 1984. With its flashy camerawork, hip clothes, and two studly leads, it made stars of Johnson (as Detective Sonny Crockett) and Philip Michael Thomas (as Detective Ricardo Tubbs). While in a hot career mode he recorded songs and his album *Heartbeat* sold more than a million copies.

At the peak of his professional popularity, Johnson found time for skiing in trendy Aspen, Colorado. There he encountered Barbra Streisand in January 1988, and the couple embarked on a heated romance. They recorded a duet together, the romantic ballad "Till I Loved You." By the time her album containing the song debuted in early 1989, their liaison was over. The reason was that Melanie Griffith had come back into his crowded life. She had married and divorced actor Steven Bauer and had borne Bauer's child, Alexander. More recently Don had convinced Griffith to undergo treatment for her out-of-control substance abuse. Afterwards they became engaged and wed in June 1989 at his twenty-acre Aspen ranch. Their daughter, Dakota, was born that October.

After *Miami Vice* went off the air in 1989, Don's career slid downward. As the mid-1990s approached, he abandoned his ten years of sobriety. His marriage to Melanie was disintegrating, and Don was becoming a reckless carouser. In March 1994 he scuffled with actor Gary Oldman at the Whiskey, a club in L.A. The next month he made an infamous, rambling phone call to a Florida radio talk show, in which his speech was slurred and his conversation incoherent. That June 1, while driving on a mountain road near Aspen with his son, Jesse, he lost control of his Jeep and it rolled into a ditch. Luckily, no one was injured.

Johnson decided it was time to take control again of his life. After drying out, he starred in the TV cop show *Nash Bridges*. As the head of a special investigation unit in San Francisco, the still hunky Don played a more mature version of his Sonny Crockett. The show, for which he was co–executive producer, bowed in March 1996 and became a hit. By then Melanie had already become interested in actor Antonio Banderas and divorced Johnson to wed her new man.

During the five seasons of *Nash Bridges*, Don's ego swelled. He dated eighteen-year-old Jodi Lyn O'Keefe, who played his daughter on the weekly program. The network was upset and the relationship faded. In 1997 two women sued Johnson for alleged sexual harassment while working on the series. He countersued. The cross-claims were settled out of court. In February 2001 there was a brief flurry when a woman filed a police report that Johnson had allegedly grabbed her and made sexually explicit comments at a San Francisco restaurant. He claimed the incident never happened. City prosecutors declined to press charges, but she later filed a civil suit.

In the late 1990s Don dated twenty-nine-year-old San Francisco socialite Kelly Phleger. They wed in April 1999 in a chic wedding and that December their daughter, Atherton Grace, was born. By spring

2001 *Nash Bridges* had been cancelled. Johnson put his $8 million San Francisco mansion on the market while he and his expanding family settled into his Apsen spread.

Having reached his fifties with a rich nest egg from past work, Johnson seemed unconcerned about the future. Probably he was just thankful to have survived his outrageous, turbulent past.

Paul Kelly

[Paul Michael Kelly]

AUGUST 9, 1899–NOVEMBER 6, 1956

Although he was an established stage star and film player for decades, this square-jawed actor is still best remembered for the 1927 bloody fist fight he had with the husband of his actress lover Dorothy Mackaye. As a result of the brawl, the man died. Not only did the headlined event create one of Hollywood's biggest scandals, but the courtroom proceedings led to Kelly being imprisoned, his once promising screen career ruined. How this bad-boy actor struggled back—to a degree—within the profession is an amazing example of fortitude.

He was born in Brooklyn, New York, the ninth child of ten of Michael D. and Nellie Therese (Murphy) Kelly. A few years later, Mr. Kelly died, which meant all the children had to find odds jobs to keep the household going. Surprisingly, Paul proved to be a major bread-winner by developing a successful acting career. He made his Broadway bow at age eight in *The Grand Army Man*. When not on the New York stage or on tour, the talented youngster began appearing in silent pictures (1911's *Captain Barnacle*) for the Vitagraph studio located near his Brooklyn home. By mid-decade he was starring for the studio in *Buddy's First Call* (1914). The next year he began a series of silent one-reelers about the Jarr family. Back on Broadway Paul was in such popular fare as *Penrod* (1918) with Helen Hayes. His professional future seemed assured.

By the early 1920s the handsome Kelly was a well-regarded stage leading man. He left the successful *Up the Ladder* (1922) to star in *Whispering Wires* (1922). By now he had renewed his friendship with young actress Dorothy Mackaye whom he'd first met a few years earlier through theatre work. She had since married the well-liked musical comedy performer Ray Raymond the prior year. (Later, questions arose whether the Raymonds were actually legally married since Ray's divorce from his first wife may not have been finalized and no record could be found of the Raymonds' alleged Mexican union.) Kelly often socialized with the couple at their home in Forest Hills, Long Island.

By 1926 the Raymonds had gone to Hollywood, and the next year Paul moved out to the West Coast. He was soon teamed with William Haines in MGM's popular *Slide, Kelly, Slide* (1927). The good-looking young actor renewed his association with the fun-loving Raymonds and the trio became part of Tinseltown's active social scene. By this point Paul realized he had fallen passionately in love with Dorothy. As such, he was distraught when she accompanied her husband to San Francisco where Raymond was doing a musical show. The lovers kept in daily communication by telegrams and letters, all filled with their secret love code. By now the abusive and alcoholic Raymond had become suspicious of the overly solicitous Kelly, who openly sided with Dorothy against her belligerent spouse.

As of early April 1927 Dorothy Mackaye and Raymond—who planned to divorce—had returned to Hollywood and she was again seeing Paul, dismissing her husband's jealous ravings. In a burst of protectiveness one evening, Kelly phoned Raymond and told him to stop ill-treating Dorothy and to refrain from besmirching Paul's reputation in Tinseltown. The already drunk Ray taunted his rival on the phone, prompting the hot-headed (and sometimes immature) Kelly to ill-advisedly rush over to the Raymonds' residence. A fight ensued—observed by the Raymonds' young daughter—in which the strapping six-foot-tall Kelly pounded the thirty-three-year-old Raymond. In the melee, the latter fell three times and the enraged Paul kicked at his fallen foe as well as bashed the man's head against the wall. After the fracas, the battered Ray managed to joke about the incident to his maid and then dragged himself to bed. The next day the badly bruised "victim" was taken to the hospital where he died a few days later of severe trauma to the brain. Dorothy persuaded a doctor friend to list the cause of Ray's death as the result of alcoholism. Nevertheless, the police investigated the suspicious death.

When Kelly was arrested on murder charges (later reduced to manslaughter), he fainted. However, during the sensational trial in which his torrid love affair with Dorothy was fully exposed to public scrutiny (despite Dorothy perjuring herself on the witness stand), he remained calm. Meanwhile, Dorothy was indicted on charges of com-

Russ Columbo being intimidated by a tough Paul Kelly (right) in *Broadway Through a Keyhole* (1933). (Courtesy of JC Archives)

pounding a felony and being an accessory after the fact for concealing the true particulars of her husband's beating. Paul was found guilty of manslaughter and ordered to serve one to ten years at San Quentin Prison, and Dorothy was sentenced to several months of incarceration.

In August 1929, twenty-five months after his imprisonment, a contrite Kelly was paroled for excellent behavior behind bars. He rejoined the already freed Dorothy. Although several of the Hollywood community had contributed to the duo's defense fund, studio executives had ostracized the pair from the film industry. Also the terms of Kelly's parole from the California penal system forbade him to earn more than $30 per week in the state or to marry without the parole board's permission. As a result, the still much-in-love couple moved out of California to New York City where they hoped to revive their acting careers on the stage.

Dorothy soon retired from show business, but Paul—determined to rebuild his career—scored a success on Broadway opposite Sylvia Sidney in *Bad Girl* (1930) and the next year he was permitted by the parole board to wed Mackaye on April 10. By 1932, with his glowing stage notices, Hollywood seemed ready to accept him. One of his first new releases was *Broadway Through a Keyhole* (1933) in which he played a tough gangster (a part that exploited his tough-guy reputation as a real-life ex-convict). He earned excellent reviews. But in the ensuing years, despite his solid talents and virile looks, he was deliberately mired in secondary roles in major films while allowed occasional lead roles in low-budget entries. He always turned in good performances, such as the 1936 quicky *The Song and Dance Man* in which he tap-danced and vocalized. But the high-level success that he should have enjoyed in the film colony was denied him. It was Hollywood's way of censuring him, not for the folly of his private life, but for being foolish enough to be caught in an act that gave the industry a taint.

During this atonement period, the once high-living Paul and Dorothy lived quietly outside the Hollywood limelight. That ended when Dorothy died in a tragic auto accident in early 1940. The next year a still-distraught Paul wed actress Claire Owen. He continued his filmmaking (mostly in poverty row entries) throughout the World War II years, but his greatest success came on Broadway. He shone in *Command Decision* (1947) and *The Country Girl* (1950), although in the screen adaptations of the two dramas, Clark Gable and Bing Crosby, respectively, received Kelly's coveted roles. Among Paul's later pictures were *Duffy of San Quentin* and *The Steel Cage* (both 1954) in which, ironically, he played the warden of the institution where he had been incarcerated in actual life.

In late 1956, having completed his role in *Bailout at 43,000* (1957), this talented man, who had eventually regained Hollywood respect if not total forgiveness, died of a heart attack.

Peter Lawford

[Peter Sydney Ernest Aylen Lawford]
SEPTEMBER 7, 1923–DECEMBER 24, 1984

For many, dapper, British-accented Lawford is best remembered as (1) President John F. Kennedy's brother-in-law who served as a liaison between amorous JFK and actress Marilyn Monroe, (2) a subordinate member of Frank Sinatra's Rat Pack, (3) a Hollywood playboy who dated many screen goddesses (Ava Gardner, Rita Hayworth, and Lana Turner) between his four marriages, and, oh yes, (4) a lightweight MGM star during the 1940s and early 1950s. But Peter had other distinguishing aspects to his ill-used life. He was a longtime alcoholic and drug addict who in the 1960s and 1970s worked hard to be Tinseltown's hippest swinger. In the process, he often made an embarrassing spectacle of himself and drove even his most loyal friends (including MGM alumnus Elizabeth Taylor) to desperation.

From the start, shocking behavior surrounded the future movie star. His grasping mother, May Sommerville Bunny, was married to Major Ernest Vaughan Aylen of the Royal Army Medical Corps. When she conceived in December 1922, Aylen was *not* the baby's father. Rather, it was the major's commanding officer, Lieutenant General Sir Sydney Lawford, who was the biological dad. To soften the potential gossip, the major remained married to May until the child was born so the offspring would be legitimate. A day after Peter's birth, the major filed for divorce. A week after the dissolution became final May wed the now single Sir Sydney. When the British newspapers played up the scandalous facts, the snobbish May was so embarrassed that she began drinking more heavily than usual. Because money was often tight in the household, Peter did not attend fancy boarding schools but was taught by tutors between family treks to Monte Carlo (Sir Sydney loved to gamble) and other points around the world, where they often imposed upon their friends' hospitality. As he grew up, Peter insisted he wanted to be an actor. He made his debut in the British-made movie *Old Bill* (1930), but thereafter, his class-conscious parents—

counseled by others—decided filmmaking was not a proper occupation for their boy. Meanwhile, the youngster had had his first sexual experiences. One of his parents' male friends had made an overt pass at the nine-year-old boy, which traumatized him; the next year he was seduced by his thirty-five-year-old German governess.

In the late 1930s when the peripatetic Lawfords were in Los Angeles, stagestruck Peter was hired to play in MGM's *Lord Jeff* (1938), starring Mickey Rooney. Thereafter, the supercilious Lawfords dragged Peter away from Tinseltown on further trips. By 1942, with World War II having curtailed their international travel, the Lawfords ended up on the West Coast again, but this time in reduced financial circumstances. Thus they were agreeable to handsome Peter, now nineteen and six feet tall, signing an MGM contract. His first picture was Greer Garson's *Mrs. Miniver* (1942), in which he was a pilot.

With so many young men away in military service, good-looking actors were much in demand on and off screen. Since the controlling May had no say over her son's acting career—the studio had quickly pushed the tyrant away—she rode roughshod over her boy's social life. Arrogant and bigoted, she brushed away any girl who showed interest in him. While this sometimes worked, when Peter began seeing MGM's blond sexpot Lana Turner, May met her match. Thereafter, in one of the most bizarre examples of perverseness, this cruel stage mother demanded a meeting with the studio's chief. She blithely announced to Louis B. Mayer, "I'm concerned that my son is a homosexual." The homophobic Mayer who, over the years, had been forced to cover over the escapades of several gay MGM stars who were box-office moneymakers, intended this time to nip the problem in the bud. An unaware Lawford was summoned to the boss's office where, to prove his manliness to the accusing Mayer, he had the mogul phone Lana. She rated the actor a nice lover and saved the day. It was not until a year later that a shocked Lawford first learned that his mother had so viciously jeopardized his career. His growing hatred of her intensified.

As a very young teenager, Peter, following his mother's example, had begun drinking. It continued throughout his MGM years (1942–52),

Peter Lawford (center) holding forth with Phil Silvers (left) and Telly Savalas (right) in *Buona Sera, Mrs. Campbell* (1969). (Courtesy of JC Archives)

helping him through moments of insecurity or as a boost in getting through the sameness of the next party that the jaded young man was attending. After being let go by the studio, Lawford freelanced, including starring in two 1950s TV series (*Dear Phoebe* and *The Thin Man*). In April 1954 he wed socialite Patricia Kennedy, the sister of John, Bobby, and Ted Kennedy. Peter brought a touch of supposed British class to the match, while she had money and social connections. They had four children (1955, 1956, 1958, and 1961). By this point Lawford, who had become a U.S. citizen in 1960, was a heavy drinker and a drug user who orbited in Frank Sinatra's jet-set crowd. As a member of Ol' Blue Eyes's posse, Peter was included in such film larks as *Ocean's Eleven* (1960) and *Sergeants 3* (1962). However, the ever amenable and frequently zonked Peter was repeatedly treated badly by the capricious, often cruel Sinatra.

With JFK's assassination in 1963, and Sinatra having put Lawford on his "out" list for imagined disloyalty, Peter was a man without industry status, especially after Patricia divorced him in 1966. Hard living, lack of exercise, and advancing age had diminished Lawford's once striking looks that had been a key to his show business success. Now it was tough to find film roles, even supporting parts or TV guest assignments. Peter had gotten hooked on Dexedrine, which he used when dieting off the flab from booze and overeating. Since then he'd graduated to heavier-duty substance abuse, further draining his diminished funds. In 1971 he married Mary Ann Rowan, daughter of comedian Dan Rowan. She was less than half his age and their union lasted but one and a half years. Inveterate party guy Lawford, who had become a perennial guest star on TV game shows, next wed twenty-five-year-old Deborah Gould, an aspiring actress. A few months after their June 1976 marriage they divorced.

By the early 1980s, decades of overdrinking and misusing drugs had left Peter with a dangerously enlarged liver and many other medical complications. He had been in and out of several substance abuse programs to little avail. Elizabeth Taylor, who had been fighting her own battles with drugs and drink, entered the Betty Ford Center in late 1983. She persuaded her longtime pal Lawford that he must follow suit. He agreed finally, but before doing so, he sold an account of Elizabeth being at the famed treatment center to a supermarket tabloid. (He badly needed the several thousand dollars they paid for the scoop.) Despite this recovery sojourn, three days after he was released from Betty Ford, Peter was getting sauced at his neighborhood bar.

His glory days long gone, Peter's Los Angeles apartment was a shrine to his show business past. Badly in debt from his expensive drug habit, he was now in such bad physical and emotional shape that he could scarcely stagger onto a soundstage to deliver the few lines of dialogue allowed him. One of his constant companions during these diminished times was model Patricia Seaton whom he had known over recent years. She insisted that she could reform him, but nothing seemed to work. The couple wed in July 1984 but five months later, at age sixty-one, he died of cardiac arrest with no money in the estate. His cemetery burial bill never paid, his cremation urn was disinterred from the Westwood Village Mortuary, and his widow, whose biography of her late spouse was about to be published, made a great fanfare of taking his remains to Marina Del Rey, California, and then boarding a boat to scatter his ashes at sea.

Rob Lowe

[Robert Hepler Lowe]

MARCH 17, 1964–

Judged against present-day global terrorism, it may not seem huge, but in 1988 it was one of the biggest news events going. A graphic, naughty videotape that movie star Lowe had made of himself and two young women frolicking in his hotel bed was stolen from his room and soon circulated around the world. The scandal made Lowe the butt of smutty jokes everywhere, prompting Arsenio Hall to quip, "Finally, a Rob Lowe movie everybody wants to see!" The disgrace of the sexcapade nearly ended the handsome Brat Packer's movie career.

Once labeled by *Entertainment Weekly* "a Rodeo Drive mannequin," hard-living bachelor Rob was known about Hollywood—like Errol Flynn, Warren Beatty, and other womanizers before him—for being afflicted with *satyriasis* (defined by *Random House Webster's College Dictionary* as "abnormal, uncontrollable sexual desire in a male"). Lowe was famous for obtaining a woman's phone number anywhere at any time, even in the ladies' powder room.

Lowe was born in 1964 in Charlottesville, Virginia, the first child of a budding trial attorney and his schoolteacher wife. Within months the family relocated to Dayton, Ohio, where in January 1968 their second son, Chad (who would become an actor also), was born.

From the moment that Rob saw the movie *Oliver!* (1968) he knew he wanted to be an actor. At eight he began performing in summer theater with regional acting groups in Dayton. In addition he appeared on local radio, TV, and in local college productions that required a youngster. (Also in 1968 the precocious, politically concerned youth was selling lemonade to raise money for Democratic presidential candidate George McGovern.)

When Rob's parents separated in 1977, Mrs. Lowe moved with her two sons to California, settling at Point Dune, a small community north of Malibu. Following Barbara Lowe's divorce from her husband, she married a psychiatrist and would mother two more sons: Micah and Justin.

Within six months of being a Californian, Lowe was registered with an L.A. talent agent. He began hanging around with such Malibu film colony offspring as Emilio Estevez and his brother Charlie Sheen, as well as Sean and Chris Penn. The group began making super 8 mm home movies on the nearby dunes and surf.

Rob's professional debut was in the short-lived TV sitcom *A New Kind of Family* (1979), which led to TV movies and *After-School Specials*. By 1981 the five-foot, eleven-inch Lowe was sufficiently famous so that, one day while driving along La Cienega Boulevard in Los Angeles, a car honked at him and the driver inquired, "Are you Rob Lowe?" It was actress Melissa Gilbert returning home from the set of TV's *Little House on the Prairie*. A romantic relationship sprung up that would endure (on and off) for six years.

After graduating from Santa Monica High School, Rob, who was dyslexic, matriculated as a film major at UCLA. Classes were to begin in the fall of 1982, but he withdrew because several acting jobs came his way. These ranged from the telefeature *Thursday's Child* (1983) to Francis Ford Coppola's *The Outsiders* (1983). The lightweight *Oxford Blues* (1984) established the actor as a throbbing sex symbol. During the making of *The Hotel New Hampshire* (1984), Lowe had an off-camera affair with coplayer Nastassja Kinski. *St. Elmo's Fire* (1985) was a paean to its Brat Pack cast, including Demi Moore who joined with Lowe in the next year's *About Last Night*. Along the way, there was also a brief romance between Lowe and Princess Stephanie of Monaco. However, in 1987 he asked Melissa Gilbert to wed him. That next March he learned by tuning in to a radio show, which she had called into, that the actress was to wed actor and playwright Bo Brinkman. The public rejection was humiliating, but nothing compared to what happened next.

In the early 1980s political activist Rob had campaigned with California Democrat Tom Hayden (and his actress wife, Jane Fonda). Thereafter, the party boy (who made $1 million a picture) spent his off-camera time speaking on civic issues such as the environment and voting. In July 1988 Hayden invited Lowe to attend the Democratic

National Convention in Atlanta, hoping that the presence of movie stars like Rob would add young glamour to the political gathering. On the afternoon of July 17, Rob, a devout baseball fan, took his video camera to the Atlanta Braves game and taped some footage. That evening he attended a bash hosted by media mogul Ted Turner. Later, along with Brat Packers Judd Nelson and Ally Sheedy, Rob visited the city's Club Rio. At the door, baby-faced Rob (who was twenty-four) was carded. That led him to assume wrongly that everyone there must be of legal age.

Rob Lowe with his wife Sheryl.
(Photo by Albert L. Ortega)

In the club Lowe had drinks and talked with several women. Among those he met were twenty-two-year-old Tara Siebert, a receptionist at a Marietta, Georgia, hair salon and sixteen-year-old Lena Jan Parsons, an assistant at the same salon. Rob invited them back to his hotel room for fun and games. Once there, he taped their entertainment, just as he had captured on the same cassette a ménage-à-trois encounter with a woman and man in Paris earlier that month. Thereafter, while he was in the bathroom, the girls left. He then noticed that $100 to $200 was missing from his wallet and the videocassette was gone as well. Rob gave the matter little further thought as he toured around the United States with presidential candidate Michael Dukakis.

About a month later, Parsons's mother discovered the show-all tape and learned about her daughter's misadventure. The matter was brought to the attention of Lowe and his attorney, and the plaintiffs were offered, but rejected, a $35,000 settlement to make the matter go away. Mrs. Parsons filed a civil suit claiming that Lowe "used his celebrity status as an inducement to females to engage in sexual intercourse, sodomy, and multiple-party sexual activity for his immediate sexual gratification, and for the purpose of making pornographic films of these activities." Later the suit was amended to allege "unlawful intercourse." Meanwhile, the local district attorney was debating whether or not to file criminal charges against Lowe. If found guilty, he would face up to twenty years in prison and a $100,000 fine. Concurrently, tape copies of Rob's Parisian and Atlanta indiscretions began circulating everywhere. Some of the footage—in edited format—even appeared on tabloid TV and cable TV shows.

In court, the presiding judge dismissed the part of the mother's lawsuit claiming emotional distress but not the other aspect, which was eventually settled out of court. Criminal charges were never filed against the star. The net result of the courtroom proceedings was that Lowe had to serve twenty hours of community service (which he did in his hometown of Dayton, Ohio) and "to stay out of trouble" for the next two years.

The worst punishment was that Rob, the star of a steamy home video, became a pariah in the film industry and the world of politics. After the exploitive *Bad Influence* was released in 1990—about a psychopath (Lowe) who videotapes a friend (James Spader) having sex with a woman—Lowe's career went down the toilet. Braving it out by refusing to go into hiding, Rob began drinking heavily. In 1990 he entered Arizona's Sierra Tucson rehab center and has been sober ever since. (He also underwent treatment for his sexual addictive behavior.) Part of his turnaround was due to his relationship with Sheryl Berkoff, a former girlfriend of Emilio Estevez. She was a makeup artist whom he had met on the set of *The Outsiders*, dated briefly, and then reencountered while making *Bad Influence*. They married in July 1991 and moved to Santa Barbara, where they are raising their two sons.

The reformed actor received a big boost by appearing in the mega hit *Wayne's World* (1992), doing solid work in the TV miniseries Stephen King's *The Stand* (1994), and providing a well-received cameo in *Austin Powers: International Man of Mystery* (1997—and its 1999 follow-up). Guest hosting on TV's *Saturday Night Live* showed that Lowe not only had retained his sense of comedy but also an ability to laugh at himself. By the fall of 1999 no one was laughing at him anymore. The rediscovered Lowe was one of the prime stars of NBC-TV's *The West Wing*. In the hit drama series, he smoothly played Sam Seaborn, the slick, concerned deputy communications director.

Having climbed back up to show business's A list, the former Brat Packer was happy at last: "My family has brought me joy I never dreamed was possible."

Dean Martin

[Dino Paul Crocetti]

JUNE 17, 1917–DECEMBER 25, 1995

There were many public Dean Martins. In his first cycle of show business success he was the engaging straight man to zany Jerry Lewis. As the amused observer of Jerry's nonstop daffiness, he might break into a love song or, just as often, join in Lewis's craziness. (Years after the team broke up in 1956, Dean commented, "Two of the greatest turnin' points in my career: first, meetin' Jerry Lewis; second, leavin' Jerry Lewis.")

As a solo act, Dean astounded Hollywood and himself by being an adept screen actor in a variety of genres: dramas (1958's *Some Come Running*), romantic comedies (1961's *All in a Night's Work*), westerns (1968's *5 Card Stud*), or disaster epics (1970's *Airport*). Martin even succeeded in a big-screen spy series (playing woman-crazy super agent Matt Helm). Then there was Dino, a key member of Frank Sinatra's Rat Pack, ready to party with Ol' Blue Eyes on screen, on stage, or in the clubs and casinos. In the recording studios Martin proved to have many lives, from his first single (1946's "Which Way Did My Heart Go?") to such later chart-toppers as "That's Amore" and his signature tune, "Everybody Needs Somebody." On TV he scored mightily with his variety series (1967–74) and his later batch of Celebrity Roasts.

As a private citizen, the five-foot, ten-inch Dean was an enigma even to those closest to him. He refused to get close to people and he wouldn't let them through his self-created barrier. Martin had been an outsider even in his earliest years. The son of an Italian immigrant, he didn't speak English till he was five, and his classmates made fun of his accent. He quit school at sixteen, tried being a boxer, labored in a steel mill, delivered bootleg liquor, and worked the numbers and craps games for local hoodlums. All the while there was only one thing he really wanted to do: be a professional singer. (Martin's idols were Harry Mills of the Mills Brothers, Bing Crosby, and Perry Como.)

From Dino Martini (his first showbiz moniker) he became Dean Martin, having had plastic surgery to reshape his too-prominent nose and building a smooth persona along the way. The struggling club singer first worked with Jerry Lewis in 1946, and their career together in several media zoomed in the 1940s and 1950s until their highly publicized split-up in 1956. Always, the two men were studies in contrast: hyperactive Jerry was obsessed with attaining success; sleepy-eyed Dean couldn't give a damn whether he succeeded or failed as long as he had a good time. The decade-younger Lewis idolized his teammate, but never really knew what made the inaccessible Martin tick.

Dean had a lot of foibles. He hated elevators (after a traumatic experience of once being trapped in one), said his prayers nightly but hardly went to Catholic Church, and had a passion for his fancy wardrobe of tailored tuxedos, cashmere sweaters, and stylish shoes. He may have enjoyed drinking Haig & Haig whiskey or a good glass of wine, but until his later years much of his reputation as a legendary lush was just part of his on-camera character. Even in adulthood, comic books (which relaxed him) were his favorite reading matter and he loved watching westerns. Most of all, no matter what the situation, he was unfazed by his celebrityhood or anyone else's. (This also applied to mobsters. Because of his work in nightclubs and his love of gambling, Dean knew a lot of underworld figures, but, unlike Sinatra, he was not duly impressed by them.) In fact, nothing seemed to amaze the self-contained man. (In the early 1980s, however, following the murder of John Lennon by a crazed fan, a concerned Dino began to pack a concealed pistol.) His biggest quirk was his I-don't-give-a-f*** attitude. It wasn't rude egotism; it was a case of I'll do my best in a given situation for the moment but if it doesn't work out, so what. I'll find something else that is fun.

Three things Dean truly loved: (1) a well-prepared Italian meal, (2) playing golf, and (3) pretty women. Of the trio, golf won out every time. As he climbed the rungs of show business success, he married three times. His first spouse, a college dropout, was Elizabeth MacDonald whom he wed in 1940. They had four children (1942, 1944, 1945, and 1948). Despite all those offspring, Martin frequently cheated

Bemused playboy Dean Martin copes with Lana Turner in *Who's Got the Action?* (1962). (Courtesy of JC Archives)

on Elizabeth. There were just too many easy temptations on the road where women swarmed after the cool crooner. One of Dean's first extracurricular celebrity dates was movie star June Allyson, then married to Dick Powell. She was not the only star to succumb to his charms in the late 1940s. Movie beauties Ann Sheridan and Lana Turner also pursued the handsome singer. Easy come, easy go was his rule with his many infidelities. But sometimes his sexual activity led to real trouble. For example, one time Dino bedded an attractive gal in Chicago not knowing that she was the property of a tough and jealous local gangster. The singer's manager saved his client's life by hustling him out of town in the nick of time.

In December 1948, Martin and Lewis were in Miami for the King Orange Jamboree Parade. Dean quickly spotted Jeanne Beiggers, a pretty twenty-one-year-old model and a former Orange Bowl Queen. Once the couple's eyes locked, it was love at first sight. It hastened the end of his marriage to Elizabeth, and in August 1949 Dino and Jeanne wed. They would have three children (1951, 1953, and 1956). But it was not the end of his philandering. Because these sexual escapades were fun but quickly forgotten, the episodes only hurt the soon-departed bed partner and, of course, Jeanne.

By the time Martin was making the comic western *Something Big* (1971) with Honor Blackman, he was in the throes of divorce. Dean had met twenty-two-year-old beauty queen Gail Renshaw in 1969 when he and his wife were about to split up. Renshaw eventually vanished, but twenty-three-year-old hair salon receptionist Catherine Mae Hawn did not. In 1972 the Martins divorced and in April 1973 Cathy and the thirty-years-older Dean married at his Bel Air, California, home. He even adopted her daughter from a prior marriage, Sasha. The union proved stormy and within three years the couple was drawing up a dissolution agreement. By then Martin was seeing Peggy Crosby, Bing Crosby's thirty-eight-year-old daughter-in-law, who had been married to the crooner's son Phillip. But this fling (one of the few of Martin's many hit-and-run dalliances to be highlighted by the media during his lifetime) evaporated in short order.

In Dean's final decades he became more reclusive, pulling away from show business acquaintances and even his close friends. The death of his son Dean Paul in 1987 in a plane crash drove the seventy-year-old Martin into a shell that no one could crack. One of the few still in his inner circle in the final years was ex-wife Jeanne who lived down the street from him. She was at his bedside, holding his hand, when he died of respiratory failure on Christmas Day 1995, twenty-nine years to the day after his beloved mother, Angela, passed on.

Steve McQueen

[Terrence Steven McQueen]
MARCH 24, 1930–NOVEMBER 7, 1980

He was the epitome of movie cool in the 1960s and 1970s. Like Marlon Brando and James Dean before him, McQueen was a rebel, but he was never a self-pitying mumbler in front of the camera. The handsome, five-foot, nine-inch blond star excelled at playing the aggressive loner (1963's *The Great Escape*) or the hostile anti-social man (1972's *The Getaway*). Frequently Steve's character was in uniform of one sort or another: naval, as in 1966's *The Sand Pebbles*; army, as in 1962's *Soldier in the Rain*; prison, as in 1973's *Papillon*; businessman, as in 1968's *The Thomas Crown Affair*; and firefighter, as in 1974's *The Towering Inferno*. Generally, his film alter ego bristled against authority.

Male filmgoers responded to McQueen's "screw-you" attitude to the world. They envied his reckless bravado on screen, whether he was riding a motorcycle over a high fence, careening his car down a steep San Francisco hill, or navigating a grueling race car course. Beyond his good looks and that impish grin, he appealed to women viewers because his intense characters were explosive men of action. Clearly, there was danger about him, which translated into palpable sexual charisma.

But most of McQueen's fans were not privy to the "real" Steve. Poorly educated and having only a limited ability to read or write (which later proved to be due to dyslexia), he was tremendously self-conscious about these failings, just as he was about his increasing deafness in one ear. It made the cocky man suspicious, standoffish, and argumentative. He could be a real pain on a film set. After working with him in *The Cincinnati Kid* (1965), esteemed director Norman Jewison rated McQueen "the most difficult actor" with whom he'd ever worked.

Steve frequently had little respect for his costars, especially if he suspected they were stealing his limelight. He thought his *Papillon* teammate Dustin Hoffman was an overacting ham, and he felt very competitive toward Paul Newman. Steve's first movie had been a bit in Newman's *Somebody up There Likes Me* (1956) and McQueen vowed one day to best his peer. When Steve switched roles from the skyscraper architect to the daring fireman in *The Towering Inferno* and Newman took over the other assignment, McQueen insisted that numerous lines of dialogue be shifted to his favor. However, it was with women in his private life that Steve displayed his greatest enmity (waiters came in second—McQueen was notorious as a stingy tipper).

Born in Beech Grove, Indiana, in 1930, he and his "dancer" mother were abandoned by his barnstormer father when the boy was six months old. Mrs. McQueen had little maternal instinct and left her child with an uncle, a hog farmer in Slater, Missouri. She would show up occasionally, but quickly returned to her wild life in Indianapolis. Angered by the recurrent abandonment, Steve grew up to be a rebellious teen. At fourteen he ran away to Los Angeles to rejoin his uncaring mother. She had remarried by now and her husband was not anxious to have McQueen around. Steve and his stepfather argued, vociferously and violently. More defiant than ever, the teenager hung out with a bad crowd and was constantly in scrapes. The stepfather convinced his wife that reform school was the only solution for Steve who had quit school in the ninth grade. She had him committed to the Boys Republic in Chino, California, in February 1945 where he was a hell-raiser.

Fourteen months later Steve's mom had relocated alone to Greenwich Village and sent for her cast-off son. Once again his expectations were dashed when he found that his alcoholic parent had a new live-in

Macho star Steve McQueen in a typical feisty pose. (Courtesy of Doug McClelland)

boyfriend and that she expected her offspring to stay with a male neighbor who was gay. Steve refused. Just before his seventeenth birthday he enlisted in the marines where he spent three years in and out of trouble and chasing women.

Once a civilian, he gravitated to acting, largely because it was a good way to meet females. He studied at the Neighborhood Playhouse, and by the time he was at the Actors Studio, he had developed a charismatic, if undisciplined, stage presence. In this period he met Neile Adam, then dancing in Broadway's *The Pajama Game*. She was far more successful than he, but she was magnetized by the motorcycle-riding, pot-smoking Steve. He followed her to California when she went under MGM contract, and they wed in November 1956. (They had two children: 1959 and 1960.) It was Neile who supported the household during the first years, but soon McQueen landed the lead in the western TV series *Wanted: Dead or Alive* (1958–61). As his success increased, so did his demanding ways on the set. His marital cheating had greatly accelerated by the time he made the big-screen entry *The Magnificent Seven* (1960). Fame brought the McQueens tangible luxuries (especially his much-loved fast cars), but he was increasingly agitated. The death of his mother in 1965 ended the love-hate relationship between parent (whom he supported) and raging child, but it didn't improve his relationships with the opposite sex.

By the late 1960s Steve was blatant in his unfaithfulness to Neile. He now had added dropping acid and using amyl nitrite to his drug habits. He was undergoing a severe midlife crisis when producing and starring in *Le Mans* (1971). From the start the set was trouble-plagued—largely due to his dictatorial ways. He seemed to survive on a regimen of sex and drugs. By now, having lost patience with him, and in retaliation for his flagrant cheating, Neile had a brief relationship with actor Maximilian Schell. Later, she erred by confessing her indiscretion to McQueen. He grew ballistic, even putting a loaded gun to her head. When she announced she was having a baby, Steve made her have an abortion, refusing to believe it was his. The couple divorced in September 1971.

Brash and vain McQueen was not single for long. Even before they started the crime drama *The Getaway* (1972), there was immediate chemistry between Steve and costar Ali MacGraw. On Texas location, Ali (married to Robert Evans, the head of Paramount Pictures, with whom she had a son in 1971) fell in love with McQueen, despite knowing that only trouble lay ahead. During filming, whenever he grew angry with Ali, he punished her by blatantly having a liaison with the first available groupie on the set. Being a lout, he often treated MacGraw badly, but she accepted it as part of the package.

The emotionally mismatched couple wed in July 1973 in Cheyenne, Wyoming, and all hell broke loose. He insisted she abandon her career, socialize only with his friends (mostly bikers and car mechanics), and refused to join her in her own cultural interests. His abusiveness—both mental and physical—accelerated, as did his mood swings, but she was too addicted to him to break free. Having abandoned moviemaking for three years and grown bushy facial hair and a pot belly—his rebellion against the Hollywood establishment—the very depressed superstar insisted on filming Henrik Ibsen's *Enemy of the People* (1977). The dry drama was, as predicted, a huge flop.

Having nearly extinguished her self-identity, Ali went back to work, making *Convoy* (1978) with Kris Kristofferson. The picture was high-profile junk and she admitted in her 1991 autobiography that she gave in to the wild environment on the set. Returning to McQueen, she hoped to make a fresh marital start. By then, however, he was living at the Beverly Wilshire Hotel (only returning home on weekends) and having an open affair with twenty-two-year-old model Barbara Mintz. In the fall of 1978 he filed for divorce, leaving forty-year-old Ali with a broken life and career.

In the late 1970s, the metamorphosing McQueen earned his pilot's license, bought a ranch house in Santa Paula, California, and began attending church and studying the Bible. He seemed to be gaining serenity. Steve married Barbara Mintz in January 1980, but only months later, he died of cancer despite undergoing a miracle cure at a Mexican clinic.

Robert Mitchum

[Robert Charles Durman Mitchum]

AUGUST 6, 1917–JULY 1, 1997

In the annals of Hollywood few stars have consistently displayed more acting acumen than Mitchum. Beefy, sleepy-eyed, and quite handsome in his earlier years, the six-foot, one-inch talent offered a natural tough style on camera that avoided all the distracting mannerisms of a Montgomery Clift, Marlon Brando, or Al Pacino. Part of Mitchum's ability to last six decades on the screen was his down-to-earth acting approach. (He said once: "I gave up being serious about making pictures years ago, around the time I made a film with Greer Garson and she took 125 takes to say 'No.'") For Robert, his success was "Largely being in the right place at the right time. . . . Every two or three years I knock off for a while. That way I'm constantly the new girl in the whorehouse." As to his trademark casualness about being a movie icon or any other type of celebrity, he sometimes quoted his one-time RKO studio boss Howard Hughes: "My God, Mitch, you're just like a pay toilet—you don't give a s*** for nothin'."

When it came to his private life, Mitchum was as deliberately casual as he was about his high-profile show business work. For example, when he wed his childhood sweetheart, Dorothy Spence, his marriage proposal was a blunt "Marry me and you'll be farting through silk." As to his unglamorous wedding ceremony in Dover, Delaware, he recalled, "We got married in a kitchen because it was the warmest room in the house."

If Robert was a man's man with his drinking and carousing, he also was quite a ladies' man. For an individual with little formal education, he had amassed a colorful vocabulary and was a wonderful raconteur. The opposite sex was constantly amazed by his gentle, sentimental side, which he displayed as often as his drunk rampaging or his lusty fornicating. In the course of making more than a hundred features, TV movies, and TV miniseries, the unpretentious celebrity had a slew of engaging leading ladies that included Jane Greer, Ava Gardner, Jane Russell, Susan Hayward, Marilyn Monroe, Deborah Kerr, Elizabeth

Taylor, and Shirley MacLaine. With a few of these and some others he had brief, but intense affairs, yet always returned eventually to his one and only wife, Dorothy, and their family.

Because Mitchum was so universally liked by the film community, much of the media, and the public, his indiscretions often were played down or even concealed during his lifetime. Sometimes, though, he was the first to spill the beans as when he unashamedly acknowledged that in his youth, while on a hobo trek through the South, he had been arrested in Savannah, Georgia, for alleged vagrancy. He had been sentenced to a chain gang in Chatham County. In 1933, about a month into his arduous sentence, he escaped and

Robert Mitchum—Hollywood's sleepy-eyed "Bad Boy." (Courtesy of JC Archives)

returned home to Delaware. By then he'd contracted blood poisoning and gangrene (a result of his prison camp shackles) and nearly lost his leg. He recovered and went about his young life, which included trekking around the country and working odd jobs. A later major brush with the law, however, almost ended Robert's successful movie career.

In 1942 Mitchum entered pictures as a stuntman in westerns, and by 1943 he had made his acting debut in a Hopalong Cassidy picture. During 1945, while briefly serving in the World War II army in the United States, Robert's movie *The Story of G.I. Joe* was released. For playing the army lieutenant killed in action, he won a Best Supporting Actor's nomination. In 1947 he was in such well-received dramas as *Crossfire* and *Out of the Past*.

For Robert, now a father of two sons, his professional outlook was bright. But there was one problem. Late in 1947 his manager and friend

Paul Behrmann was accused of defrauding a Burbank, California, housewife. Not long before that Robert and his wife had discovered that the bulk of the actor's earnings had vanished while in Behrmann's supposed safekeeping. Mitchum refused to prosecute his once pal, but now in court on this other case, he and his spouse had to testify about Behrmann's character and professional track record. Although the defendant was freed on bail from this new case, he subsequently went to jail on another similar charge. In his mind the Mitchums were responsible for his bad luck and he vowed "vengeance." After the stress of "betraying" his one-time friend, Robert and his family went back to Delaware for a breather. His family remained there when Mitchum later returned to Los Angeles.

Then came the evening of August 31, 1948. Robert and three others (including actress Lila Leeds, whom he had dated briefly) were arrested at a cottage on Ridpath Drive in the Laurel Canyon hills. The suspects were charged with the possession and use of marijuana. What today might seem harmless in comparison to the current heavy-duty drug scene created a media frenzy back in the late 1940s. There were conflicting accounts of exactly what transpired and Mitchum was convinced that somehow this situation—which smacked of a set-up—was actually Behrmann's way of gaining revenge. (The police authorities claimed, however, that they had Mitchum under surveillance for half a year because of his alleged, well-known use of grass.)

When arrested, Mitchum was so sure that this hugely publicized incident would kill his career that when he was booked at the police station that evening and asked his occupation, he shot out, "Former actor." He was also convinced that the scandal signaled the end of his shaky marriage. (It did not. His wife and two sons returned to Los Angeles to stand by him.) Robert's studio, RKO, backed him during the ordeal, mostly to protect their interests in his three unreleased new pictures. They also thought the charges might not stick and that the publicity might bolster the new Mitchum screen entries. Because of tactical delays, the much-hyped trial did not get underway until January 10, 1949.

As a result of the courtroom case, the star and Leeds were sentenced to a year in the county jail (the third party was eventually cleared). Although the defendants' sentences were suspended, the duo was placed on a two-year probation and required to spend sixty days of that time in the county jail with jail time already accumulated to be deducted. Mitchum had to stop filming *The Big Steal* (1949) and start his sentence. He began his time by mopping and cleaning cells, but a few days later he was transferred to an honor farm where he worked at the cement plant.

When released from prison on March 30, 1949, Robert was asked what jail had been like. He replied "Just like Palm Springs—without the riff-raff, of course." Syndicated columnist Earl Wilson observed, "Mitchum may even have gained something from his arrest: it was the foundation of his being a Hollywood character."

Now a free man and breathing a sigh of relief that his soundstage days were not over, Robert announced, "This has been a milestone in my life. . . . a sad lesson. It's the last time anything like this will happen to me. . . . I've learned my lesson. . . . I hope I don't get into any more trouble. But who can say what I might do tomorrow?" Indeed. Robert went on to star in many more movies. Over the years, he had more run-ins with the law, usually over drunken misbehaving. Nevertheless, the rugged individualist continued living life his way—a straight-shooting maverick to the end.

Eddie Murphy

[Edward Regan Murphy]

APRIL 3, 1961–

In July 1983 the stand-up comic told *Time* magazine: "I was in the right place at the right time and said the right thing. And had a charming smile." He had first burst onto the entertainment scene in fall 1980 as a featured player on TV's *Saturday Night Live*. In short order Murphy became a cast regular and by 1982 had costarred in the surprise big-screen hit *48 HRS*. Soon Eddie inherited the mantle of Richard Pryor, who a decade earlier had been the king of comedy.

It was a heady time for the handsome young Murphy who had grown up in New York housing projects. He was earning many millions from his films, concerts, albums, and other products and having a tough emotional adjustment to his new power and material possessions. During this time, the outspoken black superstar made escalating career demands, enjoyed an opulent lifestyle, and was, increasingly, politically incorrect in his stand-up act. By the late 1980s Murphy had gained a bad reputation within the film industry and elsewhere. Then, in the mid-1990s, just as he was repositioning himself as the new, gentler and kinder Eddie Murphy, he had a bizarre street encounter. It threatened to eradicate his still potent career.

Eddie was born in 1961 in Brooklyn's Bushwick section, the second son of Lillian (a telephone operator) and Charles Murphy (a member of the New York City Transit Authority police and an amateur comedian). When Eddie was three, his parents separated and Lillian became seriously ill, requiring lengthy hospitalization. Eddie and his two-year-older brother, Charles, were placed in foster care with a very stern woman. When Murphy was eight, his dad died. The next year Lillian wed Vernon Lynch, a loading dock foreman. The Lynches—which later included another son, Vernon Jr.—moved to a predominantly black section of Roosevelt, Long Island. Pampered by his mother, Eddie did much TV watching, studying performers whom he mimicked with ease. At school, he was a class clown with a sharp, insulting tongue.

By age fifteen Murphy was a master of ceremonies at a local talent show. The positive attention he received from the intrigued girls in the audience convinced him that show business was his destiny. He polished his act, guided by Richard Pryor's X-rated albums. Later, Eddie earned stand-up comedy bookings in neighboring communities. Because of his outside interests, Murphy almost flunked out of high school before he graduated in August 1979.

Club performances in New York City and on the road led to *Saturday Night Live*. He was hired as the token African American. By *SNL*'s 1981–82 season he was earning $4,500 a week, which later jumped to $8,500 per episode. At the time he dated Robin Givens, a Harvard Medical School student and a future actress. When Eddie was teamed with Nick Nolte in *48 HRS.*, he stole the show. His next screen vehicle, *Trading Places* (1983), was an enormous hit. His 1983 stage act (*Eddie Murphy—Delirious*) was picketed wherever it played by gay men angered by his derogatory remarks on stage. Eddie was also accused of being strongly misogynistic in his profanity-filled stand-up routines. By now the star had a five-film, $15 million deal with Paramount Pictures, which included a $44 million cash bonus.

In 1984 Murphy's first single recording ("Party All the Time") the singer wannabe vocalized about his girl liking to party a lot. It referred to his twenty-year-old fiancée, Lisa Figuerora, a college biology major. The couple broke up in 1987 with Murphy convinced that women only cared for his money. In that year's concert film, *Eddie Murphy Raw*, the motor-mouth star unleashed sexist slurs reflecting a hostility toward women. By now the megastar had moved to a $3.5 million Colonial brick mansion in Englewood Cliffs, New Jersey, which he named Bubble Hill (in street parlance *bubble* means "party"), and which many likened to Elvis Presley's ostentatious Graceland—only on a grander scale.

By the late 1980s Eddie was renowned for traveling about with his black posse (many of them relatives and friends from his youth). His steady dates had included singer Whitney Houston and actress Jasmine Guy. However, it was model Nicole Mitchell (the daughter of a black U.S. Air Force pilot and a white British homemaker) who captured his interest. Their first child was born in 1989; they wed in

March 1993. (Their fifth child was born in January 2002.) Meanwhile, Murphy had reportedly fathered other offspring, leading to at least one paternity lawsuit. In fact, court actions brought against Eddie were becoming the order of the day now that he was a wealthy, visible target.

With *Harlem Nights* (1989) and *Another 48 HRS.* (1990), the glow was off his movie career. He had angered Paramount by his forced renegotiations of his filmmaking pact, disillusioned critics with his uninspired recent vehicles, and dampened his public's enthusiasm through repetitive, indulgent performances. Among the anti-Murphy camp was filmmaker Spike Lee who insisted (although they later patched up their differences) that Eddie was not doing right by the African American community.

The much-maligned Murphy retreated to Bubble Hill in New Jersey, becoming a rich recluse, surrounded by fifty-two cronies, pals, and workers. (At the time, his wife and children mostly resided in a West Coast mansion.) When not fretting about his tarnished image, Eddie recorded vocals in his elaborate home studio.

Struggling to regain his magic touch, Murphy drew bad press for his reported tardiness and abundant self-indulgence while making 1992's *Boomerang*. Eddie provided the story, produced, and starred in *Vampire from Brooklyn* (1995) but the public wasn't biting. Then he hit pay dirt with 1996's *The Nutty Professor*. He was back on top and had mellowed into a family man who only infrequently was abrasive publicly.

Then came the May 2, 1997, incident that evoked memories of Hugh Grant's 1995 notorious encounter with a prostitute in the front seat of a BMW. Eddie's misadventure occurred in West Hollywood. At the time his wife and children were at their Sacramento residence while Murphy was based in Los Angeles. Early that Friday morning the insomnia-ridden star had driven to an all-night Hollywood newsstand to buy reading matter. Next, as Murphy drove home along Santa Monica Boulevard in his Toyota Land Cruiser, he spotted a Hawaiian-looking woman on the corner of Formosa Avenue and stopped. According to Murphy, when she told him she was "working" the street, he suggested that he give her a ride back home and forget her nocturnal activities. (Later, Eddie stated that he had a known penchant for mingling with street people, often showering them with money, hoping they'd turn their lives around.) Murphy and his passenger had driven only a few miles when they were pulled over at 4:45 A.M. by undercover cops who had been surveilling the passenger's street activities.

It developed that the female prostitute was *not* a woman, but a twenty-year-old male of Samoan extraction named Atisone Seiuli, a known transvestite prostitute. Because Murphy was doing nothing illegal at the time, he was not detained. As for Seiuli, he had broken his probation from earlier arrests by failing to get an HIV test, and was sentenced to a ninety-day jail term.

For Murphy, this unpleasant incident easily could have wrecked his planned future with family-oriented moviegoers. While Eddie's publicist announced that his client was "simply trying to be a good Samaritan," the media and topical comics refused to let the case die. Some sources soon insisted they'd located other drag queen hookers who claimed to have been intimate with the star. The actor's attorney promptly filed suits against two tabloids. Then the media coverage died.

Suddenly in April 1998 the forgotten Murphy "good-Samaritan" debacle flared up again. On April 22 Atisone Seiuli was found dead, lying facedown in a pool of blood in front of a five-story Hollywood apartment building. Media speculation that the ugly death was suicide or murder quickly faded when police concluded that the victim had locked himself out of his digs and had been attempting to swing down into his apartment's window from the roof. (After that the Murphy case again vanished until an April 26, 2001, article in *New Times Los Angeles* revisited the event. Its reportage focused on an L.A. porn actor who allegedly had been involved in a reputed hush-up of transvestites who had spoken to the tabloids about being familiar with Murphy.)

Meanwhile, with his reputation secured anew, Murphy returned to filmmaking, including *Doctor Dolittle* (1998), *Nutty Professor II: The Klumps* (2000), *Dr. Dolittle 2* (2001), and *Showtime* (2002).

Tom Neal

[Thomas Neal]

JANUARY 28, 1914–AUGUST 7, 1972

In Hollywood's amazing annals few screen actors have had a greater propensity for picking the wrong mate than Neal, a compact, burly actor best known for such 1945 features as *Detour* and *First Yank into Tokyo* and the serial *Jungle Girl* (1941). One of his romantic misjudgments almost cost him a sizeable inheritance. Another exploded into a love triangle that ruined his film career, and the third misstep landed him in prison and led to his untimely death.

Born in Evanston, Illinois, Thomas was the son of a wealthy banker, Thomas C. Neal, and his wife, Mary Martin Neal. He was the first of two children, the other being a daughter. After attending Lake Forest Academy he enrolled at Northwestern University and then at Harvard. Besides dabbling in campus dramatics, he was quite athletic. His gridiron skill as a fullback resulted in his being chosen an All-American. He was adept at other sports and turned his boxing proficiency into a brief career in the professional ring. In the fall of 1934 he arrived in New York, intent on a stage career. Unfortunately, he met Inez Martin, a buxom ex-*Ziegfeld Follies* chorine who had been the mistress of notorious gambler Arnold Rothstein. After the gangster's murder in 1928, Inez inherited Rothstein's $100,000 life insurance policy plus an additional $50,000 from contesting the deceased's will. When Tom told the press that he and Inez (nearly twice his age) were to wed, Neal's father rushed to Manhattan. He threatened to withdraw a planned $500,000 inheritance for his boy, and Inez suddenly departed for Bermuda.

Tom now refocused on Broadway, debuting in September 1935 in *If This Be Treason*. The play flopped as did his next two shows. Undaunted, the cocky, good-looking Neal moved on to Hollywood with an MGM contract. His debut was in *Out West with the Hardys* (1938) starring Mickey Rooney. Things went well for Tom at the first-class studio until he was cast in Joan Crawford's *Strange Cargo* (1940). During preproduction, Neal made sexually inappropriate remarks toward his leading lady. The brash newcomer was dropped from the picture and soon dismissed from MGM. Thereafter, he scrambled for film parts, but was saved by World War II. While actors his age were being drafted, past sports injuries kept him 4-F and available for celluloid roles. Neal worked in budget pictures for Columbia and other lesser lots. He played the Japanese lead in RKO's *Behind the Rising Sun* (1943), which was a big hit. Then it was back to starring in minor releases at poverty row studios.

In the late 1940s Neal, having inherited from his late father, wed actress Vicky Lane. They lived in Bel Air, but the joy was short lasting. By 1950 the couple divorced, with she charging he was insanely jealous. Still the cocky playboy, he soon became enamored of twenty-four-year-old Barbara Payton, a divorcée

Tom Neal as *Racket Man* (1944).
(Courtesy of JC Archives)

and actress whose figure and party girl reputation were stronger than her acting skills. She was then involved with veteran actor Franchot Tone but was intrigued by Neal. However, she changed her mind again and returned to Franchot (who was twice her age), only to switch her allegiance back to Tom. They were to marry on September 14, 1951. On September 13, he learned that Barbara and Franchot had gone nightclub hopping. A steamed Tom awaited the couple at her house when they returned around 1:30 A.M. Tone was drunk and challenged the decade-younger and far-more-fit Neal to fisticuffs. Neal tried to dissuade him, but the older man insisted. Tom knocked Franchot unconscious with his first blow and then began battering him on the front lawn. A hysterical Payton intervened and was smacked on the chin by Neal. Later Tone was rushed to the hospital with a broken nose, a fractured cheekbone, and brain concussion. Tone sued Neal for $150,000 but settled for $100,000. On September 28, 1951, Franchot and Barbara wed; several weeks later the groom filed for divorce. In spring 1952 his amended petition cited intimacy between Barbara and Tom.

The high-profile three-ring circus became a smutty Hollywood joke, which ruined Neal's once promising career. (Payton herself was soon washed up in pictures. In the early 1960s she became a public drunk and was arrested for prostitution. She died in 1967.) Tom returned to Chicago where he did a few TV soap dramas, then in the mid-1950s took another stab at Hollywood, but the studio gates were closed to him. He moved to Palm Springs, working as a restaurant night manager, and then learning the landscaping business. In 1956, now a Christian Scientist, he wed Patricia Fenton, and the next year they had a boy, Thomas Jr. Sadly, Pat died of cancer in 1958.

In 1960 Neal married twenty-four-year-old Gale Bennett, a receptionist at the Palm Springs Racquet Club. However, their union soon proved stormy. When his landscape business failed, he had to declare bankruptcy. In 1965 Tom went to Evanston to see his eight-year-old son who was living with his sister. Meanwhile, back in Palm Springs Gale filed for divorce, charging extreme cruelty. After a ten-week absence, the ex-actor returned home hoping to change Gale's mind. When she told him that a man had followed her home one day, he brought out his .45-caliber pistol and instructed her on its usage.

A little after midnight on April 2, 1965, Gale was shot to death in their home. The prosecution would claim Tom killed her while she lay sleeping. Neal insisted that while making love, a fight had erupted in which he accused her of infidelity. She had then grabbed the nearby pistol and tried to shoot him. According to Tom, while wrestling the pistol away from her, the firearm had discharged. (The gun mysteriously disappeared and was never found.) Other witnesses claimed that hours after the killing, Tom had told them he had shot his wife. (Neal insisted they had misunderstood his statements made when he was still in a daze.) Then Neal's neighbors told of hearing the couple arguing before the shooting. While Neal's defense team got the criminal charges lowered from first-degree murder, Neal was found guilty of involuntary manslaughter. In November 1965 the judge handed out a severe one-to-ten-year sentence for Neal.

After six years behind bars in California, Neal was paroled in December 1971. Photographs of the one-time playboy star revealed him to be white haired, haggard, and stooped; he looked shockingly older than his fifty-seven years. Most of the next months were spent at the modest North Hollywood apartment that he shared with his fifteen-year-old son. About 7:30 A.M. on August 7, 1972, when Neal failed to get up, his son found him dead in bed from a heart attack.

Jack Nicholson

[John Joseph Nicholson]

APRIL 22, 1937–

Back in the 1950s when Nicholson made his first screen test, the director cautioned, "I don't know what we can use you for, but if we ever do need you we'll need you real bad." Later Jack made his film debut in *The Cry Baby Killer* (1958). Since then he has appeared in more than sixty features, winning three Academy Awards (1976's *One Flew over the Cuckoo's Nest*; 1983's *Terms of Endearment*—Best Supporting Actor; 1997's *As Good as It Gets*) and being Oscar-nominated for several others. He directed a trio of films (1971's *Drive, He Said*; 1978's *Goin' South*; 1990's *The Two Jakes*), had screenwriting credit on six entries (including 1971's *Drive, He Said*), and produced four pictures (such as 1968's *Head*). Such remarkable statistics become more impressive when one considers the hectic off-camera life of "Smilin' Jack"—he of the devilish grin and those ever-present sunshades. Over the years the five-foot, nine-inch celebrity earned a reputation as one of Hollywood's *most* prodigious ladies' men, ranking up there with his good pal Warren Beatty. According to "Hollywood Madam" Heidi Fleiss, "In terms of sexual prowess, Jack is a goddamn great lover."

Besides his attention to the many, many women in his life, his allegiance to the Los Angeles Lakers basketball team was legendary. His courtside presence at their games rated him an "A" for attendance. Then there was his reported affinity for heavy partying and for substance abuse (especially alcohol and cocaine).

Nicholson was born in 1937 in Neptune, New Jersey, where he was raised by Ethel May Nicholson, a beautician, and her daughters, June and Lorraine. Ethel May's husband, an alcoholic, drifted out of the family's life when the future actor was an infant. It was not until 1974 that Jack learned (when a researcher for *Time* magazine was examining his past) that Ethel May was actually his grandmother and that his older sister June (a former chorus girl and vaudeville tap dancer) was really his mother. Nicholson never learned who his biological father was, but claimed later, "I'm not overly curious."

In high school Jack displayed a volcanic temper, once smashing up the locker room of the opposing basketball team. During these years Nicholson also performed in class plays because it was a good way to meet "chicks." By the time he graduated, his sister/mother was living in Hollywood and he followed her there. He took acting classes and later met prolific B picture filmmaker Roger Corman. The latter hired Jack for *The Cry Baby Killer*. In 1962 Nicholson married actress Sandra Knight (who was in his acting group), and the next year she gave birth to their daughter, Jennifer. (It was also in 1963 that his mother, June, passed away.) Pressured by the need to earn money, Nicholson worked long hours acting and writing screenplays. In the process his marriage came apart. A therapist suggested the couple try LSD. He found the mind-expanding experience enlightening, but she was frightened by the drug trip and turned to religion. To get away from his domestic problems, Jack worked on films in the Philippines. As his womanizing escalated, Sandra had had enough and they divorced in 1967, with she gaining custody of their child.

In this period Jack romanced statuesque, dark-haired Mimi Machu, who bore a resemblance to Sandra Knight (Mimi was tall as would be many of the women who figured strongly in Nicholson's later mating choices). Under the name I. J. Jefferson, Mimi appeared in several of Jack's movies, including *Hell's Angels on Wheels* (1967). Their competitive alliance lasted for three years, coming to an end as he gained professional fame with the trendsetting *Easy Rider* (1969). She was breaking up with the actor when, during the making of *Five Easy Pieces* (1970), he had an affair with coplayer Susan Anspach. Their son, Caleb James, was born in September 1970. However, Jack was not over Mimi and Susan was married, so it was not the right time for them. (Later, Nicholson and Anspach would have a stormy relationship, climaxing when she filed a breach-of-contract suit against him in 1995, claiming he was asking for the repayment of money he had "given" her in the late 1980s and early 1990s.)

At loose ends, Jack reencountered an old friend, Michelle Phillips (formerly of the Mamas and Papas). She had married and divorced actor Dennis Hopper earlier in 1970 and now she and Nicholson began a relationship. Gentleman Jack phoned his pal Hopper telling him the news. Dennis responded, "Best of luck, man. It's over

Max Julien (left), Susan Strasberg, and Jack Nicholson (right) in *Psych-Out* (1968). (Courtesy of Doug McClelland)

between her and me anyhow." The couple began living together in a Beverly Hills hillside house that Jack had just bought. Each party insisted they did not want to be restricted by marriage, but everything ended when she concluded he was too career oriented. More than two years after they began living together, she moved out, this time finding a haven with Jack's good buddy Warren Beatty.

In the early 1970s Jack's film career soared, and he was reaching the $1 million per movie salary level by the time of *Chinatown* (1974). Around this time Jack started seeing Anjelica Huston, daughter of esteemed director John Huston. She was taller than Jack, fourteen years his junior, and a former occasional actress who preferred modeling. Tired of "skunk-spotting" as he termed his constant searching for new female companionship, he began a relationship with smart, strong-willed Anjelica. They broke up and reunited several times, their stormy partings often prompted by his latest excess, especially his philandering. (Once when Anjelica rebuked Nicholson for his affairs with young women, he retorted, "What can I do? I'm hot.")

Some said it was retaliation for Jack's woman chasing that led Huston to hook up with actor Ryan O'Neal. Meanwhile Jack was in London to make *The Shining* (1980), and he met Margaret Trudeau, the ex-wife of the Canadian Prime Minister. Their affair began in the back seat of her limousine. However, Nicholson still pined for Anjelica, so Margaret looked elsewhere. Later she consoled herself by having a thing with O'Neal and, subsequently, reunited with Jack at a Hollywood party for new moments of passion.

While a superb actor, Jack fared less well with domesticity, scampering through relationships of various durations during the 1980s as he made such pictures as *Heartburn* (1986) and *Batman* (1989—for which he received megamillions for playing the Joker). Meanwhile, in late 1987, he met blond Rebecca Broussard, a former beauty queen from Kentucky. She had married a record producer some months before encountering Jack at an intimate party. The two of them clicked and, in the coming weeks, she and her husband ended their marriage. She took up residence in a home off of Benedict Canyon and continued her association with Jack. (Meanwhile, as far as the public knew, Nicholson and Anjelica Huston were still a close item.) Jack had two children (1990 and 1992) with Rebecca.

In 1994, the year he starred in *Wolf*, Nicholson and Broussard split up for good, leading the star to say, "I feel burned, I miss our time together—even more so because I was such a cynical man before our relationship began and now I'm even more cynical about the notion of domestic tranquility." Also that year (in March), freewheeling Jack was charged with misdemeanor assault and vandalism. It was a case of road rage—supposedly he was cut off in traffic by another driver. Reportedly Nicholson smashed the motorist's vehicle with a golf club. The victim filed a civil suit against the movie star, stating that he'd feared for his life and that he had been injured by the breaking glass. The suit was settled out of court and the criminal charges were dropped.

Then, in late 1996, the star had another legal problem when two women-for-hire alleged that not only did he not pay for their special services but that he also was not a gentleman. (The civil case that erupted was settled for $32,000.) Some weeks later, a chipper Nicholson turned up to accept his star on the Hollywood Walk of Fame. A few years ahead he would have a high-profile romance with actress Lara Flynn Boyle, thirty-three years his junior and the former date of comedian David Spade. Their romance seesawed back and forth, much to the entertainment of the supermarket tabloids.

With such a tumultuous life that so often defied logic, how better to conclude than with one of Nicholson's more famous non sequiturs, shouted as he accepted his Oscar in 1984: "All you rock people down at the Roxy and up in the Rockies, rock on!" Go figure!

Nick Nolte

[Nicolas Nolte]

FEBRUARY 8, 1941–

In four decades on the screen, this untraditional, beefy actor was twice Oscar-nominated (1991's *The Prince of Tides*; 1997's *Affliction*) and proved himself a versatile, intense performer who crawled inside offbeat roles to capture his colorful alter egos. Off camera, the hulking six-foot, one-inch star had another reputation: as a former colossal boozer and substance abuser who, in the 1990s, became a zealous health nut prone to extreme oddity. (It was not unusual for the seasoned leading man to mingle in public in green hospital scrubs or pajamas and bathrobe. The unpredictable Nick was also known for cruising along in his car while jabbing out the driver's window a leg prosthesis that had belonged to his late father.)

He was born in 1941 in Omaha, Nebraska, the second child of Frank and Helen Nolte. His dad was away serving in World War II and didn't meet his boy for three years. After the war, the Noltes lived in Ames, Iowa. The father was a traveling engineer and salesman; his mother was a fashion buyer. Imaginative Nick was a shy but mischievous child. (He once jumped off a garage roof and landed on a picket fence—straddling it.) Nolte inherited his father's gridiron skills, but was dropped from the football team in his junior year at Omaha's Benson High because of his partying activities. His enraged parents immediately sold their home and moved across town so Nick could play on a different high school squad.

When Nolte was at Arizona State on a football scholarship, his parents separated, badly upsetting their son. During this period he switched colleges frequently, reportedly quitting when he was pressured to attend classes. He supported himself by selling fake draft cards, which led to his being arrested in 1960 and convicted in 1961. His forty-five-year sentence and $75,000 fine were suspended, but he was placed on a five-year probation. (At an earlier time he had been convicted of reckless driving and sentenced to a month in jail.) Meanwhile, Nick realized he would never make it to the pros and abandoned that dream.

Since his felony conviction had made him ineligible for the draft, Nolte spent time reading and debating his future while staying with his mother in Texas. Later he discovered that acting made him feel comfortable. He signed up for drama and photography courses at Phoenix College. In 1966 he married actress Sheila Page whom he met while working at the Phoenix Little Theater. (The couple divorced in 1972.) By 1968 he was working in Excelsior, Minnesota, at the Old Log Theater, supplementing his $150 salary with modeling assignments during the day. Playwright William Inge happened to see him perform several years later and cast Nick in a Los Angeles production of *The Last Pad* (1973). Inge committed suicide the week the show opened, giving the production much notoriety.

Nolte had already done TV roles when, at age thirty-five, he signed to play the seventeen-year-old Tom Jordache in the miniseries *Rich Man, Poor Man* (1976). The show was a huge success and made Nick television's new golden boy. Holding out for a follow-up hit, he finally accepted *The Deep* (1977), but he was humiliated to have sold out to play a one-dimensional screen hunk and second fiddle to shapely Jacqueline Bisset in a wet T-shirt. Meanwhile, in 1977, after a five-year relationship, he split with galpal Karen Ecklund. She sued for palimony and the bitter contest was settled out of court. The next year, 1978, he married Sharyn Haddad, a twenty-two-year-old dancer he'd met in a Hollywood bar. His union to "Legs" ended unpleasantly in 1983. (Meanwhile, while making the unsuccessful *Cannery Row* in 1982, he reportedly had a close relationship with costar Debra Winger.)

Throughout the 1980s Nolte gained renown for tackling over-the-edge types on camera and for ferociously researching these roles. To portray the philosophical bum in *Down and Out in Beverly Hills* (1986), he literally became a nonbathing homeless type, frightening costars Bette Midler and Richard Dreyfuss. In *Farewell to the King* (1989) Nick was so zealous in prepping for his role as the deranged army deserter, who became a tribal chief in Borneo during World War II, that he overwhelmed director John Milius. To win the role of the corrupt NYPD detective in *Q & A* (1990), Nick embarked on an eating binge, gaining fifty pounds.

Nolte was a full-time boozer when he made 1984's *Grace Quigley* with Katharine Hepburn. Having had to cope decades earlier with Spencer Tracy's monumental drinking, Katharine severely chastised the besotted Nick for having fallen in every gutter in town. Gruff-voiced Nolte told the veteran screen queen: "I've got a few to go yet." Other stories of Nick's legendary self-destructive carousing included his driving a chopper madly along California roads—nude. Or the time he awoke in a Los Angeles house that he had no memory of having rented and then suddenly deciding to have tons of rocks dropped on the front lawn to see how it might look. During this reckless era of substance abuse he wed young model Rebecca Linger in 1984. A doctor's daughter, she was nineteen years his junior. Before they finally divorced in 1994 they had a child, son Brawley.

It was playing opposite Barbra Streisand in *The Prince of Tides* that won Nolte his first Academy Award nomination, made him a sex symbol at age fifty, and turned him into a hot box-office property. In a rash of quick-buck decisions that he later bitterly regretted, he starred in several high-priced properties (1994's *I Love Trouble*, 1995's *Jefferson in Paris*) that were huge flops. While making another of these fiascoes, 1994's prophetically titled *I'll Do Anything*, he met actress Vicki Lewis and they began a romance. (In 2001, after several years of joint living with Nick, Vicki moved into her own residence—three doors away from Nolte's place.)

By the mid-1990s Nolte had an epiphany about the "obscene" sums of cash he was being paid to appear in junk projects. He repositioned himself as a craftsman willing to tackle small independent films that had challenging roles. As such he signed on for 1997's *Afterglow* and *Affliction*, as well as 1999's *Simpatico*. He had also decided that now that he was a father he had to stop physically abusing his body with drink and other substances, and he attended twelve-step programs. Living on several acres of Malibu land, he developed a passion for tending his organically grown vegetables and fruits, using untraditional gardening techniques. He also became hooked on unique treatments to rejuvenate his body, unmindful of how bizarre or untested the regimens might be. As to his preference for nudity, the eccentric star reasoned, "There's nothing wrong with nudity. It just depends on where you decided to be nude."

In the twenty-first century, the movie maverick with the gravel voice (thanks to chain-smoking and heavy living) calmed down considerably off camera. He was no longer the wild Lothario of bygone years. Said Nolte in 2001: "I could have died any number of times. I did a lot of stupid and dangerous things in my younger years. I had a penchant for self-destruction."

Sean Penn

[Sean Penn]

August 17, 1960–

Thrice Oscar-nominated (1995's *Dead Man Walking*, 1999's *Sweet and Lowdown*, and 2001's *I Am Sam*) Penn proved his film acting acumen early with *Fast Times at Ridgemont High* (1982, as a spaced-out surfer dude) and *Bad Boys* (1983, as the hostile slum youth guilty of robbery and homicide). Although always deeply committed to his acting craft, Sean ached to direct movies. Unlike most actors-turned-helmers he proved his noteworthy skills with *The Indian Runner* (1991), *The Crossing Guard* (1995), and *The Pledge* (2001), the first two of which he also scripted.

Sean also excelled at other skills, including being Hollywood's king of off-screen antics. Many of these outrageous shenanigans had to do with his strong dislike of the media, his festering temper, and his strong possessiveness when in a romantic relationship. This antagonism between ultra private Sean and the inquiring press snowballed in the 1980s. The paparazzi seemed to have a knack for inciting the volatile actor into his most explosive behavior. (A favorite battle cry of his was "Get that motherf***ing camera away from me.") At no time was pugnacious, hard-drinking Penn more on the offensive than from 1985 to 1989 when he was wed to Madonna Louise Veronica Ciccone.

Penn was born in Santa Monica, California, the second of three sons of actor and director Leo Penn and former actress Eileen (Ryan) Penn. Never enthused about formal education, Sean persistently got into minor scrapes with authorities. After graduating from Santa Monica High School in 1978, he worked for two years with a Los Angeles theater group doing production, directing, and acting. He made his TV acting debut in a 1978 episode of *Barnaby Jones*. His Broadway bow came with 1981's *Heartland*. He displayed a remarkable intensity that year as a military academy student in the movie *Taps*. Thereafter, he impressed critics with performances in movies that did not match his skills (1985's *The Falcon and the Snowman*).

By now a star, his antipathy to the media had accelerated. He insisted that if any journalists were allowed on his film sets, they were to *never* be in his line of vision. On his dressing room door was the warning "Never Enter Without Knocking. Never Knock Without Need."

By early 1985 wiry, offbeat-looking Penn, a member of Hollywood's Brat Pack, had already had romantic relationships with actresses Elizabeth McGovern and Mary Stuart Masterson. That January 10, Penn was invited by director Mary Lambert to the music video set of "Like a Virgin." Its star was fast-rising music diva Madonna. Sean was intrigued with her, but the Material Girl acted cool toward him. A few days later Penn invited Madonna to a party at Warren Beatty's and their whirlwind romance began. One problem with the twosome was that she was then dating diminutive singer Prince and was not about to stop to appease jealousy-prone Sean. This

Sean Penn with his wife, actress Robin Wright Penn. (Photo by Albert L. Ortega)

led to a heated argument at Madonna's New York digs where agitated Sean allegedly smashed his hand through her apartment door.

In June 1985 when Madonna visited Penn, who was on location in Tennessee for *At Close Range* (1986), the couple who seemed to have so little in common got engaged. One day in Nashville, a British photographer sought to snap the famous duo. Sean took offense and pelted the intruder with one or more rocks and then charged after the man. Penn was charged with misdemeanor assault and battery. Eventually he was fined $100 and given a ninety-day suspended sentence. Penn's contentiousness with the media accelerated weeks later when nude photos of his wife-to-be (taken in the late 1970s) surfaced in *Penthouse* magazine.

On August 16, 1985—her twenty-seventh birthday and the day before his twenty-fifth—they were married atop an ocean bluff at a friend's lavish estate in Malibu, California. Despite precautions, news of the private event for 220 guests leaked out and press helicopters buzzed overhead throughout the ceremony. An outraged Sean—screaming at the party-crashers—allegedly fired two warning pistol shots at the hovering crafts, having earlier run down to the beach and written in the sand his personal message to the intrusive press. It read "F*** Off."

By early 1986 the honeymooners were in Hong Kong to costar in *Shanghai Surprise*. Unhappy with the movie, the unrelenting media, and coping with being wed to one of the world's most famous women, feisty Sean drank heavily throughout the project. His uncooperative behavior made him and Madonna (no longer very pleasant with journalists) media targets. When the couple flew to England to finish the picture, the British press labeled them "The Poisoned Penns."

In April 1986 the Penns were in Los Angeles. At Helena, a club in Silverlake, songwriter David Wolinski spotted Madonna and kissed his pal hello. A seething Sean punched and kicked Wolinski and beat him with a chair. The actor's wife and the club's owner yanked Penn out of the venue to cool off. The victim filed charges and in mid-July 1986 Sean was fined $1,000 and put on a year's probation. (An aghast Madonna had another taste of her husband's hot temper during their screaming match at Manhattan's Pyramid Club.)

By August 1986 the duo were in retreat in New York after the devastating opening of *Shanghai Surprise*. Every time they exited their Central Park West apartment, the press was in full pursuit. One evening, when photographer Anthony Savignano followed the Penns home from a nearby restaurant, Sean spat at the man. Reportedly, Anthony shoved the actor. In the ensuing scuffle Penn hit both Savignano and another photographer. While Savignano did not press charges, the incident became part of Sean's mounting public dossier.

As Sean began filming the cops vs. gangs drama *Colors* (1988) in spring 1987, his relationship with Madonna was cooling fast. That April 2, Jeffrey Klein, an extra on the movie set, attempted to take candid photos of the star. Penn went crazy and spit on Klein, who spit back and then was beaten by Sean. Days later Klein filed an assault charge, which could be deemed a violation of Sean's probation. A bench warrant was issued for the star's arrest. On May 1, 1987, the star turned himself in to the Los Angeles Police Department, but was released on his own recognizance pending the hearing. Meanwhile, in late May Penn was pulled over for running a red light and for speeding. He was charged with reckless and drunken driving. Now with two parole violations, he faced jail time. On June 23, 1987, he was sentenced to sixty days in jail and two years of probation and ordered to undergo counseling.

On August 1, 1987, Sean began his sentence in a private jail facility in Bridgeport, California. After five days he was allowed out to shoot a role in his father's movie *Judgment in Berlin* (1988). Then he returned to Bridgeport. Tired of the media-bashing about his so-called privileged jail treatment, Sean had himself transferred to the stark Los Angeles County Jail. (In the cell across the way from him was Richard Ramirez, the convicted Night Stalker.) To fill the long hours of confinement Sean wrote a play. After serving thirty-three days, Penn was released on September 18, 1987, for good behavior. Reportedly, when he reunited briefly with his wife, she was *not* thrilled to see him.

That November Madonna was busy in New York while Penn was in L.A. At Thanksgiving time he appeared at his wife's Manhattan apartment. Whatever transpired, on December 4, 1987, she filed for divorce, but two weeks later she withdrew her petition. For much of

1988, the unhappy couple worked far apart from one another. When Madonna became pals with comedian Sandra Bernhard, the press kidded about the scope of their relationship. Madonna and Bernhard played along with the teasing, but Penn was furious.

By the end of 1988, the Penn-Madonna marriage was reduced to heated arguments. On December 28, Madonna summoned the police to their Malibu home claiming she feared entering to collect possessions because of Sean's temper and the fact that he kept firearms on the premises. The cops arrived to find, according to Penn, him calmly eating cereal. Madonna and her several armed escorts entered the house peacefully. On January 9, 1989, Madonna filed for divorce and this time she became the ex-Mrs. Penn.

Once Penn and Madonna split, the media circus that surrounded him (thanks to her huge fame) mostly ended, although Sean did not go gently into the night as he mellowed into middle age. There were bumps in his 1990s marriage to actress Robin Wright (with whom he had two children), problems on the set of Woody Allen's *Sweet and Lowdown*, and other vocal occasions when Penn felt a studio did not see the proper light—Sean style.

Matthew Perry

[Matthew Langford Perry]

AUGUST 19, 1969–

As wise-cracking, terribly insecure Chandler Bing, he gained great fame in the TV sitcom *Friends* (1994–   ). As the hit show entered its eighth season in fall 2001, Perry was earning a whopping $750,000 per episode. Added to his past income from the program, as well as from his feature film and other work, the nearly six-foot-tall Matthew should have been bursting with happiness. However, at the time, due to past drug and alcohol addictions, he was still feeling his way back into normalcy and trying to stay out of media headlines.

Perry was born in Williamstown, Massachusetts, in 1969, the only child of actor John Bennett Perry and his wife, Suzanne, the former press secretary for the late Canadian Prime Minister Pierre Trudeau. His parents divorced when Matthew was a year old. He went with his mother to live in Ottawa, Canada, where she later married NBC-TV broadcaster Keith Morrison. As a result of a childhood accident, Perry lost the tip of the middle finger of his right hand. However, that didn't stop him from becoming a tennis whiz, both at Ashbury (a private boys school) and as a top-ranked junior player in Canada.

At age fifteen Matthew moved to Los Angeles to be with his father who had gained recognition playing the sailor in 1970s Old Spice TV commercials and since then had done a lot of small-screen work. Observing his parent work at his craft, the teenager became intrigued with acting. His feeling was enhanced by performing in theatrics at Buckley High School. While Perry continued to play tennis and rank high nationally in the sport, the lure of show business was quickly winning out. Said Matthew, "I liked the attention. I wanted the light to shine on me."

By the mid-1980s the teenager was making guest appearances on such TV fare as *Charles in Charge* and *Silver Spoons*. With his clean-cut looks and facile charm, he was in demand for teleseries—although the shows never lasted long: *Second Chance* (1987), *Sydney* (1990). By now he'd abandoned college and tennis plans and was dedicated to his acting career. He had made his big-screen debut in *A Night in the Life of Jimmy Reardon* (1988) starring River Phoenix, but most of his subsequent movie work was in telefeatures. After the failed *Home Free* (1993) TV series, Perry was featured in the TV pilot *LAX 2194* that dealt with airport baggage carriers in the future.

Meanwhile, Matthew kept being told of an upcoming TV series called (originally) *Friends Like Us* that everyone said had a perfect part for him. But he was unavailable because of *LAX 2194*. When that show failed to be picked up by a network, Perry auditioned for *Friends* and was quickly hired. During the summer break after the hit show's first season, Perry had plastic surgery to reshape his nose and redefine his chin. By that fall Matthew, who had bought a three-bedroom home in the Hollywood Hills, was back on *Friends*. In his spare time he played tennis and was starting to party heavily on the local club circuit. When Julia Roberts (then estranged from her husband Lyle Lovett) guest-starred on *Friends* in January 1996—playing Chandler's grudge-ridden school chum—there was talk briefly that the two were dating off camera.

By the close of *Friends'* third TV season in spring 1997, it was very noticeable that Perry had lost thirty-five pounds. The supermarket tabloids speculated that the flippant performer might have some dread disease. He claimed his thinness was the result of his hectic work schedule, which included making movies such as *Fools Rush In* (1997). In early June it was revealed that Perry had checked into the Hazelden Foundation of Center City, Minnesota, for treatment of a "dependency on a

A seemingly carefree Matthew Perry.
(Photo by Albert L. Ortega)

prescription medication." It was later revealed that in recent months he'd been on a combination of the prescription painkiller Vicodin, booze, cigarettes, and coffee—with little attention to food or rest. Some tabloid journalists suggested a lack of a lasting female relationship had led the affluent actor to substance abuse; others put forward that the drug addiction resulted from taking too much of the painkiller after Perry's snowmobile accident some months earlier. After a few weeks Matthew left rehab and was back in Los Angeles. By then, he was regaining some of his lost weight.

In August 1997 twenty-eight-year-old Matthew was to tape new *Friends* episodes. Instead, late that month he checked into Ottawa General Hospital (Canada) to deal with his recurring drug addiction. His mother, who lived in that city, explained, "He's just a good kid who got too much fame, money, and attention too soon."

After his latest clinic stay, Perry rejoined the hit show, and the following summer he was in Toronto making the movie *Three to Tango* (1999) with Neve Campbell. By then Matthew's waistline had gone in the opposite direction. While his TV career remained in high gear, none of Perry's feature films broke any box-office records, which frustrated the actor. Meanwhile, Matthew's weight kept escalating as the chain-smoker continued to drink and party. On the plus side, according to supermarket publications, he now had a live-in roommate. She was ex-waitress Rene Ashton, a year younger than thirty-year-old Matthew. However, by the end of 1999—a few months after they began sharing space together—they had separated.

The spring of 2000 saw Perry hospitalized again. He had lost weight and was having severe stomach pain. This time he was at Cedars-Sinai Medical Center. His two-week stay there proved to be for pancreatitis, which could lead to a chronic inflammatory condition. Partly the ailment was caused by his past drinking and drug binges, but another part was due, supposedly, to the tension of the *Friends* cast demanding a big salary hike. (The negotiations led to a new two-year pact that would bring *each* player an estimated $40 million.)

A much richer and heavier Perry left the hospital on May 20. As he was driving homeward on a narrow street in the Hollywood Hills, his green Porsche swerved (said to have been caused when he turned quickly to avoid an oncoming vehicle) ran off the road, and smashed into the front porch of a private home. Fortunately the owners were away at the time. The police reported that the unhurt actor had not been under the influence of any substance when he wrecked his vehicle.

By the fall of 2000, Matthew's roller-coaster weight—which received almost as much media attention as Oprah Winfrey's—had dropped by thirty pounds. Then the next February while he was splitting his time between *Friends* and making the movie *Servicing Sara* with Elizabeth Hurley in Dallas, Texas, it was said that he'd suffered another pancreatitis attack. Within weeks, however, it was made known he'd entered a rehab facility in Marina Del Rey, southwest of Los Angeles. By late March Perry was back on the TV sitcom set to film his character's wedding to Monica Geller (played by Courteney Cox Arquette). Reportedly some of the *Friends* squad offered the actor tough love regarding his recurring substance abuse. Then, on April 19, 2001, he was involved in another auto accident that banged up his new BMW car. The incident occurred in west Los Angeles, but it was the other driver (a seventy-five-year-old woman) who was at fault.

As Perry wise-cracked through the 2001–02 season of *Friends*, fat watchers were quick to report that Matthew had climbed over the 200-pound threshold and was moving higher. Such has been the up-and-down life of an extremely rich TV star.

River Phoenix

[River Jude Bottom]

AUGUST 23, 1970–OCTOBER 31, 1993

The drug overdose death of Phoenix in 1993 badly shook the public. Even today, many still have not gotten over the heartbreak. The loss affected people on several deep levels. Here was a superbly talented, Oscar-nominated actor dead at twenty-three, so much of his promise yet unrealized. In addition, the late star had grown up in the public eye and many felt as if they had been intimate witnesses to his maturation. Then too, there was a profound sense of sadness that this human being, wise beyond his years in some ways, could have fallen prey to destructive substance abuse. Most of all, many who knew only the public River, associated the appealing young man with vegetarianism, ecological causes, spiritual goodness, and pure living. When it was generally revealed after his death that he had been indulging in drugs for a long time, many felt betrayed. It was hard to fathom that this "innocent" artist was full of human frailties that led to his abrupt death on a West Hollywood sidewalk.

Like Abraham Lincoln the future movie star was born in a log cabin, but this one was a communal house on a mint farm in Madras, Oregon. Phoenix's father had been a carpenter, and his mother a secretary in New York City. The hippie couple had first met in Los Angeles in 1968 and teamed together working as itinerant fruit pickers. The "Jude" part of his name derived from the river of life described in Hermann Hesse's *Siddhartha* (1922). By the time the boy was two, his parents had joined the Children of God, a strongly counterculture sect. The family—which later included River's siblings Joaquin, Summer, Rain, and Liberty—relocated to South America where John was the cult's Archbishop of Venezuela. By 1977 they had become disillusioned with, and left, the Children of God, and had settled in central Florida. In was at this time that they changed the family name to Phoenix. During this period of readjustment to a more conventional life, the family survived many tough financial times and the children received very spotty educations. Often, River and Rain would perform songs on the streets to beg coins.

As a child River was drawn to music and proved eager to perfect his skills. By 1978 he and seven-year-old Rain were singing publicly and often winning local talent events. Soon the family had moved to Los Angeles where the parents hoped that their children could get into show business and, once famous, they could recruit others to the family's beliefs. It wasn't too long before cute Phoenix was playing his guitar during the audience warm-up sessions on a Los Angeles–based TV game show. He had a big break when he was hired to play Guthrie McFadden, the youngest brother on the teleseries *Seven Brides for Seven Brothers* (1982–83). Later the young actor did commercials, but he hated the phoniness of that part of the business.

Now a "seasoned" entertainer, River made his first theatrical feature, *Explorers* (1985), cast as a nerdy, smart youngster. However, it was the notable *Stand by Me* (1986), based on Stephen King's novella, that gave River national attention. In *The Mosquito Coast* (1986), set in a Caribbean jungle, Phoenix was seen as the son of Harrison Ford. It was on this picture that Phoenix first worked with actress Martha Plimpton, then age fifteen.

On the surface it seemed that River was dealing well with his growing success, pleased that he could help his family by being the household's breadwinner. However, he was conflicted by such responsibilities. He was also upset by the growing gulf between his parents as his mother monitored her son's career closely while the father was withdrawing from their lifestyle of material success. It was in this period that Phoenix began experimenting with cocaine. He kept such extracurricular activity from his parents—and the public. River grew adept at disguising his activities.

Phoenix had his first leading role in *A Night in the Life of Jimmy Reardon* (1988), which inappropriately cast him as a girl-chasing teen. Much more successful was that year's *Running on Empty*, for which he was Oscar-nominated as Best Supporting Actor for playing the son of 1960s radicals on the lam. Martha Plimpton, his real-life romance, appeared as his love interest.

Off camera River was struggling with his growing fame and escalating guilt concerning his childhood ambition of helping to save the world, which was proving to be an impossible goal. Provoked by the temptations available to a popular, good-looking movie actor on the rise, the conflicted teenager escaped into cocaine and other recreational drugs, including hallucinogenics. Never one to do things by half measures, he grew excessive in his private life of substance abuse while in public he projected a strong image as a proselytizer for the purer aspects of a God-filled life.

By the later 1980s the Phoenix family was again based in Florida, but there was growing dissention between the parents as to the course of River's life—should he continue his Hollywood career (which supported the household) or abandon the crass life and return to fundamentals in Florida. Torn between opposing forces, the actor's drug use, drinking, and cigarette smoking increased—all activities alien to his public image. He sought distraction in Aleka's Attic, the band that he had helped to form.

By the time that Phoenix, now a major screen personality, costarred with pal Keanu Reeves in *My Own Private Idaho* (1991), River's fractured life had escalated badly. Some observers insisted that Phoenix, known for digging into his screen roles, had delved so deeply into his part as the drug-using male hustler in *Idaho*, that he had been unable to pull out of the substance abuse that reportedly occurred during the movie's filming.

In the period thereafter, Phoenix slipped frequently into a new off-camera guise, completely different from the wholesome heartthrob that the public so adored. Increasingly his interviews contained statements that seemed arrogant and crude. Martha Plimpton withdrew from River's life and singer and musician Suzanne Solgot, who shared a Gainesville, Florida, apartment with Phoenix, was often a fixture of the star's life.

As the early 1990s proceeded, those who mingled with the off-camera Phoenix were taken aback by the "new" River. While still a strong environmentalist (especially dedicated to animal rights), he now seemed a lost person who had given in to life's bad side and would not or could not find a way out through recovery. Also he was choosing peculiar screen projects in which to appear, ranging from the bizarre western *Silent Tongue* (1993) to *The Thing Called Love* (1993). The latter, directed by Peter Bogdanovich and set in Nashville, had Samantha Mathis (River's new girlfriend) as his costar. Several people noted River's repeated drug use and incoherence throughout the production. Back in Hollywood the word spread that the young star had become unreliable. There were many sightings of him high and unable to function normally. While he participated in occasional twelve-step meetings, he mostly remained in denial about his snowballing problems.

By mid-1993 River, who had grown increasingly moody, was working on *Dark Blood*, which was being filmed largely in the Utah desert. By late October everyone was back in L.A. to shoot interior sequences. One of these was River's character's death scenes. On Saturday, October 30, 1993, after working on the soundstage, River returned to his Los Angeles hotel room and the start of a night of partying. It ended with his visit to the Viper Room, the Sunset Boulevard club partly owned by actor and musician Johnny Depp. There River ingested heroin, Valium, and other drugs. The combination proved deadly. On the street outside the club, he went into convulsions. He was rushed to a nearby hospital where he was pronounced dead. His battles with his dark side were finally over.

Elvis Presley

[Elvis Aron Presley]

JANUARY 8, 1935–AUGUST 16, 1977

As a legendary pop culture phenomenon of the 1950s, the "King" remains enthroned. During his reign, he changed the world's taste in music through his bumping and grinding rock 'n' roll, and he changed the way a pop star was perceived and lived. His overall impact was overwhelming. So great was his popularity that when he died, many fans refused to accept his demise. His flow of recordings made tremendous amounts of money, and if his more than thirty Hollywood movies were mostly interchangeable pabulum, they were lighthearted fun.

Over the years many books were written about the tragically self-destructive Elvis. Several of them revealed new pieces in the puzzle of his amazing life that saw a simple southern country boy turned into a massive legend, a fable that kept on growing even after he died. What is perhaps most intriguing about this bigger-than-life star was his enormous appetite for food and drugs. Both of these orgiastic habits helped him through the ordeal that stardom had become to him. Each of these excesses brought him closer to his drug-induced finale at age forty-two.

Besides food and drugs, Elvis's overindulged lifestyle included his gaudy wardrobe, special hairstyle, beloved Graceland mansion, jet planes, Cadillac cars, gun collection, and an entourage of good ol' boys. While he cavorted, his rapscallion manager, Colonel Tom Parker, and others negotiated the deals that kept Presley's career moving onward. Throughout his three decades in the limelight, when he was not in the recording studios, the soundstages, performing in concert, or lost in a drug daze, Elvis had a parade of female companions—both before and after his "storybook" marriage to Priscilla Beaulieu.

Elvis Aron Presley was born in Tupelo, Mississippi, in 1935, thirty-five minutes after his identical twin brother, Jesse Garon, died. When Elvis was thirteen, the family moved to Memphis where he completed his schooling. At one time he was a movie theater usher, then a truck driver. He began singing as The Hillbilly Cat, and made recordings for a regional label before being signed by RCA in 1955. The pelvis-gyrating Presley became an industry phenomenon, leading to his screen debut in the western *Love Me Tender* (1956). The movie new-comer was at his musical best in *Jailhouse Rock* (1957) and displayed a dramatic breadth in *King Creole* (1958). After his year-and-a-half military service ended in 1960, Parker's cash cow returned to moviemaking, a big-screen career that ended with a western (1969's *Charro!*) and a concert film (1972's *Elvis on Tour*). Five years later, thanks to his punishing intake of drugs, Presley was gone, dead on the bathroom floor at Graceland.

The most important woman in Elvis's life was his mother, Gladys, who'd bought him his first guitar when he was twelve. When she died in 1958, he was bereft and it further complicated his approach to females, which had long been tied into his vision of the idealized woman—his mother. (Supposedly this psychological association was one of the reasons that when his wife, Priscilla, became a mother, his sexual interest in her greatly diminished.)

Presley still had some of his raw redneck ways when he arrived in Hollywood in 1956. He quickly became infatuated with his *Love Me Tender* costar Debra Paget. However, the actress resisted his advances, encouraged by her parents who felt he wasn't in her league. While Debra went on to wed and divorce singer and actor David Street in 1958, motorcycle-riding Elvis turned to rising screen star Natalie Wood. She was in her post–*Rebel Without a Cause* (1955) wild period and was intrigued by the polite Presley who made her feel so every-day normal. But the novelty wore off after she visited Elvis in his hometown of Memphis. There she discovered how unsophisticated he truly was.

Presley was still naive in the ways of the world while on military duty in Germany in the late 1950s. As the idol of millions of scream-ing teenage girls, he, in turn, was attracted to such youths. He dated a German typist, Margrit Buergin, when he was first based overseas. He called the sixteen-year-old his "Little Puppy" and bestowed a diamond-encrusted gold watch on her at Christmas. Meanwhile Elvis had met another German at the army post movies. She was Elisabeth Stefaniak and was a few years older than Margrit. He hired her to handle his fan mail. One day she was riding in a car with Elvis's dad when the vehicle skidded off the road. She was taken to the hospital to have her injuries treated. When Elvis showed up later he was in a foul, suspicious mood. He snarled at the patient, who was still in shock, "What were you and my daddy doin' that caused that wreck?" She insisted she had been doing nothing wrong, but he wasn't inclined to believe her. (She later married one of Presley's army buddies.)

The Pelvis's young American fans were glad when he turned to a young miss from his homeland. Fourteen-year-old Priscilla Beaulieu, his "teen angel," was the stepdaughter of an air force captain stationed in Germany. Elvis was enchanted with her, despite the age gap. When she turned sixteen and he was back in the United States, her parents gave permission for Priscilla to come to the United States, ostensibly with Presley's dad, Vernon, to chaperone her at Graceland and elsewhere. (Actually, Presley had summoned Priscilla stateside because of his recently ended "romance" with young Anita Wood, a hostess of a Memphis TV dance show. She had balked at being under his control and they parted company without their relationship being consummated. Thereafter, he brought Priscilla to Tennessee to prove to Anita that he could find someone better than she.)

Priscilla spent four years in limbo as Elvis's guest/companion/ fairytale princess. Finally, purportedly at her father's insistence, the couple "decided" to get married. The gaudy festivities were held in Las Vegas in May 1967. Nine months and a few days thereafter, daughter Lisa Marie (who later married and divorced singer Michael Jackson) was born.

Before and during his marriage to Priscilla, Elvis was frequently on the move and he always found willing female companionship. During the making of *Viva Las Vegas* (1964) he became entranced with his sex kitten costar, Ann-Margret, and pursued her. Their affair ended abruptly for no specified reason, but he always had a soft spot for the vivacious songstress. On the soundstages Elvis also met pert Deborah Walley (one of the movies' Gidgets) who was his leading lady in *Spin-out* (1966). Their whirlwind courtship included Presley's sharing of drugs with the willing student. While shooting *Speedway* (1968) with Nancy Sinatra, Elvis (who had recently married Priscilla) and the daughter of Frank Sinatra shared a marvelous rapport. On the set they

HOLLYWOOD BAD BOYS

played juvenile pranks on one another. When the picture wrapped, Presley gave Nancy a kiss good-bye. It was the end of their almost-affair.

Meanwhile, Priscilla had grown tired of being on the sidelines and began her own extramarital relationship—only months after pressuring Elvis to wed her. The new man in her life was Mike Stone, a Hawaiian karate instructor. In 1972, angered by her spouse's escalating extracurricular activity, she told him about her ties to Stone and that she intended to leave him for Mike. The Presleys divorced in October 1973, but Stone remained at the top of Elvis's hate list for the rest of the singer's life.

In 1972 Elvis and Priscilla were in the throes of divorce. At this juncture, the bloated, often drug-hazed star met Miss Tennessee. Linda Thompson was not only a virgin, but bright and entertaining. The couple clicked and for the next year Presley remained faithful to her, a record of sorts. Thereafter he resumed his careless old ways of indulging his whims with other women, which put a bad crimp in his situation with Linda. But she proved to be resilient and their relationship continued. On several occasions when the King of Rock 'n' Roll was engulfed in drugs, Linda saved his life. (There was the time he nodded off at dinner, slumping head first into a soup bowl. She yanked his head back and saved him from drowning!) The duo finally split in 1976.

Presley had first met Ginger Alden of Memphis when she was five. Her mother had brought her to the Graceland shrine where Elvis had patted her head. Fifteen years later the attractive woman became his mansion consort. Unlike others in his life, Ginger did not yield to his caprices and the more she remained strong, the more he was intrigued with her. At the end of January 1977 he proposed to her—in his favorite space, his Graceland bathroom. She consented to be Mrs. Presley number two. However, months later, in mid-August, she awoke one day at Graceland to find Elvis dead in the adjoining bathroom. The book he'd been reading when he passed away was *The Scientific Search for the Face of Jesus* (1972) by Frank O. Adams.

Richard Pryor

[Richard Franklin Lennox Thomas Pryor]

DECEMBER 1, 1940–

As a stand-up comic, Pryor was influenced by Lenny Bruce, Dick Gregory, and Bill Cosby (just as later comedians like Eddie Murphy and Robin Williams would benefit from the inventive, edgy, and groundbreaking Pryor). Richard would become renowned for his distinctive brand of profane comedy, full of irreverent characters and salty street language that pushed the limits of censorship. He carved new boundaries for a mainstream comedian in the 1960s and 1970s, especially in a white world not accustomed to an African American telling truths—often in rough, raging, ever-questioning language. As a social commentator, Pryor made the black experience known in an era that had yet to treat the racial minority with equality.

Over decades of professional and personal highs and lows, Richard overcame many daunting challenges (including racial basis). None, however, imperiled his survival more than his reckless, oversized addictions. He seemingly couldn't stop chasing women. (On the subject of the opposite sex, he once said, "When a man hits a woman, one of two things happens. Either she hauls a** in the opposite direction or she becomes yours.") There was also his insatiable attraction to cocaine. His voracious appetite for the white powder led him into mayhem, on stage and off. Physically it punished his body and contributed to his mild heart attack in 1977, a much more severe one in 1990, and his heart surgery the following year. But a decade earlier, in June 1980, he had come very close to dying. As he admitted later, it was not (as the media was told initially) an accidental self-immolation when he lit his pipe while freebasing. Rather, the heavily depressed and cocaine-zonked Pryor had doused himself with cognac and then flicked on his pocket lighter. It set him ablaze resulting in third-degree burns around most of his upper body. That he survived such a punishing ordeal was a miracle.

He was born Richard Franklin Lennox Thomas Pryor in Peoria, Illinois, in 1940. His mother would disappear on drinking binges for months at a time. He was four years old before he first saw his father, who had been away in World War II military service. Pryor was raised by his paternal grandmother, Marie, who operated several bars and brothels in town. As a result the boy learned too much about life at an early age. In the classroom hyperactive Richard became noted as the class clown. After school the youngster often went to the local community center where he was drawn to the drama group and found delight in being before audiences. At age fifteen, after an altercation at school, he was expelled. In 1957 the fast-living Pryor, who was working odd jobs, fathered his first child, a girl. The next year he enlisted in the army and served for two years, part of that time based in West Germany.

By his early twenties, the five-foot, ten-inch Richard was working on the black club circuit developing his comic characters, many of them based on the winos, whores, and pimps around whom he had grown up. Already much of the $50 he earned weekly was going for drugs—at first marijuana and uppers, later on harder stuff. He also found himself having constant run-ins with law authorities, who distrusted and often jailed the foul-mouthed, agitated comedian, a black stranger in their predominately white towns.

When Richard got his girlfriend Patricia Price pregnant, he married her in 1961 just before she gave birth to their son, Richard Jr. Soon thereafter he took off—this time to New York where he gained a foothold entertaining in Greenwich Village venues and eventually on TV variety shows. By the end of the 1960s he was playing Las Vegas and had released his first comedy album, *Richard Pryor*, which was full of his trademark raw and profane comedy. Having divorced his first wife, he married and divorced again in the late sixties; from that union he had a daughter. By now he was very hooked on cocaine. As with sex, he just couldn't get enough.

In 1970 Pryor, angered with himself for becoming too "white" a comic, stormed off the stage at the Aladdin Hotel in Las Vegas and regrouped in the hippie environment of Berkeley, California. When he emerged he had found his true comic voice—rough and raunchy. Having made his film debut in *The Busy Body* (1967), he spent much of the early 1970s making blaxploitation films like *The Mack* (1973).

The stand-up comedian holding forth in concert for *Richard Pryor: Live on the Sunset Strip* (1982). (Courtesy of JC Archives)

On a far higher note was his role as Piano Man with Diana Ross in *Lady Sings the Blues* (1972) and his script contributions to *Blazing Saddles* (1974). Pryor continued to score with his albums (1975's *Is It Something I Said?*), his movies (1976's *Silver Streak*—teamed with Gene Wilder), and his one-man concerts. In 1976 he signed a long-term multimillion-dollar pact with Universal Pictures—the biggest deal yet for an African American screen talent.

In 1977 Richard married black model Deboragh McGuire and they had a daughter; the couple ended their abusive relationship in 1979. Meanwhile, the drugs, the booze, his anger with the world, and his sorrow over the late 1970s death of his father and his grandmother, led him to make poor career decisions.

In addition, the addiction haze continued to control his romantic relationships, such as when, after another big fight with his new woman (Jennifer Lee—they would marry and divorce in the early 1980s), the paranoid star threatened to shoot her with his .357 revolver. In typical fashion the couple made up a few minutes later with Richard telling his girlfriend, "I'm glad you didn't make me kill you." To the severely addicted man, nothing was ever his fault. He was always the "innocent" victim. Sometimes he went through an entire kilo of drugs in a weekend.

Even after his near-death experience in 1980 Pryor continued using cocaine. After a severe arrhythmia landed him in the hospital, he knew it was his heavy drug usage that had almost destroyed him. He also grasped finally—but did not act on it—that he was a cocaine addict. He tried therapy to understand his substance abuses. The star made the autobiographical movie *Jo Jo Dancer, Your Life Is Calling* (1986) in which he not only starred, but produced, directed, and wrote. However, it took another shocking discovery to wake him up at last and calm him down—medical tests revealed that he was suffering from multiple sclerosis. In the late 1980s his health continued to decline as he grew thinner, slower of movement, and so forth, but it wasn't until he endured quadruple bypass surgery in 1991 that he went public with his MS diagnosis. By then he had remarried and was soon to divorce Flynn BeLaine to whom he was first wed from 1986 to 1987.

In the 1990s, increasingly ravaged by his illness and forced to be wheelchair-bound, Pryor gave up drug usage and his self-destructive behavior. He performed his act occasionally. He wrote his autobiography (1995's *Pryor Convictions and Other Life Sentences*), was the subject of many testimonials (including receiving the first Mark Twain Prize in celebration of American humor in 1998), and turned to ex-wife Jennifer Lee for emotional support in his fragile times.

By now, Pryor, once the brokenhearted comedian and a victim of excesses, had learned a new rule in life: "I always remember to keep some sunshine on my face."

George Raft

[George Ranft]

SEPTEMBER 27, 1895–NOVEMBER 24, 1980

Hollywood has long been fascinated with gangster movies, and some denizens of Tinseltown have delighted in associating with mobsters. But rarely did the film community welcome into its own as a screen star such a bona fide mob underling as Raft who always maintained links with his criminal pals. In Raft's early years as an entertainer his gangland affiliations sparked fascination; in later life his past associations with the criminal world caused him grief.

German-born Conrad Ranft and his Italian wife, Eva, were living in Hell's Kitchen (the toughest part of New York City's West Side) when Eva gave birth to George in 1895, the first of their five children (four boys and a girl). The father worked at a Coney Island concession, the mother toiled at a laundry. In rough Hell's Kitchen the only chance of survival was membership in a local gang. George joined the Gophers and quit school by age seven. Later he became best friends with the son of a family from England who had just arrived in Hell's Kitchen. The lad was Owney Madden who grew up to be a notorious gangster.

In 1907 the Ranfts moved uptown to Broadway and 116th Street. Away from the Gophers, the teen's biggest diversion was attending the home games of the New York Highlanders (later the Yankees). When George refused to go back to school, he fought with his father and left home. Thereafter, the homeless young man picked fruit in upstate New York, shoveled snow, or hung around the Highlanders. He also was a frequent visitor to Sing Sing Prison in Ossining, New York, where Owney Madden was incarcerated for a murder conviction.

At loose ends, George joined a semiprofessional ball team based in Springfield, Massachusetts, but soon realized he was not a star player. Back in New York, George Raft, as he was now known, became a professional boxer, but was frequently pulverized by his opponents. To earn a living, he expanded his pickpocketing activities from sports crowds to dance halls. There he became a fancy dresser and a dancer.

He soon perfected as a specialty a superfast Charleston, a skill that led to paying jobs entertaining at clubs. Sometimes he worked as a taxi dancer (customers would pay a "fare" to dance with him at dance halls) and gigolo in Manhattan or toured in vaudeville with a dance act. Popular with women, he frequently brawled with their angered boyfriends.

In early 1923, back in New York City, he married Grayce Mulrooney, a secretary. Their love match soon fizzled, but she would not divorce him. The next year, during the height of Prohibition, Owney Madden was released from prison and he and George continued their friendship. Owney signed on with a major bootlegger. Through Madden's new contacts in Manhattan clubs, Raft got many dance engagements. Other times he helped Owney and his pals (who included mobster Dutch Schultz) in their frequently dangerous bootlegging activities and other criminal endeavors.

In 1927 George had been in the Broadway revue *Padlocks of 1927* with Texas Guinan. When she went to Hollywood to make *Queen of the Night Clubs* (1929), George accompanied her and was given a small role in the film. After a few other parts in pictures, George returned to New York. When Madden had to leave town during a gang war, he had Raft drive him to California and told his pal he should switch to a safer career—making movies.

Before long, Raft appeared in the gangster yarn *Quick Millions* (1931). Meanwhile, the Los Angeles police were not happy to have Owney Madden's pal in town. Raft's underworld ties were further publicized when he was arrested along with a visiting

Grace Bradley and George Raft in a publicity pose for *Stolen Harmony* (1935).
(Courtesy of JC Archives)

stranger who proved to be the brother of Chicago mobster Al Capone. George's efficient lawyer got the two sprung from an L.A. jail.

Raft's screen career was cemented when he was cast as an Al Capone–like character in *Scarface: The Shame of the Nation* (1932). Before long he signed a contract at Paramount Pictures and appeared in such vehicles as *Night After Night* (1932), and musicals like *Bolero* (1934) and *Every Night at Eight* (1935). Increasingly impressed by his own fame, Raft grew temperamental about accepting "unworthy" screen assignments so he moved over to Warner Bros. in 1939 where he joined Jimmy Cagney in *Each Dawn I Die* (1939). Thereafter, the finicky Raft turned down making *The Maltese Falcon* (1941), *High Sierra* (1941), and *Casablanca* (1942). Humphrey Bogart was glad for such roles and they made him a major star.

During the 1930s gentlemanly, soft-touch Raft was a movie colony favorite. Friends sympathized that his New York City–based wife Grayce would not divorce him so he could marry transplanted Chicago socialite, Virginia Pine. The two lived openly together, which was considered shocking at the time. By 1939 Raft was courting Norma Shearer, the movie star widow of an MGM magnate. When that amazing coupling of the sophisticate and the lowbrow cooled down, the still-married George very openly dated future World War II pin-up queen Betty Grable. (Their affair ended and she married big band leader Harry James in 1943.) By 1945 George was working at RKO in lesser features. Meanwhile, Raft had established a close friendship with Benjamin "Bugsy" Siegel, a notorious East Coast gangster who had come to California in 1937 to widen the mob's influence. Recurrently Raft's ties to Siegel got him on the bad side of the law. In June 1947 Siegel was shot to death in Beverly Hills, and the press was quick to note that George had met with Bugsy earlier that fateful evening.

By the early 1950s Raft's screen career was fading. His comeback in a 1953 TV series, *I Am the Law*, failed, and his last decent screen role was as a poker-faced gang boss in *Some Like It Hot* (1959) with Marilyn Monroe. That same year his Havana, Cuba, gambling club was shut down by Fidel Castro's regime and he was not reimbursed. To replenish his bank account he sold the screen rights to his life, leading to a low-budget 1961 entry starring Ray Danton. Thereafter he was pressured by the IRS for back taxes and suffered another setback when, in the mid-1960s, because of his underworld connections, he was denied entry to England to manage a classy London gambling club. One of Raft's last screen parts was a cameo in Mae West's screen finale, *Sextette* (1978). With George's death in 1980, Hollywood lost one of its most famous on- and off-camera tough guys.

Wallace Reid

[William Wallace Reid]
APRIL 15, 1891–JANUARY 18, 1923

In some people's estimation it does *not* matter why a person becomes addicted to drugs or alcohol, but merely that the individual is a substance abuser. For them there is no room for explanation. As for Reid, one of Hollywood's most handsome, congenial, and popular stars of the silent era, it was a case of innocently being hooked on morphine (and later liquor—which was his own doing) and being unable to shake the deadly habit. Whether or not that revealed a lack of character, his untimely passing was, nevertheless, a major shock to his many fans. It left many wondering how could a man who had everything (good looks, a family, a lucrative film contract, and great fame) squander his great luck?

Born into a theatrical family in 1891 in St. Louis, Reid accompanied his parents as they performed around America. He made his acting debut at age four, and enjoyed it. However, shortly thereafter, his parents separated (and later divorced). His mother did not want her boy to become too enamored of the theater and kept him away from it. This meant he saw little of his father in his early years because the latter was always on the road starring in, writing, or directing a new stage production. In 1909, having graduated from boarding school in Pennsylvania, Wallace found employment at a Wyoming hotel run by the sister of Buffalo Bill Cody (a pal of Reid's dad). The next year, the twenty-year-old joined his father who was then scripting and directing movies for the Selig Studios in Chicago. With his strong jaw and all-American good looks it was not long before this athletic young Adonis was performing in front of the silent film camera (1910's *The Phoenix*). Returning to New York City (where he had grown up), the multitalented Wallace worked at several movie firms: acting, writing, directing, and photographing. Away from moviemaking, he was a poet, musician, composer, and athlete, not to mention his abilities with the automobile (racer, mechanic, and so on) or on the dance floor.

In 1912 Reid followed the ever-growing film industry to Los Angeles, where he worked for Universal Pictures. He much preferred directing one- and two-reelers to acting. He became enamored of a fellow Universal employee, seventeen-year-old Dorothy Davenport, and they wed on October 13, 1913. (The couple would become parents of William Wallace Jr. and adopt a daughter, Betty Ann.) In D. W. Griffith's Civil War saga, *The Birth of a Nation* (1915), Wallace played a strapping blacksmith as well as the Christ image in the finale's tableau.

Paramount Pictures signed the six-foot, one-inch, 180-pound actor to a studio pact. It was not long before Reid was earning more than $156,000 annually (a great fee then). Congenial Reid proved to be a workaholic: it was not unusual for him to star in eight to nine silent features a year. On camera he was always very optimistic, charming, and unassuming and was more entertaining than his slight vehicles (for instance, 1917's *The Squaw Man's Son*, 1918's *Rimrock Jones*). The studio paired him with an assortment of fashionable leading ladies including Bebe Daniels and Gloria Swanson. Fearful of losing their moneymaker, Paramount convinced Reid not to enlist in World War I, just as they had diverted him from racing cars at the Indianapolis Speedway.

During the filming of *The Valley of the Giants* (1919) in the High Sierras, the train carrying the cast and crew derailed. Despite his own injuries, the star helped many aboard to safety. In the accident Reid gashed his head (which triggered later persistent headaches) and injured the base of his spine. So that filming could continue, the picture's on-set doctor ordered the pain-racked Wallace to receive daily dosages of morphine. Once back in Hollywood, the actor was confined to bed for three months and was administered more morphine. Thereafter, when Reid attempted to kick his drug habit, he discovered he couldn't. Severely depressed, he began to drink heavily. It was not long before rumors spread throughout the movie colony (but not to the public) that Reid was drug addicted. Paramount, however, did not relent on his work schedule. For example, in 1921, the year an industry survey ranked Wallace as the number one male box-office star, he was in six features.

Wallace Reid (left) with Sylvia Ashton and William Gaden in *The Love Special* (1921). (Courtesy of JC Archives)

As Reid began the farce *Thirty Days*—his ninth 1922 release—it was quite obvious to everyone on the set how gaunt and weak he had become. Verging on delirium he could hardly navigate through his celluloid role. Nevertheless, demanding studio executives pressed him onward, until Wallace collapsed on the set and broke into tears. An ambulance took him home. The superstar was soon transferred to a local sanitarium and told his friend, Paramount filmmaker Cecil B. DeMille, "I'll either come out cured—or I won't come out." Realizing the secret of her husband's addiction could no longer be contained, Dorothy Reid informed the press just before Christmas of the situation. (However, Wallace was not told that the public had been let in on his grave condition.)

By the start of 1923 the dangerously ill Reid—who was kept in a padded cell when he went into a thrashing frenzy as he went through withdrawal—contracted influenza. His constitution was already severely weakened (he had lost sixty pounds) and he was in and out of a coma. On January 18, 1923, around 1:00 P.M., the matinee idol screamed out "God . . . I . . . Please!" and then expired, a victim of lung and kidney congestion.

After his death, Wallace's widow (who never remarried) appeared in two antidrug pictures that she cofinanced. Of her late spouse she once said, "He was much loved. He had so many talents—the gods were overly kind, but they also made him vulnerable, his own worst enemy, to compensate for their lavishness."

Brad Renfro

[Brad Barron Renfro]
JULY 25, 1982–

In Hollywood's Golden Age, if a child star misbehaved or rebelled against studio or family bosses, it was discreetly kept from the public. More recently there have been many instances of a young performer getting into scrapes, especially when the good times ended after their hit shows were cancelled and/or they had grown up: Todd Bridges (*Diff'rent Strokes*), Adam Rich (*Eight Is Enough*), and Danny Bonaduce (*The Partridge Family*). These postsuccess misadventures were well documented by the media. With today's relaxed moral standards, the situation has changed. Even when young stars' indiscretions occur *during* their peak performing years, and these episodes are recorded at the time by the press, few if any career repercussions result. Take the case of the extremely talented Renfro.

Born in Knoxville, Tennessee, in 1982, Brad was the only child of Mark Renfro (who worked in a blueprint factory) and his wife. When Brad was nearly six, his parents divorced. His mother moved to Michigan, remarried, and later moved back to Knoxville. Meanwhile Brad lived with his grandmother Joanne (a church secretary) and his father (who moved out when he remarried). A feisty youngster, Brad regarded his grandmother Jo-Jo as his "ma'maw," and he found solace in classic rock and blues music, as well as his guitar playing. He began smoking when he was eleven.

Also at age eleven, Renfro came to the attention of casting director Mali Finn. She was searching the South for a young boy to play the lead in the screen adaptation of John Grisham's bestseller *The Client*. The boy displayed such natural talent in an impromptu audition that a few months later—with his grandmother on hand—he was in Los Angeles working with director Joel Schumacher and the picture's star Susan Sarandon. The newcomer proved impressive in that hit movie and was equally noteworthy in the touching AIDS drama *The Cure* (1995), and then did well in a comic turn as Huck Finn in *Tom and Huck* (1995). His repertoire of screen work led to his winning the *Hollywood Reporter*'s YoungStar Award and being included by *People* magazine in its "Top 30 Under 30" roundup of young talent.

Whenever he wasn't making a picture, Brad returned to his humble surroundings in East Knoxville, claiming he wanted to stay level-headed and not be led astray by Hollywood's wild life. Meanwhile, the extremely bright youngster—known as Pagey, Renfreak, or Fro to friends—was becoming disinterested in school and had become mischievous. (Reflecting on not being greatly disciplined as a youth Renfro said the reason "nobody ever told me to shut up and take out the garbage is because they know what my response would be—and I made sure they knew that. . . . Whether or not it was true.") It was director Joel Schumacher who suggested that the gifted Brad transfer to a Nashville Montessori school where he attended classes when not being tutored on film sets. At one point in 1997 Brad was reported to be dating teen actress Gaby Hoffman.

Continuing his successful film career, Brad had the lead in *Telling Lies in America* (1997) with Kevin Bacon and was the essence of contemporary evil in *Apt Pupil* (1998), based on a Stephen King novella. In the fall of 1998, shortly before the release of that well-received thriller, Renfro was arrested in Knoxville while joyriding with his cousin in the early A.M. for driving under the influence of marijuana. He was also charged with the possession of marijuana and a packet of cocaine. He was released into his grandmother's custody. Later, in his plea bargaining to have the charges dropped, he agreed to enter a drug rehab program and to be subjected to random drug tests over the next six months. Later, the guitar enthusiast, who was at ease with a harmonica and played in a local band (40/04), said of his blemished reputation, "We all make mistakes as kids and I'm still a kid. I've messed up a bit. But I try to do better. I'm not the bad boy people think I am."

There was a two-year gap before Brad's next pictures, a trio of films in 2000 (including *Skipped Parts* with Jennifer Jason Leigh). Then on August 28, 2000, the brown-eyed, brown-haired Renfro was back in trouble. He and a friend (twenty-four-year-old Harold Bond) climbed aboard a $175,000 yacht berthed at the Holiday Harbor marina in Fort Lauderdale, Florida. They came aboard the forty-five-foot vessel around 3:40 A.M. and reportedly Renfro started one of the two engines. He gave the engine a burst of gas and it zoomed out a few feet, then slammed back into the dock. The duo repeated the same action a few more times, not realizing (they were allegedly under the influence at the time) that the *Time Out* was still tied to the dock! By this point the engine had quit functioning and people on nearby crafts at the marina had called the police. Held at bay by the 911 callers until the law arrived, Renfro and his cohort were taken to the Broward County Jail where they were each charged with one count of third-degree grand theft and criminal mischief (while the police were investigating whether he and his partner were under the influence at the time). Brad posted $10,000 bail after spending much of a day behind bars.

On January 4, 2001, a Florida judge sentenced Renfro to two years' probation, plus the repair costs ($4,204.55) for the vessel and police fees ($141.02—investigative costs). During the sentencing hearing Brad said, "I don't have any excuses or fast one-liners to pull out of my shoes." In reporting the botched heist and its aftermath, much of the media had found the dumb incident amusing, adding to Brad's reputation as a nondangerous bad boy.

A day after being released from jail in August 2000, Brad reported to the Fort Lauderdale, Florida, set of *Bully* (2001), a picture being directed by Larry Clark and for which Renfro was a producer. Brad played one of several Florida youths who murder the town's bully. (When asked later if he felt he and the cast had been exploited in making the highly controversial *Bully*, Renfro allowed, "It's kind of hard to exploit or embarrass Old Brad Renfro. I've done a good job of that my damn self.") Other films that year featuring the five-foot, eleven-inch Renfro included the R-rated *Tart* and the well-received *Ghost World* with Thora Birch and Steve Buscemi.

But the constantly busy actor found occasion to get into more mischief. Around 1:00 A.M. on May 16, 2001, Brad and a friend were riding along in their car in Knoxville, when a Knox County sheriff's deputy stopped them for a failure to signal when changing lanes. The nineteen-year-old Renfro acknowledged to the police that he had been drinking earlier. Brad was arrested, booked, and released on $500 bond. His acquaintance was not arrested. Later, in July 2001, Renfro had to miss the Los Angeles premiere of *Bully* to appear in Florida court to answer charges that he had violated his probation in the 2000 yacht incident by using alcohol and/or drugs. Luckily, Brad was able to smooth over the situation with the judicial system.

Brad's legal problems, however, were not over. On January 14, 2002, he was arrested not far from his Knoxville, Tennessee, home on charges of driving without his license and for public intoxication. Three weeks later, Renfro surrendered himself to Florida authorities for having again violated his probation. He was offered the option of three months in a rehab facility or nine months in jail. Renfro chose the former alternative and was warned that if he did not complete the prescribed program he would find himself behind bars for nine months.

Ironically, one of Renfro's upcoming screen releases, *American Girl* (2002), dealt with convicts and their families having a picnic.

Burt Reynolds

[Burton Leon Reynolds Jr.]

FEBRUARY 11, 1936–

Over a prolific career that began in the late 1950s, Reynolds had more peaks and valleys than the Rocky Mountains. Among his artistic high points were *Deliverance* (1972), *Starting Over* (1979), and *Boogie Nights* (1997)—for which he was Oscar-nominated for Best Supporting Actor. But he also reached a popular peak with *Smokey and the Bandit* (1977), which created a big-screen franchise. Yet even at the zenith of his box-office clout, Burt could jest, "I've become the number one box-office star in the world not *because* of my movies—but *in spite* of them." Over the years he also made many stinkers: *Stick* (1985), *Heat* (1987), and *Rent-a-Cop* (1988). As for such junk entries, Reynolds offered, "A lot of directors don't realize the hardest thing to do is to make chicken salad out of chicken s***. I've done that a lot."

It is this sense of humor and perspective about his talents and his screen output that got Reynolds through several professional dry stretches. There were the times he had to cope with jokes about his bad toupees, his marital problems with wife Loni Anderson, or his trendsetting nude centerfold in the April 1972 issue of *Cosmopolitan* magazine. Somehow the six-foot-tall bad boy with the wicked smile got through it all.

Reynolds was born in Lansing, Michigan, and had an older sister, Nancy. His mother was a former nurse and his father was a policeman. In 1946 the family relocated to Riviera, Florida, where his disciplinarian father was the town sheriff and his mother operated a small restaurant. A few years later Mr. Reynolds became the sheriff of West Palm Beach. Buddy—as Burt was called—entered the local high school. There, to overcome bigotry because he was part Native American, he became a tough jock, scoring well on the gridiron. By age fourteen he'd lost his virginity. During his high school years he got a local prom queen pregnant. (The girl had an abortion.)

When it came time for college, Reynolds's football skills prompted fourteen scholarship offers. He matriculated at Florida State University in Tallahassee. In the fall of 1955 he tore his knee cartilage during a ball game, ending his football career. That Christmas, reckless Buddy crashed his father's car. The nineteen-year-old flatlined, but was revived. After transferring to Palm Beach Jr. College in 1956, he became interested in theater, leading to a scholarship at an upstate New York theater group. He moved on to a small role in a Manhattan stage revival. Thereafter the athletic Burt moved to Los Angeles, surviving by working as a TV stuntman.

Good-looking and young, Burt accepted a seven-year contract at Universal Studios and was cast in the TV series *Riverboat*. Because he was perceived as a troublemaker with a smart mouth, he was dropped midway through the show's first season (1959–60), and months later was released from his studio contract. Freelancing, he was hired (1962–65) to play a mute, half-breed blacksmith on *Gunsmoke*, but the lack of acting challenge on the western program left Burt frustrated. Meanwhile he had married British actress Judy Carne in 1963. While her career zoomed upward, his stagnated. It caused dissention (Carne claimed Reynolds physically abused her) and the couple divorced in 1966.

Freewheeling, outspoken Reynolds played in two more TV series, both short-lived, and was seen in several unmemorable B movies. In 1971 everything turned around for Burt. He was a surprise guest on Dinah Shore's TV talk show. The chemistry between the fifty-three-year-old Dinah and nineteen-year-younger Burt was palpable to the audience. Their fairytale but genuine romance did wonders for Burt's career. His status climbed even higher in 1972 when 1.6 million *Cosmopolitan* readers saw Reynolds's nude centerfold, while moviegoers that year were impressed by his macho dramatics in *Deliverance*. On the downside, while on location for *The Man Who Loved Cat Dancing* (1973), a young publicity man died of a gunshot wound. The deceased had been obsessed with costar Sarah Miles and was convinced she was having an affair with Burt. The coroner's inquest determined the man had died of a self-inflicted wound. Reynolds was cleared of any complicity, but rumors about the messy situation persisted for a long time.

Much to the public's disappointment the love affair between Burt and Dinah ended in 1976, either because of her fear of growing old in his arms and/or because she had become overly possessive of him. The two, nevertheless, remained good friends.

On the professional front, Reynolds once said, "I want to direct two times a year. You can only hold your stomach in for so many years." He had already directed on TV, but his first crack at handling a feature was the dismal but popular redneck entry, *Gator* (1976). Now reaching his career pinnacle with *Smokey and the Bandit*, he embarked on a long-term romance with the film's costar, Sally Field, who would make three additional pictures with him. The couple seemed to have everything going for them: Burt was Hollywood's highest-paid star while Field was an Oscar winner (1979's *Norma Rae*). The match fell through, however, partly because she disliked being a trophy girlfriend, and he felt overshadowed by her.

With movies like *The Cannonball Run* (1981) and *The Man Who Loved Women* (1983), the 1980s were not kind to Reynolds. He found solace in his dinner theater and acting school in Jupiter, Florida, and his womanizing. (His staff had a routine before a visit by one of the star's women. It included checking everything in the house—from dresser drawers to the bath towels—to be sure there was no evidence of the previous female visitor. To personalize everything, photos and other trinkets of the arriving girlfriend were retrieved from marked cartons and displayed appropriately.)

Before long Burt's steady became twice-divorced Loni Anderson, costar of the TV series *WKRP in Cincinnati* (1978–82). The press labeled them the "beefcake and the cheesecake." Unpublicized at the time were their many problems, which ranged from Burt's desire to rekindle a romance with Sally Field to his ongoing drug dependency. His substance abuse began in the early 1980s when he got hooked on painkillers to counteract body aches from many filmmaking injuries. He went cold turkey on his own but then became dependent again when he suffered a fractured jaw on the set of *City Heat* (1984). The injury affected his inner ear and he had troubled chewing. He lost weight and rumors spread that he had AIDS. By now he was addicted to the painkiller Halcion and his life was hell. Again he went through drug withdrawal on his own and eventually, after many medical consultations, found a solution to his rare jaw problem. However, his years of tremendous mood swings on and off the set, his unexplained ailments, and his rash career decisions (such as turning down the role in 1983's *Terms of Endearment* that won Jack Nicholson an Oscar) had greatly diminished his industry standing. Besides, by now, the public had newer, younger favorites.

In April 1988 Burt and Loni were finally married and the following year they adopted a son, Quinton. Reynolds's sagging career got a tremendous boost when he starred in the hit TV sitcom *Evening Shade* (1990–94). Once again, however, there were much-reported conflicts on the set between Burt and management. The year the show was cancelled, Dinah Shore had died of cancer, Burt had collapsed on the TV soundstage, and he had been mugged. As a capper to 1994, he and Anderson ended their thirteen-year-long relationship. Loni claimed that she first learned of the split when two sheriffs served her with papers, and the law enforcers relayed Burt's order that she vacate the premises immediately. The media had a blast with the messy breakup, quoting Reynolds extensively on the subject. To the supermarket tabloids, he revealed or suggested many problems in the marriage. In the process, information about Reynolds's long-term girlfriend Pam Seals became public knowledge. In the sticky divorce negotiations Anderson ended up with, among other items, $26,000 monthly alimony and child support.

With his time-consuming divorce over, Reynolds discovered that his career had bottomed out. He settled for taking a character role (as the debauched politician) in the Demi Moore vehicle *Striptease* (1996) for a fraction of his past salaries. Later in 1996 Burt, who had made many millions, now owed more than $10 million to his creditors. He filed for bankruptcy and scaled back his lifestyle substantially.

Thanks to his resourceful performance as the porn filmmaker in *Boogie Nights*, he won a Golden Globe in early 1998. It gave him the respect he had longed for over the decades. Thereafter he alternated between major studio releases (1999's *Mystery, Alaska*) and journeyman assignments (2001's *Hollywood Sign*). He continued to live life by the philosophy: "You can kill, you can maim people, but to be boring is truly a sin. And God will punish you for that."

Mickey Rourke

[Philip André Rourke Jr.]

SEPTEMBER 16, 1953?–

One of Hollywood's most offbeat, colorful personalities has to be Rourke. Persistently enigmatic about his tough and troubled early life, he later became renowned for the amount of plastic surgery he underwent to refine his facial features. In fact—and not just because of aging—his countenance in the late 1990s bore little physical resemblance to the original.

Mickey gained his acting reputation in several arty pictures—1983's *Rumble Fish*, 1984's *The Pope of Greenwich Village*, 1985's *Year of the Dragon*—in which the naturalistic performer was far more persuasive than the flawed productions. He developed a cult following in the United States and, especially, abroad, which led Tinseltown producers to issue him healthy paychecks. When his industry standing waned, he regained visibility with two sexually explicit and steamy features: *9½ Weeks* (1986) and *Wild Orchid* (1990). Thereafter the rough guy returned to his first love—professional boxing. For him, participating in the ring took precedence over everything, including his love of motorcycles. At about this time he said, "I don't care about sex anymore. It's been years since I made love. Nowadays I so much prefer motorcycles."

Rourke was born around 1953 (sources list anywhere from 1950 to 1958) in Schenectady, New York, the oldest of three children. His parents had a troubled marriage, and when he was seven he joined his mother, grandmother, brother, and sister in moving to Miami, Florida. The trauma of leaving his father (a country club caretaker and amateur bodybuilder) deeply affected Rourke. In Miami the grandmother opened a launderette in the dangerous Liberty City section of town, and the family lived in rooms behind the business. About a year later, Rourke's mother remarried and he suddenly gained five stepbrothers. Unhappy with his new relations, he escaped into daydreaming and, conversely, becoming a rowdy tough guy on the mean streets.

Unmotivated in school, Mickey hung out with his tough pals and got into activities he will not discuss. His one outlet was boxing, but at the time—to his lasting regret—he was too undisciplined to become a successful prizefighter. In his mid-teens his parents moved to Miami Beach, and once again Rourke didn't fit in, this time with a more affluent neighborhood. By the time he finished high school in 1971, he was a frequent user of drugs. At nineteen he realized his boxing ambitions were hopeless and he borrowed money from his sister to move to New York. The year was 1972. He scrounged around town (often living on stolen candy bars and bags of chips), working odd jobs (parking lot attendant). For a time he studied cosmetology. He floundered until he began acting lessons, complementing his self-education through reading. His best pal through much of this period was "Little Eddie," a four-foot, six-inch tough Cuban whom he had known in Miami.

Leather-jacketed Mickey Rourke, Hollywood's "Tough Boy" star. (Courtesy of JC Archives)

By 1978 Rourke was in California working as a bouncer in a Hollywood transvestite club. It took seventy-eight auditions before someone hired him in the film business—he won a bit in the 1979 film *1941*. By 1980 he had small roles in TV movies and such colossal flops as *Heaven's Gate*. His playing the professional arsonist in *Body Heat* (1981) and especially his performance in *Diner* (1982) launched his film career. The five-foot, eleven-inch actor wed actress and dancer Debra Feuer in 1982. As with so much of Rourke's life, the marriage was unconventional in that they spent little time living together. Mickey preferred to hang with his male pals and ride his chopper. By the time the union ended in the later 1980s, Rourke had engaged in several extramarital affairs. He had also developed a reputation for being difficult on film sets.

While rejecting leads in such pictures as 1984's *Beverly Hills Cop* and 1986's *Top Gun*, he made what proved to be flops like *A Prayer for the Dying* (1987) and *Homeboy* (1988), and his career was nosediving. The European coproduction *Francesca* (1989), in which he played Saint Francis of Assisi, vanished quickly except for the hue and cry that ensued when the British press accused Rourke of being an IRA sympathizer for announcing he was donating most of his $1–3 million film salary to "certain causes in Ireland." A few years later Mickey, who spent impulsively and supported a posse of unsavory hangers-on, admitted that he was often broke. He just couldn't manage his income, which included million-dollar endorsement deals from Japanese commercials.

Another side of the enigmatic Rourke was his involvement in sideline businesses that included a Beverly Hills hair salon (which he part-owned) and a Beverly Hills soda shop he and his brother operated. These establishments contrasted to his sparse living quarters that often proved to be an unimposing rented space with autographed photos of boxers tacked around the walls.

By the early 1990s when Mickey belatedly attempted a boxing comeback, he was considered plain peculiar by the film industry. His four-year effort in the ring failed and he returned to acting. Meanwhile he married former model Carré Otis, his X-rated *Wild Orchid* costar. At one point early in their union, she was hospitalized for severe depression. In 1991, while on location with Mickey in New Mexico, she was rushed to a hospital emergency room with a bullet wound in her shoulder. She insisted that a .357 Magnum had accidentally discharged while moving a bag that contained the weapon. On July 18, 1994, Rourke was arrested by the Los Angeles Police Department for allegedly having slapped and kicked his wife in her agent's office. He said he was innocent of the misdemeanor spousal abuse charges. When Otis later made herself unavailable to testify in court, the proceedings were dropped. By then the couple had separated.

This had not been Mickey's first tangle with the police. On January 4, 1994, the cops arrived at the actor's establishment, Mickey's Place, in Miami Beach to disperse an angry crowd gathered in front of the club. Rourke, "highly agitated and clenching his fists," was taken into custody for resisting arrest and was held for several hours. The disposition of his case required he do community service—in his case, teaching boxing to inner-city youths.

The rest of 1994 was equally disruptive for Rourke. He was hospitalized voluntarily for psychiatric observation, and at another time was admitted to Cedars-Sinai Medical Center as a potential suicide candidate. In November that year he was in the news for allegedly doing $20,000 worth of damages when he trashed his megaexpensive suite at the Trump Plaza Hotel in New York.

By early 1995, Rourke and Otis both happened to be in New York City where she was reactivating her modeling career. She claimed that Mickey was stalking her. At one Manhattan fashion industry festivity Rourke persuaded rapper/actor Tupac Shakur to take a bottle of champagne to his wife's table. By midyear Rourke and Otis were living together again, but then divorced in 1998. By late 2001 they had become platonic friends who got together occasionally for dinner and a chat.

Once a star, by the late 1990s the now almost unrecognizable Rourke had turned to character roles, proving to be gritty and effective in his mature years: *The Rainmaker* (1997), *Shades* (1997), *The Pledge* (2001), *Once upon a Time in Mexico* (2002).

Tupac Shakur

[Lesane Parish Crooks]

JUNE 16, 1971–SEPTEMBER 13, 1996

In his brief lifetime Shakur was often confrontational and reckless. Certainly his brash behavior was not unique for a thuggish street-smart guy. He was one more volatile young man who carried anger and hostility within him, often leading to explosive temperament. However, Tupac's outstanding artistic abilities gave distinction to this intense and confident individual. With his persuasive performing, the African American Shakur rose to prominence not only as a songster rapper, but as a skillful screen actor. Then, at age twenty-five he was violently murdered. His killing climaxed years of bad-guy behavior and brushes with the law that merged his offstage and onstage images. For his fans—then and now—his death vested Tupac with icon status that continues to grow.

Shakur was born in New York City in 1971. His mother, Alice Faye Williams, had been married to Lumumba Abdul Shakur, a Black Panther. In 1969 she was among Black Panther members arrested for an alleged conspiracy to blow up New York City buildings. While out on bail in 1970, Alice had a relationship with William "Billy" Garland, another Panther. (The affair led to Lumumba divorcing her.) By 1971, a now-pregnant Alice was behind bars in Manhattan. Later, she was acquitted of the charges. A month thereafter she gave birth to her baby boy. (Years later, when providing information to the police regarding Tupac's death, the family listed Shakur with an aka of Lesane Parish Crooks, although the source of the surname was not made known.) Soon thereafter, Garland and the boy's mother split. When the boy was still a tot, his mother married Mutulu Shakur and assumed the name Afeni Shakur, and her offspring became known as Tupac Amaru Shakur.

In 1981 Mutulu allegedly was involved in an armored truck robbery and homicides, and he went underground. (He was captured in 1986 and sentenced to sixty years behind bars.) Meanwhile, the young Tupac moved frequently within Harlem and the Bronx with Afeni and his stepsister, Sekyiwa. By the time he was a teenager, he was writing poetry. His mother enrolled him in Harlem's 127th Street Ensemble and at age thirteen Shakur performed in a stage production of *A Raisin in the Sun* at the Apollo Theater.

When Tupac was fifteen, Afeni moved her family to Baltimore, Maryland, where he attended the School for the Arts, majoring in acting and dance. During this period he wrote his first rap number. In 1988, because of escalating gang violence in their neighborhood, Afeni sent her children to stay with a family friend in Marin City, California, north of San Francisco. Later she joined them in the ghetto there but became bogged down in a self-admitted drug haze. Soon Shakur left home, preferring to live with friends in an abandoned building. When he was seventeen he quit high school, working odd jobs (including selling drugs) to get by.

Despite his unsavory existence, Shakur never forgot his artistic interests and began joining and forming rap groups. In 1990 he auditioned for Digital Underground and was hired as one of their dancers and roadies. He made his recording debut on the group's 1991 album *This Is an E Release*. His own album—his solo debut as a gangsta rapper—was *2Pacalypse Now* (1991). When in spring 1992 a Texas state trooper was killed by a young man who claimed that listening to "Souja's Story" (a track on Tupac's album) had inspired his vicious deed, an outcry ensued to have Shakur's disc removed from stores. The controversy helped to build the artist's outlaw reputation and boosted album sales.

While still part of Digital Underground, Tupac (billed as 2Pac Shakur) had made his movie debut in *Nothing but Trouble* (1991). It was in the ghetto drama *Juice* (1992), however, that critics and filmgoers really noticed the versatile, six-foot-tall Tupac. Meanwhile, he had engendered headlines of another type when a youngster died in the crossfire between Tupac's posse and a rival group back in Marin City.

In these years the media coverage of Shakur (who had relocated to Los Angeles and then to Atlanta, Georgia) alternated between reviews of his albums and movies and his mounting confrontations with the law. At one point the notorious entertainer had court appearances

Tupac Shakur at the September 1993 first annual Minority Motion Picture Awards in Los Angeles. (Photo by Albert L. Ortega)

scheduled in California, New York, Georgia, and Michigan. Charges against him included such items as: battery of a woman who had asked for an autograph; a claim that he attempted to smash a fellow rapper with a baseball bat at a concert; accusations that one of his nightclub performances had incited the audience to near riot and, during the melee, a woman patron had been shot by a stray bullet. On October 31, 1993, Tupac was charged with shooting two off-duty police officers in Atlanta. However, the case was later dropped. Some months after being fired from the film *Menace II Society* (1993) for being disruptive on the set, Shakur encountered its directors (Albert and Allen Hughes) and a fight erupted. Convicted of misdemeanor assault and battery in February 1994, Shakur served fifteen days in Los Angeles County jail and another such term with the California Department of Transportation road crew.

Shakur may have scored with his performance opposite Janet Jackson in *Poetic Justice*, but the swaggering, tattooed, hard-living celebrity made a bad impression when he and buddies were charged with alleged sexual assault (later reduced to sexual abuse) of a young woman in New York City. While out on bail, Tupac went to a recording studio in Manhattan's Times Square to rap on another's album. As he and his entourage entered the building's lobby on November 30, 1994, two men shot and robbed him. Despite severe injuries, he survived and then had to deal with his sentence in the sexual abuse case. He was to serve one and a half to four and a half years at the Clinton Correctional facility in Danemora, New York. During his prison stay, Tupac told the media that he had decided to abandon his thug lifestyle and that he had even stopped marijuana smoking. While incarcerated, the rapper and movie actor wed college student Keisha Morris in a marriage that *Vanity Fair* magazine labeled as a "jailhouse convenience." (The union was later annulled.)

After eight months Shakur was released from prison pending an appeal. He quickly found himself embroiled in a feud between Death Row Records (for whom he now recorded) and its leader (Marion "Suge" Knight) and such rivals as Bad Boy Records (led by Sean "Puffy" Combs). Meanwhile, Tupac founded Euphanasia, a firm to control his movie and music careers. He became engaged to Kidada Jones, the daughter of music mogul Quincy Jones.

During this period Shakur became increasingly convinced he would not live till old age. Then on the night of September 7, 1996, while driving in Las Vegas with Suge Knight, a quartet of unknown assailants driving in a Cadillac shot at them. Suge was not hurt but Tupac was badly injured in the drive-by shooting. He underwent emergency surgery and remained in a coma for several days before dying on September 13.

Shakur's death was mourned by fans around the world. Several new, as well as compilation, albums were released to good sales. (His spring 2001 double album *Until the End of Time* reached number one on the charts and went triple platinum in sales.) Several more movies with Tupac also came out, including *Gridlock'd* and *Gang Related* (both 1997). Since her son's death, Afeni, along with Tupac's attorney, coadministers the late star's $8 million to $10 million estate, copes with the lawsuits that popped up after Tupac's passing, and deals with the cultlike status of Tupac's legendary mystique. (In the December 2001 cable TV movie: *Too Legit: The MC Hammer Story*, Lamont Bentley played Tupac in this small-screen biography of rapper MC Hammer and his associates/friends. In January 2002, the Nick Broomfield–directed documentary *Biggie and Tupac* debuted at the Sundance Film Festival. It dealt with the filmmaker's investigation of the still unsolved murders of Shakur and a rival rap star, Christopher Wallace [aka The Notorious B.I.G. or "Biggie" Smalls]. Meanwhile, MTV Films and Amaru Entertainment were planning to produce a feature-length documentary about Shakur.)

In death Shakur became a martyr to gangsta rap and the tough lifestyle he lived and rapped about.

Charlie Sheen

[Carlos Irwin Estevez]

SEPTEMBER 3, 1965–

First he was known as actor Martin Sheen's son; then he was described as the kid brother of Hollywood Brat Packer Emilio Estevez. Later—thanks to starring roles in *Platoon* (1986) and *Wall Street* (1987)—five-foot, ten-inch Charlie was hailed as the most promising new actor of his generation. In 1990, to demonstrate his "sensitive" side, he published a book of poems titled *A Peace of My Mind*. Later in his roller-coaster movie career, Sheen appeared in such cinema junk as *Loose Women* (1996) and *No Code of Conduct* (1998). For a long time these two film titles represented (respectively) his favorite type of female companion and his arrogant, volatile, unmannered mode of behavior. He became a perennial headliner in the supermarket tabloids that detailed his latest bad-boy exploits. Sheen's explosions at pursuing paparazzi became legendary.

Charlie was born in New York City, the third of four children (all of whom became performers) to stage and TV actor Martin Sheen and his artist wife, Betty. By 1968 the family had relocated to Point Dune in Malibu, California, because of Martin Sheen's burgeoning film career. When the future actor was ten, he had a bit with Martin in the TV movie *The Execution of Private Slovik*. That made him consider an acting career. However, while on location with his dad for *Apocalypse Now* (1979), he watched his parent suffer a near-fatal heart attack and decided instead to become a professional baseball player. (He even had a batting cage installed in the family's backyard.)

Meanwhile, big brother Emilio had started making TV movies, and the highly competitive younger brother began getting on the wrong side of the law. At sixteen, with a new 329 BMW to tool around in, Charlie went wild. He was arrested for the use of marijuana, but his family got him out of the scrape. Next he embarked on a spree of misusing other people's charge card numbers to order merchandise. When the cops apprehended him (in front of his senior year art class), the Sheens made restitution. On the romantic front, when Charlie was sixteen he dated actress Robin Wright (who years later wed actor Sean Penn). Then he and high school girlfriend Paula Profit had a child (Cassandra) born out of wedlock. Soon, the couple broke up. Back at school, the perpetual truant was caught buying exam answers and being overly confrontational with one of his teachers. Sheen was expelled, at which point he decided becoming an actor would be expedient.

Using the professional name of Charlie Sheen made him seem less ethnic and opened professional doors as Martin Sheen's son. His first top-billed role was in *The Wraith* (1986), and he got to live his dream by playing a baseball player in both *Eight Men Out* (1988) and *Major League* (1989). With his newfound fame, he became a voracious party animal. (He recalled later, "I'd hoped to be a very recognizable celebrity. I thought that's what it was about: the women, the money, the fame, all the bulls***.")

Sheen's career momentum was derailed with drivel like *Courage Mountain* (1989) and *Navy SEALS* (1990). His use of drugs and booze accelerated and it affected his ability to perform on movie sets. The actor became so engulfed in substance abuse that in August 1990, after a family intervention, he spent a month in a rehab clinic. By the next year Charlie was insisting, "I've settled down considerably and it feels good." He dated Eddie Murphy's ex, Charlotte Lewis. His involvement with actress Kelly Preston ended, reportedly, when he "accidentally" shot her in the arm.

Charlie had a professional comeback with the highly successful comedy *Hot Shots!* (1991). Now back in the game, Sheen was again spending freely on women, cars, and party fun. He was famous for his list of Tinseltown's hottest women (each rated by him). He flaunted a relationship with porn star Ginger Lynn Allen. As would come out in the scandal and 1994 trial of Hollywood madam Heidi Fleiss, Sheen also had a penchant for prostitutes. For example, in a fifteen-month span between 1991 and 1993, the actor expended more than $53,000 on twenty-seven get-togethers with various of Heidi's girls. (Red-faced Charlie was one of the few Tinseltown celebrities to be named during Fleiss's legal mess, and it didn't help his screen career. He observed, "[Studios] won't hire you, even though you screwed the same whores and ate the bullet for it. Yet they pull you aside at a party and say you're their hero for the things you do.")

In September 1995 after dating for only a few weeks, he married model Donna Peele, but the union fell apart after six months. Soon Sheen, who had become a born-again Christian, was rumored to be out of control again. His career decelerated with such films as *The Arrival* (1996), leading Charlie to observe, "I went from making multimillion-dollar deals on movies and having sex with *Playboy* Playmates to being unemployable and doing it with a pregnant prostitute with Caesarean scars in a bar in Mexico."

In late 1996 a day after reportedly smashing a woman friend's car with a baseball bat, Charlie was arrested for allegedly assaulting his ex-girlfriend Brittany Ashland at his Malibu Lake home. She claimed she was pushed to the marble floor and knocked unconscious. The next February he was charged with misdemeanor battery. He pleaded no contest and was sentenced to three hundred hours of community service and placed on probation until June 1999.

May 1998 saw Sheen being rushed to a hospital in Thousand Oaks, California, for a severe drug overdose. After being released, he checked into the Malibu-based Promises, a rehab center. A day later, he took off. Practicing tough love, Martin Sheen signed a warrant for his son's arrest. Charlie was apprehended by the cops for drinking and using medications. The actor, who had the choice of substance abuse treatment or jail time, re-entered Promises in June. He was placed on drug probation until June 2000. With the court's permission he was released from rehab in November 1998.

Later, in need of work, he accepted his brother's offer to costar in the cable TV movie *Rated X* (2000). It unflinchingly detailed two siblings who produce X-rated porno films, with one (Sheen's character) succumbing to drug addiction and being fatally shot by his brother during an argument. Having led a life very separate from Emilio over the past decade, it was an opportunity for the two brothers to reconnect.

At this critical juncture in his professional and private life, former bad boy Charlie was hired to replace ailing Michael J. Fox in the TV sitcom *Spin City* (1996–   ) in the lead opposite Heather Locklear. Sheen debuted in the show in fall 2000 in a tailor-made role as politico

Charley Crawford, a ladies man with a bad past. Obviously, it was a case of art imitating life.

Being cast in *Spin City* proved to be fortuitous for both the trouble-prone Sheen and for the sitcom itself (which was sagging in home audience ratings). Charlie's presence in the series did much to revive the show's zip and viewers' interest in the offering. As a result, the comedy program was renewed for the 2001-02 season and, in January 2002, Sheen received a Golden Globe as Best Comedic Actor in a TV series. That same month he announced his engagement to actress Denise Richards. He first met the thirty-year-old performer when they made the big-screen comedy *Good Advice* (2001) and then furthered their relationship when she guested on *Spin City*.

Here was a case of a notorious Hollywood bad boy cleaning up his act and gaining professional and personal rewards in the process. While appreciating his newfound success, Sheen acknowledged that some worldly matters still perplexed him: "If I've learned anything, it's that I know nothing about women. But I've [stopped] trying to figure them out."

O. J. Simpson

[Orenthal James Simpson]

JULY 9, 1947–

Sometimes catastrophes, like 2001's terrorist attacks on America, bring a country together; other times tragedies can sharply divide a nation. In the case of O. J. Simpson, accused in the 1994 homicides of his ex-wife Nicole Brown Simpson and her friend Ronald Goldman, the high-profile trial seemed to split the country more along racial lines than the case "facts." Until then, former football great Simpson had been a national idol, prized first for his gridiron achievements and later as a handsome personality who was a screen actor, a TV sports commentator, and a major product spokesperson.

In 1995, as the lengthy "trial of the century" played out in the Los Angeles courtroom, the public learned of another side of the well-groomed celebrity whose most recent feature film, *Naked Gun 33⅓: The Final Insult* (1994), had presented him as an L.A. police detective.

Simpson was born in 1947 in San Francisco, the third child in a family where the father was often absent (he would leave the household by the time Simpson was four) and the mother was a graveyard-shift hospital orderly. The Simpsons lived in a housing project in the Potrero Hill part of town. As a child Orenthal suffered from rickets and wore homemade braces on his legs. The determined Simpson not only kept himself mobile, but he forced himself to run, whether playing baseball (his goal was to be a professional player) or football. As a member of a local street gang (the Persian Kings), he was always on the move—from cops, from teachers, from the tough ghetto lifestyle. When not involved in extracurricular pranks or worse, he played football at Galileo High School. Deciding against joining the army, he attended City College of San Francisco, gaining admission on his athletic prowess, not his academic grades. As a hard-playing running back he was named Junior College All-American. With his athletic accomplishments, "Juice" (his sports nickname) entered the University of Southern California on a sports scholarship. In his second year there he won the prestigious Heisman Trophy. In the National Foot-

O. J. Simpson caught in the middle of a discussion between Elizabeth Montgomery (left) and Rosalind Cash (right) for the TV movie *A Killing Affair* (1977). (Courtesy of JC Archives)

ball League's 1969 draft, O.J. signed with the Buffalo Bills with a $350,000 four-year contract.

In June 1967 Simpson had married his high school sweetheart, Marguerite Whitley. Their first child was born in 1968, and their second in 1970. As time passed there was increasing friction between the couple. She preferred living in their fancy California home with their children and wanted him home more. She was against his re-signing with the Buffalo Bills, but, nevertheless, he renewed with the team. Being out of town so often, O.J. found entertainment and companionship elsewhere—with his looks and success he drew women to him.

Like football great Jim Brown who had already parlayed his sports celebrityhood into an action film career, Simpson had his eyes on Hollywood. The six-foot, one inch, 212-pound sports great was a natural for the movies. Thus, during football's off-season he made his screen debut in *The Towering Inferno* (1974), a big-priced disaster saga starring Paul Newman and Steve McQueen. Unlike other African American performers in that decade, O.J. did not become part of the black action film cycle. Rather he performed in more mainstream pictures. In *The Cassandra Crossing* (1976) he hobnobbed with costars Sophia Loren and Ava Gardner. Later he was part of the prestigious TV miniseries *Roots* (1977). When he reteamed with Loren in *Firepower* (1979), there were rumors of an off-camera romance, just as when he had paired with Elizabeth Montgomery for the telefeature *A Killing Affair* (1977). Also during this period Simpson was a TV sports commentator and gained lucrative endorsement deals from such major players as Hertz and Foster Grant sunglasses.

In 1977 thirty-year-old O.J. left the Buffalo Bills and spent his final two seasons of pro ball with the San Francisco 49ers, paid $773,000 annually. Also that year the Simpsons' third child, Aaren, was born. But their marriage was now mostly in name only. They separated officially in September 1978 and in March of the next year he filed for divorce. While their attorneys were divvying up O.J.'s sizeable net worth, the couple's almost two-year-old daughter, Aaren, drowned in the family's swimming pool in August 1979.

Now retired from the football field, O.J. intensified his presence as a TV sports commentator and product endorser, and—through his own production company—developed acting properties for himself. The TV movie *Goldie and the Boxer* (1979) was so popular that it led to *Goldie and the Boxer Go to Hollywood* (1981). Meanwhile the playboy-about-town had found a new romance. He had met vivacious blond Nicole Brown in June 1977 at the Beverly Hills club (The Daisy) where she waitressed. She was an eighteen-year-old from Laguna Beach, California. The interracial couple began dating and months later began living together. As time went on, besides his Brentwood mansion, they would stay at his Laguna Beach oceanfront home, or, later, at his condo on New York's fashionable Upper East Side. The couple led an active life, ignoring the slurs about their interracial pairing. Engaged in 1982, the couple married in early 1985—the year he was inducted into the Football Hall of Fame—and they had two children (1985 and 1988). As before, Simpson was frequently on the road or when in Los Angeles was still a high-spirited party animal who left Nicole home to care for their children.

In 1988 O.J. played a police detective in the satirical *Naked Gun: From the Files of Police Squad!* The following year Simpson was on the other side of the law. After returning home from a New Year's Eve party in the early morning of January 1, 1989, Nicole summoned the Los Angeles cops to the Simpsons' Brentwood compound. She complained of physical and verbal abuse from O.J. Reportedly this was the ninth occasion that the police had come to the Simpson house because of claimed domestic violence. This time the celebrity was charged with spousal abuse. He had to pay a $200 fine, donate $500 to a battered women's shelter, do 120 hours of community service, and undertake a two-year probation. Things did not improve between the Simpsons and in March 1992 she filed for a divorce. Thereafter, O.J. tried repeatedly to reestablish their relationship, even though he was dating model/actress Paula Barbieri. During this period, on October 25, 1993, Nicole reported to 911 that her ex-husband was outside (and then inside) her condo shouting obscenities and threatening physical violence against her.

On June 12, 1994, Nicole and O.J. had attended separately a dance recital for their nine-year-old daughter, Sydney, in West Los Angeles. That evening around 10:30 P.M. Nicole and her friend Ron Goldman were stabbed to death outside her Brentwood condo while her two children slept inside. The next morning the bodies were discovered and the media maelstrom began. The fracas included O.J.'s "flight" in his white Ford Bronco before the reportedly suicidal man surrendered to the police. Entering a plea of not guilty to the charges of two counts of murder with special circumstances, he utilized a dream team of A-list lawyers to defend him. After a lengthy trial he was found not guilty in October 1995. (In 1997, O.J. lost a multimillion-dollar wrongful death civil suit brought by the victims' families.)

As a result of the murder trial, Simpson lost his endorsement contracts, broke up with Paula Barbieri, reportedly went into debt to meet partial payment of the 1997 civil suit, endured many hearings and appeals regarding the custody of his two children by Nicole, relocated to Florida, and, despite legal action, saw his murder trial made into a

TV miniseries (*An American Tragedy*). Meanwhile, in May 2000. he was in the news again when he was involved in a loud argument at his hotel with his then girlfriend, twenty-five-year-old blond beautician Christie Prody. This time he was not the aggressor and he declined to press charges. Months later she alleged that Simpson, now her ex-boyfriend, had broken into her Miami apartment and, in addition, was stalking her.

In October 2001 O.J. was in court yet again, this time in Florida on a charge of felony auto burglary and misdemeanor battery. The prior December, in the upscale Miami suburb of Kendall, Simpson had reportedly run a stop sign in his Lincoln Navigator and the plaintiff, who had been forced to suddenly brake his vehicle, had then honked and flicked his car lights at Simpson. O.J. had supposedly gotten incensed and in a heated discussion with the other driver, O.J. had either brushed against or pulled off the man's eyeglasses and in the process purportedly scratched the plaintiff's face. After two hours of deliberation, the multiethnic jury found O.J. not guilty of the road-rage charges that could have sent Simpson to prison for sixteen years. In thanking the jury, Simpson held his hand over his heart.

In early December 2001, just when it seemed that Simpson was finally out of the headlines for a while, he suddenly cropped up in the news yet again. This time, members of the FBI and the Drug Enforcement Administration had reportedly searched his suburban Miami home as part of an ongoing broad investigation that one media source described as an "Ecstasy drug and money-laundering ring and the sale of pirated satellite TV decoder equipment." O.J.'s house was one of several sites the officials searched in the Miami area. At the time no charges were filed against Simpson.

The saga of O. J. Simpson rolls ever onward.

Frank Sinatra

[Francis Albert Sinatra]

DECEMBER 12, 1915–MAY 14, 1998

As a song stylist he was peerless, whether redefining an old classic ("I Get a Kick Out of You") with a new interpretation or rendering one of his sparkling signature tunes such as "New York, New York." Another of Sinatra's trademark songs, "My Way," best described the manner in which the super crooner lived life. Once the singing idol solidified his fame in the 1940s, he set his own ground rules, traveled with his own cheering section (the fabled Rat Pack), and even employed his own special, colorful "ring-a-ding-ding" language. At times egocentric, volatile, stubborn, and vengeful, he could, on the other hand, be extremely loyal, generous, and gentlemanly. As he was excessive in his talent, so he was in the energy he put into his massively self-indulgent lifestyle. When he needed to calm down, he had several alternative remedies (besides a quick get-together with a "broad"): "Basically, I'm for anything that gets you through the night—be it prayer, tranquilizers, or a bottle of Jack Daniels."

By the early World War II years the crooner had a massive fan clique (especially the screaming bobbysoxers), and had evolved from being a big band singer to a solo artist who outshone his own idol, Bing Crosby. Within a few years of making movies, his successes in that venue (1945's *Anchors Aweigh*, 1949's *On the Town*) confirmed that Frank's special chemistry with audiences worked just as effectively on the big screen as it had in other mediums. But then came a career tumble in the early 1950s. He leaped back with a dramatic role in *From Here to Eternity* (1953), winning a Best Supporting Actor Oscar in the process. Thereafter, when not goofing off on camera, he reconfirmed his acting capabilities with striking performances in such pictures as *Some Came Running* (1958) and *The Manchurian Candidate* (1962). His last full-length screen role, 1980's *The First Deadly Sin*, found him in a favorite celluloid guise—as a tough cop.

Throughout much of his adult life Sinatra was reputed to have (strong) ties to organized crime. He always insisted such accusations were media fabrications based on his being Italian American. He also theorized that it was impossible for an entertainer to work (let alone be the high-rolling gambler that he was) in clubs or in Las Vegas in the old days without rubbing shoulders with crime figures who had financial stakes in such operations. In addition, the star insisted that he often didn't know the backgrounds of the disreputable people he'd met over the years. (This was the rationalization used to explain the well-circulated photo of Frank posing with "the big boys" after a 1976 concert at the Westchester Premiere Theater.)

In actuality, Frank was the kind of guy from a working-class background who found the world of organized crime to be glamorous. It led, for example, to his arranged 1947 visit to Havana, Cuba, to meet infamous mobster Lucky Luciano. (Years later, Luciano reportedly asked Sinatra's help to get Lucky's life story made into a movie.) There was also Sinatra's much-touted (but much-denied) acquaintanceship with underworld top dog Sam Giancana, the kingpin who wanted the singer to intercede with John F. and Bobby Kennedy for special favors in the early 1960s. The scope of Frank's real-life association with Sam was documented by the FBI in 1962 and led President Kennedy to cancel vacation plans to stay at the crooner's Palm Springs digs. The next year, 1963, Frank's ties to Sam led to the revocation of Sinatra's gambling license at the Cal-Neva Lodge (of which he was a part owner). He finally regained it in 1981 after several hours of testimony before the Nevada Gaming Commission. Many sources viewed Frank's explanation of his alleged underworld contacts as a rewriting of history—Sinatra style, of course.

Born in 1915 in Hoboken, New Jersey, to Italian-born parents, street-tough Sinatra developed an early dislike of formal education, which led him to quit high school. He first performed with a local singing group, and then as a saloon singer in northern New Jersey. Big band leader Harry James heard Frank perform on radio and hired him. Sinatra later moved on to Tommy Dorsey's band, remaining with that group until 1942. Thereafter he was on his own and his career went into high gear. So did his good times with a slew of women.

As the chauvinistic playboy of the Western world, Ol' Blue Eyes— whether married at the time or not—spent years chasing and bedding women. His charisma and his reputation for being well endowed and having lots of stamina were tantalizing drawing cards that made conquests easy for swingin' Sinatra. As such, he was the envy of most men, who reasoned that Frankie had the best of all possible worlds—domesticity when he chose or a quickie get-together with a lovely when the urge hit him. It was generally assumed that Sinatra was an expert on dealing with the opposite sex. However, he disagreed: First of all, as to quantity: "If I had as many affairs as you fellows [reporters] claim, I'd be speaking to you today from a jar in the Harvard Medical School." As to the quality of his romantic interactions: "I'm supposed to have a Ph.D. on the subject of women. Truth is, I've flunked more often than not. I'm very fond of women. I admire them. But, like all men, I don't understand them."

In February 1939 Frank married Nancy Barbato, his longtime girlfriend. (They would have three children: 1940, 1944, and 1948.) During this period he carried on with other women, often staying out all night to party. Even when his philandering led to domestic squabbles, Sinatra patched up the differences with Nancy—for the sake of the children, the church, his career, and especially because his forceful mother, Dolly, believed in the institution of family. In the late 1940s, when Frank was established in Hollywood, he and Nancy split up officially for the first time. He transferred operations to his new apartment where he and his cronies partied through the wee hours of the morning. He was seen frequently in the company of gorgeous Lana Turner and also with a lesser screen siren, Marilyn Maxwell. Later, the celebrity moved back home.

By the late 1940s Sinatra had fallen under the spell of screen goddess Ava Gardner, another MGM star. She had been twice married and although she had insecurities about her "poor white trash" southern background, she was an increasingly tough lady when it came to indulging her caprices. When the skinny crooner and Gardner fell in love he was still married, which led to much squabbling between the hard-drinking, bickering lovebirds. Finally, in 1951 Frank and Nancy divorced and he wed Ava. She was at the peak of her beauty and her screen career was still rising, while he was in a slump and had almost lost his voice. Now she was the one who babied him, but the narcissistic movie enchantress had her limits. They boozed, brawled, and played the field (to satisfy their whims and to get revenge on the other). The duo finally separated in 1954 (divorcing in 1957). The big blow-up in 1954 occurred at Frank's Palm Springs abode where Ava, Lana Turner, and others were in attendance that day. Sinatra walked in, overheard a statement, assumed it was about him, and fireworks began. What also finally severed their marriage ties—beyond their indiscretions, jealousies, insecurities, and the demands of their individual careers—was that Gardner's mothering instinct was no longer needed once Frank had regained his professional momentum.

Frank Sinatra making his point to Patrice Wymore in *Ocean's Eleven* (1960). (Courtesy of JC Archives)

In the post-Ava period Sinatra was at the top of his power and charm. Among other couplings, he had flings with an assortment of movie lovelies. It had been Natalie Wood's mother who pushed her young daughter at Sinatra in the 1950s, hoping it would help the girl's screen career. He was years older than Wood and their romance was short-lived, but they remained good friends. As such, he cast her as his leading lady in 1958's *Kings Go Forth*. The singer was more serious about Lauren Bacall, the widow of his good chum Humphrey Bogart. Supposedly, the thought of marriage scared him off. He was great pals with emotionally needy megastar Judy Garland in the 1950s, and he also hung around with the likes of shapely Angie Dickinson, Jill St. John, and Anita Ekberg. Along the way, he had encounters with Marlene Dietrich (who called Sinatra "the Mercedes Benz of men!"), and he was seen out and about with Marilyn Monroe and Kim Novak. In addition, there was vocalist Jill Corey and statuesque dancer-turned-actress Juliet Prowse, who appeared with Frank in *Can-Can* (1960). The crooner also hooked up with well-known party girl Judith Campbell Exner, which caused a rumpus later when it was learned that the swinger had introduced her both to gangster Sam Giancana and to John F. Kennedy.

By the mid-1960s Sinatra was still riding high professionally with a stream of hit albums and popular movies (1965's *Von Ryan's Express*). However, as he approached age fifty he had a midlife crisis. Part of the problem was his headline-making romance with nineteen-year-old Mia Farrow. Bosomy Ava Gardner, who remained Frank's lifelong friend, was so amused that her ex-spouse was marrying someone as thin and waiflike as Mia that she remarked, "I always knew he'd end up with a man." As everyone anticipated, the age gap and the highly incompatible lifestyles of the newlyweds were too much to overcome. Farrow was bored with his set of friends; he didn't dig her hippie generation cohorts. In 1968 the couple divorced.

During subsequent years Sinatra had a 1975 minicourtship of Jacqueline Onassis. (She dropped him, supposedly, after learning Frank's full part in his long-ago setting up of JFK on Hollywood dates.) Then in July 1976, sixty-one-year-old Sinatra wed Barbara Marx. The forty-six-year-old was the ex-wife of Zeppo Marx (of the Marx Brothers), and over the years there was little love lost between Barbara and Frank's offspring from his first wife, Nancy.

In 1998 Sinatra died of heart and kidney failure and cancer. At age eighty-two, the five-foot, eleven-inch star had worn himself out. He was buried in Desert Memorial Park in Cathedral City, California. The legend on his tombstone reads "The Best Is Yet to Come."

Christian Slater

[Christian Michael Leonard Hawkins]
AUGUST 18, 1969–

In *Heathers* (1989), one of his best early performances, reviewers noted the similarities (facial look and mannerisms) between cocky young Slater (with those devilish arched eyebrows) and established star Jack Nicholson. Also in this period Hollywood observers constantly confused Christian with the year-younger actor River Phoenix. By the 1990s, having made a screen name for himself in *Pump Up the Volume* (1990) and *Robin Hood: Prince of Thieves* (1991), interviewers were describing Slater as the "young Warren Beatty." That comparison concerned Christian's penchant for romancing his leading ladies: Valentina Vargas of 1986's *The Name of the Rose*, Winona Ryder of *Heathers*, Samantha Mathis of *Pump Up the Volume*, Patricia Arquette of 1993's *True Romance*. In other matters—Slater's reckless substance abuse and partying in the late 1980s and much of the 1990s—the five-foot, eight-inch performer was following in the footsteps of such legendary Hollywood rogues as John Barrymore and Errol Flynn.

Born in Manhattan in 1969, Slater was the only child of actor Michael Hawkins and his wife, Mary Jo (Slater) Hawkins, who was a former actress turned casting agent. Professionally, his father had used other names, including Michael D. Gainsborough and Garson de Bremenilo. It is show business lore that when Christian was still an infant, his mother took her three-month-old baby onto the stage of an empty theater, held the baby high, and informed him dramatically, "This is your life, my son." He began ad modeling when he was six months old, and she got him a one-day bit in the daytime TV soap opera *One Life to Live* when he was seven. Three years later he embarked on a nine-month tour of *The Music Man* starring Dick Van Dyke. Christian played the young brother of Marian, the librarian. By then, his parents had divorced and he had adopted the stage name of Christian Slater. During the early 1980s he alternated between stage and TV work and an occasional feature film (1986's *Twisted*). Never much for formal education, Slater dropped out of New York's High School of Performing Arts months before graduation.

The budding star was precocious in other ways. He began smoking when he was fourteen, lost his virginity to an older woman soon thereafter, appeared nude on screen in *The Name of the Rose*, and was already dabbling in cocaine and other drugs ranging from ecstasy to mushrooms. By the age of seventeen he and his mother had relocated to Los Angeles, and he was living with a girlfriend and his mom. Already a drinker, he claimed it was not until he made 1988's *Tucker: The Man and His Dream* with Jeff Bridges that he realized his fondness for booze should be classified as alcoholism. By the next year, he had moved to his own pad and began the shoot of *Heathers*, while dating coplayer Kim Walker. By project's end he was romancing costar Winona Ryder.

Slater had the bad habit of drinking and driving and earned a DUI in early 1988 in Los Angeles. The incident, however, failed to slow down his addiction ("I squeezed alcohol dry," he said), partying, or bar-hopping practices. Christian received a second DUI in West Hollywood on December 29, 1989. During this new brush with the law the police had to give pursuit. In the screeching melee, Slater, who had passengers in the car, drove down a back alley, and then slammed his Saab 900 into a telephone pole. He jumped out and while clambering up a chain-link fence, tossed one of his cowboy boots at a police officer. On April 2, 1990, Christian pleaded no contest, spent ten days in jail, was fined $1,400, and placed on five years' probation. He claimed the nightmarish incident was a wake-up call: "I learned that I don't have to be intoxicated to feel OK." The new Slater changed his circle of friends to nondrinking buddies, attended twelve-step meetings, and wore a triangle-in-a-circle pendant that signified "Peace, Serenity, and Strength."

Never part of Hollywood's infamous Brat Pack, he did join group member Emilio Estevez for the western *Young Guns II* (1990). In *Kuffs* (1992) Christian received solo star billing, but the action caper bombed. By now he had patched up his relationship with his mother, but he and his father (then living in L.A.) had little communication.

At the time Christian was dating aspiring screenwriter Nina Huang, six years his senior.

Slater replaced the late River Phoenix in *Interview with the Vampire* (1994). Soon after it was released, Christian was back in the headlines. On December 23, 1994, he was flying from New York to Los Angeles. At John F. Kennedy Airport he checked his luggage and proceeded to the boarding location. He was carrying a black nylon bag that he set down on the conveyor belt to pass through the metal detector. Seconds later he was handcuffed and under arrest for possession of a handgun. His effects contained a 7.65 Baretta semiautomatic pistol. Conviction of criminal possession would require an up-to-seven-year prison term. Hours later—now it was Christmas Eve—he was taken to Queens Criminal Court where he was released under his own recognizance.

Christian Slater on the Hollywood scene.
(Photo by Albert L. Ortega)

By March 17, 1995, the actor and his lawyer had negotiated a plea bargain with the local Queens County assistant district attorney. The charge for trying to carry the licensed, empty gun aboard the flight was lowered to attempted weapon possession—a misdemeanor. Slater was sentenced to three days of community service (with the Children's Health Project).

Two months later Slater was back in the news when Nina Huang, to whom he was once engaged, sued Christian for palimony, claiming she had placed her career on hold during their relationship. (In April 1995 the actor had told Nina to move out of the San Fernando Valley home they shared when he began seeing a prior flame, supermodel Christy Turlington.) Huang's suit was settled out of court in early 1996.

Slater's film career started up again when he teamed with John Travolta for the thriller *Broken Arrow* (1996), although the arty *Julian Po* (1997) did nothing to further it. Then came Sunday, August 10, 1997, and it was like old times. Christian was at a rowdy party in a posh Westwood, California, high-rise condo building. In the wee hours of Monday morning, he got into an argument there with his galpal Michelle Jonas. Allegedly the out-of-control actor punched her in the face and then bit her male friend in the chest when the latter came to her aid. Police were summoned and reportedly the actor, then without shirt or shoes, scuffled with them. He was charged with assault with a deadly weapon (for trying to grab one officer's loaded gun) and for using drugs (cocaine). He was released on $50,000 bail. A month later the felony charges were dropped. In December 1997 Christian pled no contest to the charges and was sentenced to ninety days in jail (starting in January 1998), plus an additional three months in a residential drug treatment program. For a several-thousand-dollar fee, he was permitted to serve his time at the "luxury" La Verne Public Safety Facility in La Verne, California. One of his jobs during his stay there was washing police vehicles. He was released after fifty-nine days for good behavior.

After that Slater returned to Broadway and thereafter appeared in such films as *The Contender* (2000) and *Windtalkers* (2002). Married to producer Ryan Haddon in February 2000, Slater fathered two children (1999 and 2001). Hollywood's former wild man seemed to have been tamed.

Carl "Alfalfa" Switzer

[Carl Dean Switzer]

AUGUST 7, 1927–JANUARY 21, 1959

In any profession it is a difficult experience to outlive one's usefulness, but in show business it is especially tough for those who once were major film and/or TV players. Now, having passed their career prime, they must endure seeing their screen work in reruns, home videos, and such—painful reminders of when they were "somebody." This unpleasant situation is even worse for ex-child stars who have their full adulthoods to cope with their former fame. One of the most tragic examples of used-to-be child celebrities is Carl Switzer, once a mainstay of the enormously popular Our Gang movie series in the 1930s. With his trademark cowlick and squeaky voice (that squealed off-key whenever he sang), the freckle-faced "Alfalfa" (as he was nicknamed) was extremely popular in his day. Between 1935 and 1940 he made sixty-one Our Gang short subjects.

Switzer was born in 1927 on a farm in Paris, Illinois. Carl and his two-year-older brother, Harold, frequently sang at local events. In early 1935 the boys visited their grandparents in Southern California. One day the rambunctious duo visited the Hal Roach studio where the beloved Our Gang comedy shorts were produced. The country kids had no legitimate means of getting onto the film lot, but they noticed that the studio cafeteria was situated just outside the gate. One noontime the youngsters made an appearance there. Dressed in coveralls, the country siblings offered an impromptu round of hillbilly songs. Hal Roach, producer of the series, was impressed by their nerve, and hastily rewrote the screenplay of an Our Gang entry (1935's *Beginner's Luck*) then in production to include the brothers. Harold, called "Slim" or "Deadpan," stayed with the series for some seasons, but usually as a background character. Alfalfa, however, quickly developed a strong following, rivaling Spanky McFarland as the focus of the mischievous on-screen youngsters.

By the end of 1940 the thirteen-year-old Alfalfa had departed the Gang, too tall and gangling to be part any longer of the adolescent

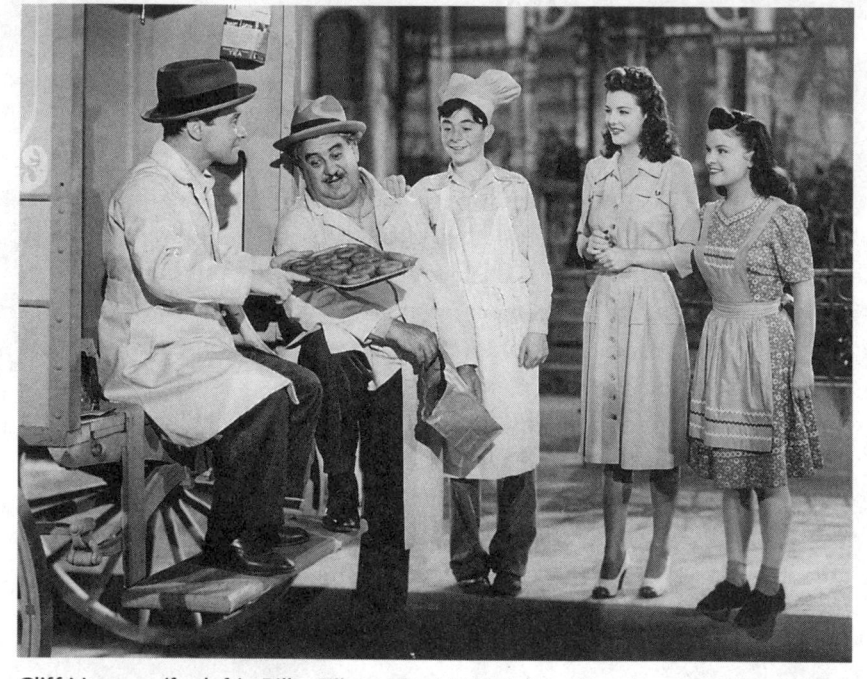

Cliff Nazarro (far left), Billy Gilbert, Carl "Alfalfa" Switzer (center), Marjorie Lord, and Mary Lee in *Shantytown* (1943). (Courtesy of JC Archives)

group's on-camera mischief. Switzer quickly discovered that his past fame was a hindrance. Most casting offices, remembering his famed celluloid persona, couldn't envision him in other roles. It frustrated the young man who just wanted a chance to work. Occasionally he got tiny movie parts: *My Favorite Blonde* (1942), *Going My Way* (1944). He was also part of the Gas House Kids movie series in the mid-1940s, but only three of these low-budget entries were made. To make ends meet, Carl earned a modest livelihood as a bartender or sometimes as a hunting (fishing and game) guide.

In 1954 he wed the daughter of a well-to-do farmer from Wichita, Kansas. The always restless, hot-tempered Switzer tried to settle down, but the union ended in five weeks. The ex-wife remarried and it was years before her son learned that Alfalfa was his actual dad. Meanwhile, angered by his bad luck, Carl began drinking heavily.

When intoxicated, he became boastful and belligerent, which often led to barroom scuffles. Cowboy star Roy Rogers, who had been a hunting client of Switzer, cast him on his TV series a few times between 1952 and 1955, and there were a few big-screen acting assignments including 1954's *Track of the Cat* and 1956's *The Ten Commandments*. Ever hoping for a comeback, the thirty-year-old thought his small role in *The Defiant Ones* (1958) might turn things around. Instead the Tony Curtis–Sidney Poitier drama was his acting finale.

As a youngster Carl often lost his temper when things did not go his way. As an adult he was constantly getting into scrapes. In early 1958 he was shot at by an unknown assailant in a Los Angeles parking lot as he entered his car. On January 21, 1959, Switzer and a pal (bit actor Jack Piott) rushed to the bungalow home of Moses S. "Bud" Stiltz in the San Fernando Valley. Carl was steamed that he had laid out $50 in reward money to retrieve Stiltz's hunting dog. Now Alfalfa wanted to be compensated for that sum, even though it was he who had lost the canine. Since phone calls to Stiltz had not worked, he burst into the man's living room. During the subsequent argument, the drunken intruder seized a nearby heavy clock and smashed it over Stiltz's head. The blow cut the victim badly over his eye. While Switzer's pal remained an observer, Stiltz darted into his bedroom to retrieve his gun with Alfalfa in fast pursuit. In a struggle for the weapon it went off, leading Stiltz's fiancée and her three children (who were crouched with her in the bedroom) to retreat to a neighbor's house. Next, Carl reportedly drew his hunting knife (some reports state a jackknife) and yelled he was going to demolish his opponent. When he charged his prey, Stiltz fired. The bullet entered Carl's stomach and he sank to the ground, dead.

Carl was buried at Hollywood Memorial Park Cemetery (now called Hollywood Forever). His grave marker, besides his name, carries a profile drawing of Petey (the Our Gang dog) and two Masonic symbols. At Stiltz's trial, the jury concluded it was "justifiable homicide."

When Carl Switzer's dad passed away in 1960, he was buried next to Alfalfa. In April 1967 Alfalfa's brother Harold, who then had an appliance franchise, got into a dispute with a customer. After killing the man, Harold later committed suicide. He was also interred at the same Hollywood cemetery. (For years, Alfalfa's mother and sister, who lived in San Diego, drove up regularly to tend the graves.)

Thus was the sad finale of two former child actors—one a star—who could never deal with life successfully after Hollywood rejected them. A strange postscript, however, to Carl's demise occurred in early 2001 when the *Ventura* (California) *County Star* published an article regarding Switzer's long-ago death. In the piece, Tom Corrigan, the stepson of Bud Stiltz, claimed that the facts in the case as put forth in the coroner's inquest decades earlier were not as he believed they had actually happened. In Corrigan's chronology of the facts Carl had come by Stiltz's place with his friend Jack Piott to demand a $50 reimbursement. Switzer had gotten into a scuffle with Bud who was brandishing a .38-caliber revolver. In the ruckus that followed, a shot fired from Stiltz's gun hit the wall and broke some plaster. According to Corrigan, his two younger sisters then ran to a neighbor's house to call the police, while Tom himself went outside. As such, fourteen-year-old Corrigan was not a witness when the next shot was fired. But when the teenager went back inside the fatally wounded Carl was already falling to the ground. Right thereafter Tom observed a closed penknife at the victim's side, which he assumed had fallen out of the deceased's pocket. Supposedly, said Corrigan, only the pleading of his own mother (Bud's wife)—who was present during the incident—and the quick arrival of the police prevented Stiltz from shooting the cowering Piott. Corrigan also told the *Ventura County Star* journalist for the 2001 article that, shortly after the killing, a police detective (since deceased) had asked Tom if he would tell a judge what he had witnessed. The teenager had agreed to do so, but he was never called upon to appear in court. Only days after the shooting, Stiltz was cleared by the coroner's jury. Thereafter, per Corrigan, every Christmas until Bud died in 1984 Stiltz received a holiday card signed "Alfie."

William Desmond Taylor

[William Cunningham Deane Tanner]

April 26, 1867?–February 1, 1922

In the early 1920s Paramount Pictures had a run of extremely bad luck involving several of its key talents. In September 1921 rotund comedian Roscoe "Fatty" Arbuckle was involved in the death of a young "actress" in San Francisco. As played out, the sex scandal ruined his grade-A career. In January 1923 handsome studio star Wallace Reid died in agony at age thirty-one in a Los Angeles sanitarium while undergoing drug withdrawal. Sandwiched in between these two costly disasters was the murder of Paramount film director William Desmond Taylor. It was a high-profile case so enmeshed in studio interference with the crime site, bribed law officers, missing evidence, and lying suspects that eight decades later it still has not been resolved officially or forgotten by Tinseltown observers. (More recently, several writers have sought—in novel or nonfiction format—to piece together the particulars in the baffling homicide.) At the center of the case was, of course, the aristocratic movie director whose shadowy past was as full of contradictory, colorful facts as his shocking murder and the amazing cover-up it engendered.

The future filmmaker was born in Carlow, Ireland, in 1867 (or 1872 or 1877). The son of hard-working Irish Catholics, William gravitated to the stage, which angered his conservative father. Eventually, the young man was shipped to a ranch in Kansas, hoping the discipline there would turn him into a gentleman. That failed, and, after returning to Ireland briefly, he ended up in New York City where he developed a stage career. Three years later, he mysteriously quit the profession and wound up in Alaska. Thereafter he turned up in New York in 1901 and married a member of the theatrical group the Floradora Sextette, a woman whose greatest attraction was her family's wealth. They had a daughter, Ethel Daisy. However, in October 1908 William inexplicably vanished from the Fifth Avenue antique shop that he and his wife, Ethel May, operated, winding up in Alaska yet again. By 1912 he was acting in San Francisco under the name of

William Desmond Taylor. A year later the adventurer was in Hollywood where he maneuvered bit roles in the movies. Soon he was featured in such silent pictures as *Tainted Money* (1914) and *An Eye for an Eye* (1915). Already he had begun directing films, such as *The Judge's Wife* (1914) and *A Woman Scorned* (1915).

Taylor enlisted in the Canadian army in 1918 but World War I ended before he could ship off to France. By the early 1920s he was ensconced as a respected director at Paramount. Unbeknownst to the public, this successful sophisticate was dating and mentoring popular comedian Mabel Normand, helping her deal with her drug addiction. He was also carrying on a clandestine romance with teenage actress Mary Miles Minter who had been featured in several of Taylor's movies in 1920. (In addition there was gossip that Taylor might have been bisexual or homosexual. This rumor spread further when it came out that the director's valet, Henry Peavey, had been caught by the police soliciting young men in downtown Los Angeles days before the director's death. In fact, Taylor was scheduled to appear at Peavey's hearing on February 2. This situation led some sources to theorize that Peavey, who left Los Angeles soon after his employer's demise, had been procuring dates for his boss.)

As the "facts" were reconstructed by the Los Angeles police, on the day of his murder Taylor had worked at Paramount. He was home at his Alvarado Street digs by early evening, when he phoned actor Antonio Moreno at the Los Angeles Athletic Club at 7:00 P.M. About five minutes later Mabel Normand's limousine arrived at Taylor's bungalow; she left around 7:45 P.M. carrying a book on Freud he gave her. Soon after her departure, Taylor was felled by a single bullet to the chest. An individual in men's clothing was seen leaving the premises directly thereafter, but no identification could be made.

Within hours the studio sent key employees to the death site, allegedly removing unspecified items and leaving others. Meanwhile Peavey, the servant, was instructed to put the place in order. Initially it had been the plan to list Taylor's death as the result of a severe stomach disorder that led to hemorrhaging. But the bullet hole (from a .38-caliber pistol) in the corpse ruled that out.

Before long, love notes from Normand and very personal effects of Minter were discovered on the premises. They both were questioned, but no charges were brought against them, nor against Minter's shrewish, controlling stage mother, a former actress named Charlotte Shelby. Also interrogated were Antonio Moreno as well as Edward Sands, the former valet to Taylor who some suggested had been blackmailing the filmmaker.

Film director William Desmond Taylor some months before his still officially unsolved murder in 1922. (Courtesy of JC Archives)

The cast of characters in the killing would soon include good police investigators hamstrung or mysteriously taken off the high-profile case, and bad police department members over the years who, supposedly, were bribed to leave the matter alone. The scandal generated by the unsolved murder (which many believe was committed by Charlotte Shelby) ruined Minter and Normand's screen careers. Forty-five years later veteran film director King Vidor investigated the facts of Taylor's murder case on his own, hoping to use the details as the basis of a new movie he would write and direct. After weeks of inquiry and note taking, he locked away his findings in a strongbox and dropped the planned picture. Following Vidor's death in 1982, the director's biographer, Sidney Kirkpatrick, uncovered these notes, which he utilized for his book *A Cast of Killers* (1986).

Today the prolific silent film actor and director remains a major footnote in Hollywood's history, a cipher whose life and death are filled with contradictory facts, vivid personalities, and vibrant situations—none of which has yet yielded the truth in this bizarre caper.

Lawrence Tierney

[Lawrence Tierney]

MARCH 15, 1919–FEBRUARY 26, 2002

Hollywood has long thrived on creating movie stars from raw material, molding performers into screen images that are frequently far afield from their off-camera personae. An exception to this Tinseltown rule was Tierney, the cold-blooded gangster in *Dillinger* (1945) and other such classic 1940s film noir pictures as *The Devil Thumbs a Ride* (1947) and *Born to Kill* (1947). He was an aggressive sort both before and after his movie successes. Particularly, in the 1950s, this pugnacious individual had many confrontations with and arrests by the police, proving that his celluloid tough guys were similar to the real-life man with the Irish temper who had trouble dealing with fame, women, and booze.

Tierney grew up in Yonkers and then Brooklyn, the older brother of Jerry Tierney, who became movie actor Scotty Brady (1924–85; also a heavy drinker), and Edward Tierney (1928–83) who acted briefly as Ed Tracy. Their father was at one time a night watchman. Lawrence was a track and field star at Boys High School, which led to a scholarship to Manhattan College and a chance to join a national champion cross-country team sponsored by the New York Athletic Club. In summers and after college he held jobs ranging from sandhog to punch press operator and accountant. As a youngster, brash Lawrence had been an avid moviegoer and was convinced he could do better than those on the screen. He had a chance to prove himself in school and amateur productions. The square-jawed, dour-looking Tierney was spotted by modeling agency executives, which led to his posing for Sears & Roebuck and Montgomery Ward catalogs, and a job with the John Robert Powers Agency. This, in turn, led to a stock contract with RKO Pictures.

Once in Hollywood, the insistent but polite Tierney played several small roles and then went aggressively after the key part of the legendary gangster in *Dillinger*. The low-budget picture was a surprise hit and Lawrence received strong reviews. Thereafter, he jumped from combat yarns to westerns (never quite losing his New York accent) but was best in tough-guy assignments such as *San Quentin* (1946) and *Bodyguard* (1948). In Cecil B. DeMille's circus extravaganza, *The Greatest Show on Earth* (1952), Tierney played another villain.

Meanwhile, away from the soundstages the six-foot, 185-pound Tierney was getting a severe bad boy's reputation as a binge drinker often in trouble. In August 1950 he was sentenced to ninety days behind bars for fracturing a man's jaw; a few months later he was in the news again for kicking a New York City cop. By then he had racked up more than a dozen contretemps with the law due to drunk and disorderly conduct. In 1952, after freelancing in Hollywood, he was set for an actor's pact at Paramount, but he got into a nightclub fracas and that ended the potential long-term contract. (He played his last real leading-man role in the inconsequential *Female Jungle*, a 1954 independent entry with Jayne Mansfield.) More contrary behavior and arrests occurred so that when he was taken into custody in August 1955 for disorderly conduct at Ocean Beach, Fire Island, New York, one newspaper quipped that the actor "has been arrested more times [sixteen] than Dillinger, the one-time public enemy whom he portrayed on the screen."

By April 1957 with charges of drunk driving, simple assault, and driving without a license against him, he was out of work and staying in a rented room in the Bronx (sometimes he had day work in construction). A few months later he was charged with breaking down a woman's apartment door but released on $500 bail. With further run-ins with the police,

Lawrence Tierney—Hollywood leading man of budget films. (Courtesy of Echo Book Shop)

Lawrence served time (sixty-six days) for breaking a college student's jaw during a heated argument. In January 1960, Lawrence's mother, Maria, was found dead in her Hollywood apartment (with a bottle of sleeping tablets found nearby); Tierney had been arrested earlier that morning for breaking into a woman's apartment and striking her boyfriend.

With such a busy personal and court life, little wonder that Tierney was off the screen from 1956 to 1962. (Along the way, he was married briefly and had two children. He also had a daughter by the woman who later married his youngest brother, Edward.) He was in *A Child Is Waiting* (1963) and *Custer of the West* (1967), and notching up more arrests—in October 1963 for disorderly conduct and in April 1964 for third-degree assault, and others. In August 1970 a supermarket tabloid recorded that Tierney was attending Alcoholics Anonymous. In mid-January 1973 he attracted media coverage when he was stabbed outside a Ninth Avenue bar in New York City, an assault that required surgery. More positive, but sad, was the 1974 report that the once leading man was driving a horse-drawn carriage in Central Park. Even further bad headlines haunted Tierney. In June 1975 the *New York Times* recorded, "A young woman who had been drinking with Lawrence Tierney, the former actor, in her fourth floor [Manhattan] apartment . . . jumped or fell to her death according to the police. Detectives said that Bonnie Jones, twenty-four years old, landed on a second floor setback. She died in Roosevelt Hospital." The death was ruled a suicide.

By the late 1970s, the veteran actor had done a turnabout and was earning new screen work (*Blood Rage*). Later, he had a recurring role as a police sergeant (!) on TV's *Hill Street Blues* in 1981. He was also a cop in the mainstream feature *Prizzi's Honor* (1985) and had a good role in the film noir *Tough Guys Don't Dance* (1987). In his seventies, he was quite active in small roles in feature films (1992's *Reservoir Dogs*, 1993's *Red*, 1997's *American Hero*) and appeared frequently on TV (including playing Julia Louis-Dreyfus's dad in a 1991 episode of *Seinfeld* and, the same year, portraying a sheriff in the TV-movie remake of *Dillinger*).

In the late 1990s, Tierney suffered a series of strokes. In early 2002 he contracted pneumonia and was admitted to an L.A. nursing home. He died in his sleep on February 26, 2002, at the age of eighty-two. He was survived by his daughter, Elizabeth Tierney, of Park City, Utah. A few years earlier, when reviewing his tumultuous life, the actor (then having been sober for about five years) said, "I finally wised up. I'd say it was about time. Heck, I threw away about seven careers through drink."

Spencer Tracy

[Spencer Bonaventure Tracy]
APRIL 5, 1900–JUNE 10, 1967

Hollywood's Golden Age produced many male superstars, including Clark Gable, James Cagney, and Henry Fonda. None, however, was more gilt-edged than Tracy, who, in his lengthy film career, won two Academy Awards (1937's *Captains Courageous* and 1938's *Boys Town*) and seven additional Oscar nominations—all in the Best Actor category. More than his peers, the rugged, down-to-earth Tracy was appreciated for his captivating naturalistic acting. By the time he joined MGM in 1935, his box-office magnetism was so prized that the studio went through Herculean efforts over the coming years to keep his movie image as clean as possible. Sometimes, as with the married Tracy's longtime relationship (1942–67) with Oscar-winning, single Katharine Hepburn, the studio was joined by the movie colony and the press in discreetly keeping the extracurricular romance from the public. On the other hand, Hollywood was less successful in masking Spencer's longtime alcoholism from public scrutiny, especially in his earlier years on the West Coast. His addiction was so detrimental that it often turned Spencer the measured observer into a ferocious drunk. In such a foul mood he would destroy a soundstage set. Or he might attempt to strangle his older brother, Carroll, and throw him out of the window of the Beverly Wilshire Hotel, just because his sibling was trying to calm Spencer down.

Spencer Bonaventure Tracy was born in 1900 in Milwaukee, Wisconsin. His father, John, was a devout Irish Catholic with a drinking problem and a tendency toward violence; his mother, Carrie, was Protestant. The Tracys' first son, Carroll, had been born in 1896. As a child, Spencer attended more than a dozen schools, not always because his family moved a lot as their fortunes rose and fell, but mainly because the boy was frequently truant or disruptive. Yet when he attended the local Marquette Academy, Tracy grew intently interested in Catholicism and for a time considered becoming a priest. Later, after a World War I navy stint, Spencer attended Ripon College in Wisconsin. On campus the premed student participated in the debating team, which led to an interest in acting. He left Ripon and attended the American Academy of Dramatic Arts in New York City. Before graduating in 1923, he made his Broadway debut in *R.U.R.* (1922). Later, while part of a stock company in White Plains, New York, he fell in love with budding actress Louise Treadwell (an Episcopalian) and married her in September 1923. The next year their son, John, was born. When it was discovered that the baby was incurably deaf, the parents' lives changed forever.

Louise masked her grief by devotedly helping her boy learn to cope. In contrast, Spencer, following in the tradition of his father and his brother, turned to heavy drinking during this crisis. Eventually Tracy emerged from his slump and devoted himself to advancing his career so he could afford to provide for the boy's treatment and well-being. Alternating between stock and Broadway, Spencer was a standout in the New York run of *The Last Mile* (1930), a prison drama. This led to his starring as a gangster in Fox Films' *Up the River* (1930). He soon signed a contract with the studio.

Once based in Southern California, Spencer began having brushes with the law. For example, one time in late 1930 he was erratically backing out of a driveway (between a gambling club and a whorehouse) on the Sunset Strip. When he resisted police arrest, he was taken to the county jail until the studio engineered a quick release. Anything might trigger a Tracy binge. He could go for periods without a drink, then he might start fretting over son John (who had just recovered from a polio attack) or the poor caliber of his Fox projects. It only took a drink or two for him to take on a costar with whom he was miffed or a studio coworker who had innocently taken his parking space. The actor's propensity for violence, like his drinking problem, seemed to be a case of like father, like son.

Things improved with the Tracys when Louise gave birth in 1932 to a healthy girl, Susan. Then, however, life took a sharp turn when Spencer was loaned to Columbia Pictures. During the making of *A Man's Castle* (1933) Tracy became enamored of his twenty-year-old costar, Loretta Young. As a result, Tracy and his wife temporarily separated. Eventually Young announced that, because she and Spencer

Spencer Tracy and Katharine Hepburn in one of their costarring vehicles, *Pat and Mike* (1952). (Courtesy of JC Archives)

were both Roman Catholic, they had agreed not to see one another socially again. Nevertheless, the clandestine relationship continued for a while before Tracy returned home. As would be his practice later with Hepburn, the Catholic Tracy would not divorce his wife, but he would not give up his latest lady love either. Caught in his own dilemma, Tracy took out his frustration and aggression on others.

During the early 1930s Tracy would disappear from the studio lot for days at a time—often in the midst of shooting a picture. He'd later reappear looking like a smelly skid row reject. Sometimes on these binges he'd end up in a strange city (such as Yuma, Arizona) forcing the studio to retrieve him and make amends with the local law. Once when Tracy got "that" look in his eyes at Fox, the director cleared the soundstage while the actor, a notorious insomniac, sunk into a sleeping fit. Locking Spencer in the building, everyone waited outside for the "all clear" signal. But suddenly, the performer came awake and began smashing objects and toppling the walls of the set.

By 1935 a weary Fox Films did not renew cantankerous Spencer's contract. However, MGM gambled on signing him. Tracy stayed on his best behavior—for a time. For one thing, he was now happier with his screen projects (which led him to two back-to-back Oscars) and his new studio's respectful treatment of him. Things had stabilized at home for the sake of the children. And when Tracy fell off the wagon, Metro-Goldwyn-Mayer immediately protected their multi-Oscar-winning star. Then too, MGM had very efficient methods to cover over their contractee's misdeeds. For such emergencies with Tracy and other stars, the studio maintained an official-looking ambulance with uniformed employees to pick up key MGM players when they made nuisances of themselves in public.

Sometimes during his MGM tenure (1935–55) something would set Tracy off and he would disappear from the studio. One time after vanishing, he returned from having spent a "lost weekend" at a Brooklyn hotel, trying to drive out the devil within while away from the media's watchful eyes. On another occasion, shortly after his failed Broadway comeback in 1946's *The Rugged Path*, Spencer went on a tremendous bender in Manhattan. The studio tracked him down, had him admitted to Doctors Hospital and, to keep prying eyes away, had him assigned to a private room on the obstetrics/gynecology floor. However, a "pal" stupidly brought Spencer some liquor and it ignited a round of delirium tremors that required Spencer to be restrained with a straitjacket while the drying-out process began again. This major relapse kept Tracy off the screen for a year. To cover up, the studio created a fictional ailment to excuse Tracy's absence from Hollywood.

As Tracy grew older, he did not get much better at managing his substance abuse or the accompanying destructive outbursts (he had a bad one during the making of 1956's *The Mountain*). However, he usually had Katharine Hepburn on hand (they made nine films together) to calm him down or, better yet, to divert an oncoming destructive drinking mood. In Tracy's last decade of life he suffered from heart problems, and only a few weeks after he and Katharine completed *Guess Who's Coming to Dinner* in 1967, the fine actor with the uncontrollable inner fury passed away.

Rudolph Valentino

[Rodolfo Alfonso Raffaelo Pierre Philibert Guglielmi di
Valentina d'Antonguolla]

MAY 6, 1895–AUGUST 23, 1926

Valentino was so much a phenomenon of his time that it is difficult
today to truly appreciate the extraordinary impact he made on 1920s
moviegoers. Many of his silent features (1922's *The Young Rajah*,
1924's *A Sainted Devil*) were a crass disservice to the box-office magnet who had gained screen immortality with two 1921 releases: *The
Four Horsemen of the Apocalypse* and *The Sheik*. However, even in
his lesser vehicles audiences (especially women) flocked to the theaters
to behold the swarthy, lithe, and flamboyant Valentino, with his
intense eyes, flaring nostrils, and slicked-back hair. When the most
famous of Hollywood's Latin Lovers died suddenly at age thirty-one
in 1926, the mass hysteria was genuine, albeit orchestrated to an even
higher pitch by crafty Hollywood executives. But few mourners knew
what it had taken for Valentino to become a movie star.

Valentino was born in 1895 in Castellaneta in southern Italy, the
second of three children of a veterinarian and his French-descended
schoolteacher wife. When Rodolfo was twelve, his father died and the
middle-class family moved to Taranto. The undisciplined youth was
enrolled in military school but he remained free spirited. He later
abandoned premed studies, planning to join the military. However,
such aspirations were too bold for his unwealthy family and, instead,
he was trained in agriculture. Wanting a more glamorous life, Rudy
trekked to Paris where he improved his dancing skills and indulged
his wastrel tendencies among the bohemian set. By late 1913 his exasperated mother had barred him from her house, but she paid for his
steerage-class voyage to the United States.

In New York the dreamy newcomer was but another impoverished
immigrant who had yet to master the English language. Struggling to
survive, he worked as an assistant gardener, a busboy, and a petty
thief. Having honed his dancing skills, he became a gigolo, one of the

breed who danced the waltz and the daring tango with rich customers in the fancier Manhattan clubs. With his swarthy good looks, the preening immigrant (known as "Rudy the Peacock") was soon much in demand among wealthy women who compensated him for his services in the boudoir. He developed a routine of paid bedroom trysts after the afternoon tea dances and then after the evening activities. Before long, the once penniless twenty-year-old was living on the Upper East Side, in a chic apartment filled with gifts from his pampering clients. (Reputedly, some of his customers were males.)

As his popularity with the social set grew, he was introduced to Bianca de Saulles, the wealthy Chilean spouse of a philandering American. A torrid love affair quickly ensued. Meanwhile, the city's police

Rudolph Valentino (right) with Karl Dane in *The Son of the Sheik* (1926), Valentino's last film. (Courtesy of JC Archives)

department was investigating the prostitution racket among the gigolos on the cabaret scene. Wanting to be "pure" for Bianca, Rudy abandoned the salons and partnered for a time with Bonnie Glass in an exhibition dance act on Broadway and on an East Coast tour. Later, in a scheme hatched with Bianca, the Italian export introduced his hated new dance partner (Joan Sawyer) to Mr. de Saulles. The two hit it off and Rudy later testified in divorce court about Bianca's unfaithful spouse being with Sawyer. But de Saulles had his revenge. He implicated Rudy with the notorious Mrs. Georgia Thym, an enterprising society madam who reportedly blackmailed her wealthy clientele. The police held Valentino for questioning for several days. Not long thereafter, Bianca de Saulles shot her ex-husband over the custody of their offspring. At this juncture Rudy fled town and joined a touring stage musical. Eventually he landed in Los Angeles.

Two New York actor pals, Norman Kerry and Mae Murray, helped Rudy break into the film business where he worked as an extra. When screen work was scarce for the foreigner, he returned to his old habits: exhibition dancing (sometimes in questionable establishments), private dance lessons, and bedding rich customers. (He was also reputed to hang out at the swank Torch Club, a gay venue in Los Angeles.)

In 1919 Rudy wed lesbian actress Jean Acker, but they almost immediately separated and were divorced in 1922. Because the marriage had not been consummated, Rudy became the butt of jokes in Hollywood. Through a platonic friendship with highly respected scenarist June Mathis the actor was hired for the lead in *The Four Horsemen of the Apocalypse*, the 1921 epic that made him a star. His success resulted in Rudy, who now was called Rudolph Valentino, becoming even more self-absorbed and temperamental.

The Sheik (1921) and *Blood and Sand* (1922) sealed Valentino's meteoric screen climb. Meanwhile he had come under the sway of bisexual (or lesbian) Natacha Rambova—the former Winifred Hudnut—an exotic movie costume and art designer. Becoming her "love slave," he and Natacha traipsed to Mexico in May 1922 to wed, not realizing that his divorce from Acker was not yet final. He was jailed on bigamy charges and left to stew for hours in a crowded cell by his studio who wanted to teach their uncooperative box-office magnet some humility. Later, he was let off the legal hook when he admitted in court that he and his "bride" had not shared the bed in her hotel room on their wedding night. In March 1923 the twosome remarried and thereafter his dominating spouse made every decision for her too-pliant husband. Before long she had alienated his studio, and for a while he was away from the screen. When the bullying Natacha stormed off to New York, Valentino had a grandiose mansion (Falcon's Lair) built, hoping to win her back. However, she was bored with her mate and sued for divorce in Paris in January 1926.

Abandoned by two wives, the humiliated screen lover began a highly publicized "romance" with Polish-born Pola Negri, the exotic

Continental movie star who had relocated to Hollywood. Meanwhile, Valentino and his studio were contending with a backlash from American men who were tired of being compared unfavorably to Valentino by their idol-struck wives. Rumors about Rudolph's effeminacy and his sexual preferences abounded, leading one Chicago journalist to label Rudy a "pink powder puff."

Having completed *The Son of the Sheik* (1926), which tested well with audiences, Valentino went to New York to promote the picture. By the time he reached Manhattan he was suffering from severe stomach pains. On August 16, 1926, he was admitted to Polyclinic Hospital where it was discovered that his appendix had ruptured and uremic poisoning was spreading throughout his body. On August 23 he died, setting off a nationwide frenzy among his fans. Few then or later appreciated the means or the extent to which ambitious Valentino had gone to reach the apex of Tinseltown.

Jean-Claude Van Damme

[Jean-Claude Camille François Van Varenberg]
OCTOBER 18, 1960–

Known as "The Muscle from Brussels," "Hot Damme," "Van Dammage," and such, this five-foot, eight-inch personality burst onto the international filmmaking scene in the mid-1980s. The 185-pound Belgian had a forty-inch chest and could kick as high as six feet into the air. With vehicles like *Bloodsport* (1988) and *Kickboxer* (1989) he made his presence felt in the arena of martial arts and action movies whose stars then included the older Arnold Schwarzenegger, Sylvester Stallone, Chuck Norris, and Steven Seagal. Trained as a ballet dancer, along with martial arts, the square-jawed Jean-Claude proclaimed, "I am the Fred Astaire of karate."

Van Damme's growing fan base didn't mind if his heavy accent converted dialogue like "focus" into "fuh-kus." After all, besides his superior martial arts skills, he was handsome and had a well-proportioned (not exaggerated) upper body. Not only did he kick butt on camera, but generally he displayed his own, well-shaped, bare backside as well.

Brawny Van Damme built himself into a big-screen institution, churning out two to three films a year. The narcissistic star was soon proclaiming himself a magnet for women, and he seemed determined to prove the point whether or not he was married at the time. On camera he sought to expand his acting range by revealing his sensitive side. In real life he proved his human frailty when it became known in the 1990s that he had succumbed to drug addiction. Even more shocking, during this bad time, the fitness fanatic permitted his famed torso—his shrine of success—to slacken.

He was born Jean-Claude Van Varenberg in 1960 near Willebroek, Belgium, to Roman Catholic parents. Soon after, the family (which included an older child, Veronique) moved to Brussels where the father worked as an accountant. As a youngster, Jean-Claude was frail, sensitive, and picked on by his peers. When he was ten, his dad took him to a karate class, hoping the discipline would toughen him. Thereafter, not only did the boy work out there, but he was drawn also to music and painting, played the piano, and—for five years—danced ballet. When a French dance company offered him a position, he chose karate because it was "more fun." Another of his passions was the cinema and he dreamed of becoming a movie star.

At sixteen—the year he earned a black belt in Shotokan—the strong-willed teen quit school and left home. He did well modeling in Brussels, Paris, and Hong Kong. When he was eighteen, he began winning karate awards and martial arts competitions, and obtained a black belt in kickboxing. In France he won bits in a few small movies, one of which was *Monaco Forever*, released in 1984, in which he had a brief role as a homosexual.

In 1982 Jean-Claude sold his gym (which he had owned for a few years), placed the bulk of the proceeds into a European bank—promising himself not to touch it—and, with about $800, flew to Los Angeles. There he survived with such jobs as a pizza deliverer and a bouncer in a Newport Beach nightclub. He improved his English by watching TV when not training at a gym. This regimen lasted for three years, by which time he'd adopted the surname of a family friend, Van Damme. During this period the émigré married Maria Rodriguez. Their union developed into arguments and they divorced in 1984. Two years later he would wed Cynthia Derderian of Newport Beach, a relationship that lasted only seven months.

In 1985 Jean-Claude answered a casting call and was hired for the second-billed role of Ivan, a villainous Russian karate champion in the low-budget entry *No Retreat, No Surrender* (1986). Around this time he met bodybuilder Gladys Portugues. They wed in 1986 and had two children (1987 and 1990).

Never lacking boldness, audacious Jean-Claude approached film producers and directors wherever he saw them. In the parking lot of an L.A. restaurant, he encountered Menahem Golan, then the head of Cannon Films. Van Damme exhibited his 360-degree, six-foot leg jump over the mogul's head and suggested that he be hired for one of Golan's upcoming movies. The impressed filmmaker soon complied and three weeks later Jean-Claude was in Hong Kong filming *Bloodsport* (1988) at a $50,000 salary. The movie was a big moneymaker. Jean-Claude's next film, *Black Eagle* (1988), was the newcomer's final role as a villain. He was now on his way to becoming an international star.

By this point the highly visible Jean-Claude was having his problems with the law. In 1989 he was sued for, allegedly, "willfully" gouging the eye of an extra in a swordfight while making that year's *Cyborg*. The plaintiff won more than $487,000. In early 1991 Van Damme was involved in a $2 million breach-of-contract suit involving a European coproduction in which he was supposed to have starred. In September 1991 the star, now earning upward of $600,000 per film, was stopped on Arizona's Interstate 40 for driving 108 mph in a 65 mph posted zone.

In 1992 Van Damme's roving eyes proved hazardous to his third marriage. He was in Hong Kong at the Regent Hotel, as was twenty-six-year-old former model and dancer Darcy LaPier. She was the wife of much older Ron Rice, the suntan lotion entrepreneur. Darcy had been on the prowl for Jean-Claude for a time. On this occasion she phoned his room, inviting him to her penthouse suite. He arrived in his robe. When she opened the door, the soundtrack to the movie *Bugsy* was playing. He went in and the rest became international gossip when Van Damme and Gladys divorced.

In late 1993 a lawsuit was filed by a New Orleans woman alleging that in 1992 Van Damme had coerced her into performing oral sex on him at a local hotel. The case was settled out of court. In February 1994 Jean-Claude and Darcy wed in a Buddhist ceremony in Bangkok, Thailand. Van Damme spent a small fortune upgrading his lifestyle to accommodate his bride. Nevertheless, domestic discord soon began. She claimed that he was a "control freak" and was against her becoming an actress. He alleged that once, in Bali, she assaulted him with an end table. In 1995 the couple argued in Sun Valley, Idaho, and she called 911 (but no charges were filed). In August 1996 she telephoned the Santa Monica, California, police after another contretemps. On that occasion it was Van Damme who made a police report on his spouse. Already Darcy had filed for divorce twice (in 1994 and again in 1996) as had Jean-Claude himself, but they always reconciled. During one of the couple's splits in late 1994, Van Damme made up, briefly, with wife number three, and then began dating actress Tatum O'Neal.

During his tumultuous marriage to Darcy and while his career was stagnating with such entries as *Street Fighter* (1994) and *Sudden*

Death (1995), Van Damme began using cocaine in increasing dosages, reasoning it increased his sexual prowess. Reportedly his consumption increased after the birth of his third child, Nicholas, in 1995. Absorbed in his sex drive, his pending directorial debut (1996's *The Quest*), and the pressure of competing with Hong Kong action stars like Jackie Chan, Van Damme began to ignore his daily training ritual. He began losing weight. Later he said, "I did so much damage to myself. . . ." By December 1996 out-of-control Jean-Claude was undergoing treatment at the Exodus drug rehab center in Los Angeles. The action star explained, "I feel I've been a role model to children . . . and couldn't live with myself if I didn't regain my health and conquer this thing."

While Van Damme was getting clean and sober, his wife number four had returned to her ex-husband and filed yet again for divorce. The vituperative legal split had each party accusing the other of cocaine usage and violence. In January 1998 Darcy received handsome spousal and child support awards. That February, Van Damme was in New York where he brawled with a former employee, Chuck Zito, at an East Side Manhattan club. In this encounter Zito proved to be the victor, which did nothing for Jean-Claude's ego or screen reputation.

Van Damme had remained friendly with Gladys Portugues and the couple remarried on June 25, 1999, in his hometown in Belgium. Yet, by that September he was in hot water again, arrested in Los Angeles for drunken driving and being without his license. He was taken to jail. At the time of being stopped by the police he was in the company of a pretty brunette. When the case came to court, Van Damme was sentenced to three years' probation, fined $1,200, and ordered into a ninety-day alcohol education program.

By early 2000 Jean-Claude was again the happy family man, proclaiming from his west San Fernando Valley home that he shared with Gladys and their two children: "I've been a wild man. But all that's behind me. This is where I love to be. In my home. It's my church, my castle, my refuge." As for his films, after a two-year absence he returned to the screen with *Replicant* (2001), which went directly to video. Nevertheless, he continued to grind out new entries thereafter.

Jan-Michael Vincent

[Jan-Michael Vincent]

July 15, 1944–

Rarely has a Hollywood Golden Boy tumbled so often or so deeply as Vincent. With his spectacular looks, physique, and rebel attitude, he had everything going for him as the star of *Buster and Billie* (1974), *White Line Fever* (1975), and *Baby Blue Marine* (1976). In his best screen showcase, 1978's *Big Wednesday*, he was the personification of the handsome and reckless California surfer dude. Then his career and his personal life began to implode. By the mid-1980s while he was crashing and burning through his TV series, *Airwolf*, costar Deborah Pratt asked him why he was throwing away his once-bright career with booze, bad behavior, and such. His reply was, "Because I don't understand my talent, and I don't know why people like me."

He was born in the farming community of Hanford, California, where his father owned a billboard company. Until the fifth grade, he was a typical nice kid. Then he grew rebellious, running away from home, setting off bombs in school, and creating mayhem in many ways. In high school he was on the swim team, surfed, built his own hot rod, and got into a lot of fights (possibly as a means of asserting himself). He also had developed a penchant for getting drunk. One such intoxication at a school football game led to a clash with the police. The morning after Vincent graduated from high school, he returned home with a hangover from an all-night party. When his father insisted he was now expected to join the family business, Jan-Michael promptly left home. He enrolled at Ventura College, but after casual participation as an art major for four semesters, he headed for the surfing waters of Mexico.

Back in California Jan-Michael was in the National Guard for a time and then while working half-heartedly for his dad's business, he was discovered by a television ad agent, which led to acting assignments. His first picture, *Los Bandidos* (1967), got him a contract at Universal Studios where he popped up in TV series (1968's *The Banana Splits Adventure Hour*), feature films (1969's *The Unde-*

feated), and TV movies (1970's *Tribes*). Meanwhile, in 1968 he wed Bonnie Foreman whom he'd met in college and who shared his love of surfing. For his portrayal of Robert Mitchum's son in *Going Home* (1971), Vincent received a Golden Globe nomination as Best Supporting Actor. By 1973, the year he became a poster boy starring in *The World's Greatest Athlete*, he was the father of daughter Amber. By then, his marriage was falling apart. The couple separated in 1978 and eventually divorced in 1984.

As Jan-Michael and Bonnie split up, he met a teenage high school student at a beach party. He was thirty-four and Joanne Robinson was half his age. Her parents were against the relationship, so they dated secretly. He often helped her cut classes so they could go surfing. During this period, while living in the Malibu area, the actor was arrested on charges of growing forty-one marijuana plants in his home, but got past that incident.

In 1983 the still boyish-looking Vincent had a career reprieve when cast again as Robert Mitchum's son, this time in the TV miniseries *The Winds of War*. Off camera that year Jan-Michael was detained by the police for driving under the influence in Malibu and was put on probation. In June 1984 he was in an altercation with a customer at a Malibu bar and restaurant. In October 1985 the golden bad boy was in the news again, now accused of hitting a woman (a friend of his wife-to-be, Joanne) in the face and breaking her nose. It was the third time in fifteen months that battery charges had been made against him. He was eventually acquitted of these allegations, but in the meantime was sentenced to thirty days in jail for violating probation from a 1983 drunk-driving conviction. He entered a rehab program to show the court that he meant to break his drunk-driving syndrome and was given a reprieve against the jail sentence.

During TV's *Airwolf* (1984–86), the show's star spent much of his time drinking (and, supposedly, doing drugs) and causing problems on the set. The year the program was cancelled he married Joanne.

Now into his forties and his looks further diminished by rough partying, Jan-Michael was reduced to appearing in such celluloid junk as *Alienator* (1989) and *Xtro II: The Second Encounter* (1990). In April 1988 having recently ended his four-year probation period for another

Jan-Michael Vincent (center) taking the law into his own hands against Victor Brandt (right) as Judson Pratt (left) looks on in *Vigilante Force* (1975). (Courtesy of Doug McClelland)

drunken-driving conviction, he and his wife were stopped by sheriff's deputies in Agoura Hills because of an expired car registration. In the process fifteen white amphetamine tablets were alleged to be discovered in Vincent's briefcase in the car and the actor (but not his wife) was arrested. He was released on $1,000 bail. Charges were dropped when lab testing revealed that the tablets were actually caffeine.

By November 1991 *Globe* tabloid headlines were insisting "Airwolf Hunk Is a Down-&-Out Drunk." The feature detailed that Vincent had lost his Malibu beach retreat, had quit staying with his in-laws because of their no-drinking rule, and had supposedly shown up at his wife's rehab graduation sipping a bottle of booze.

By 1994 Vincent's wife Joanne was recounting to the *National Enquirer* and other such publications a laundry list of repeated physical, emotional, and sexual abuses that she purportedly suffered at the hands of her spouse, whom she claimed was frequently drunk and had even stomped her kitten to death in one of his rages. Jan-Michael countered, "Man I'm freakin' over this thing. . . . Yeah, I've been verbally abusive in the past, but that's where it stops. . . ." During this period she sought court protection from her husband, restraining him from coming near her abode, but she failed to show up for the hearing.

Now reduced to brief appearances in direct-to-cable items like *Red Line* (1996), Jan-Michael had been through a brief relationship with a would-be actress in 1995 (who turned around and sued him for a huge amount for physically abusing her while she was pregnant and reputedly causing a miscarriage), and seen his wife file for divorce the next year. Reports insisted—and photos confirmed—that the once star was a wasted shell of his former self.

The seeming nadir of his downward spiral occurred on August 26, 1996, in Mission Viejo, in Orange County, California. According to one account, he was following his current girlfriend, a waitress, to her mother's home when his car rear-ended her auto. The impact caused his vehicle to slam into a traffic signal. (Another version insisted the couple had been arguing before she took off in her car; with he angrily following her in his and jamming into her vehicle.) While the woman and her two young sons were unhurt, Vincent suffered a broken neck and facial lacerations. Once hospitalized, it was determined that his death-defying injury would not leave him paralyzed, although problems occurred during his recovery that resulted in his having a very raspy voice. Later, after he was released from the hospital in fair condition, police blood tests determined that Jan-Michael's alcohol level had been .18 percent at the time of the accident and he was charged with drunken driving. He ended this episode on probation, was placed in yet another intensive rehab program, and swore (again) to give up drinking. Thereafter he made a few token low-budget movie appearances.

By September 1999 Jan-Michael was in court again, pleading guilty to three counts of public drunkenness. He was ordered to pay an $800 fine, enter a six-month rehab program, and serve a three-year probation. In mid-July 2000 he was taken into custody in Orange County for missing a court date for a January 2000 incident where he was publicly drunk. He was freed on bail pending a September 14, 2000, trial. Ten days later he was busted for alleged domestic violence against his current fiancée, Patricia Christ. That September he was sentenced to sixty days in jail. He served his time at a Culver City facility, cutting his sentence in half by doing janitorial duties when not confined to a locked room. From there he was to go back to rehab to complete yet another substance abuse program.

When asked not so long ago how he was coping with his problem-plagued life, Jan-Michael said, "I'm just hanging on, by white knuckles. That's being honest."

Mark Wahlberg

[Mark Robert Michael Wahlberg]

JUNE 5, 1971–

In one decade Wahlberg went from being a tough, unknown New Englander to a rap star of the bubblegum set to a world-famous Calvin Klein underwear model and onward to greater success as a major film star. The progression was all the more amazing when Mark's troubled past (including a stay behind bars and other legal scrapes) is considered.

Wahlberg was born in 1971 in Dorchester, Massachusetts. He was the ninth child in an overcrowded, three-bedroom household. From two previous marriages Alma (a registered nurse) had had six children, and with Mark's father (a truck and then bus driver) she had three. Dorchester was a tough neighborhood in which to grow up, full of racial clashes and economic hardship. There were times when the German–Irish Catholic Wahlbergs barely scraped by. When Mark was eleven his parents divorced and the trauma led the youngster to become rebellious, including self-tattooing a shamrock on his left leg.

When Mark was thirteen, his slightly older brother Donnie auditioned for a music group being packaged by two Bostonians. Donnie insisted that Mark be made part of the act, soon called New Kids on the Block. Ambitious Donnie thrived on leading the white rap group to popularity, but Mark, more interested in playing basketball and having fun, quit the New Kids. Meanwhile, in the classroom he was not faring well, a result of disinterest and truancy. Mark failed his freshman year at Copley High and had to repeat the grade. By age fifteen he had quit school in favor of the fast track among punks. By now he had developed a violent streak, often reflected in outbursts aimed at minorities.

The teenage Wahlberg was running with a rough crowd. As he acknowledged later, these were guys who thrived on joy riding, rolling drunks, and, supposedly, engineering liquor store robberies. One evening, when Mark was sixteen, he and his cohorts discovered a stash of the drug "angel dust" in a friend's freezer. The adventurous

Wahlberg and his confederates smoked this PCP and soon were elevated into an enraged state. Deciding they wanted some booze, they went in search of a still-open liquor store. When they couldn't find one, they became desperate. They spotted an Asian man on the street carrying a beer. When he would not give it up, Mark reportedly grabbed a long pole and beat the victim into submission. (One account of the aggression—perhaps embellished to make Mark seem tougher—had Walhberg attacking the beer-carrying Vietnamese man and, in the process, poking out the victim's eye, as he screamed "Vietnam f****** s***!")

When Mark was picked up by the police on an attempted murder charge (later reduced to assault and battery), it came to light that two years earlier he and other white friends on bicycles had chased several African American schoolgirls while hurling racial epithets at them. For whatever reason, the attackers were not punished then, but now Mark's offense was a different story. When the case came before the judge, Wahlberg was offered an option. He could be treated as a juvenile offender and remain in an institution for wayward youths until he was eighteen. Or, if judged as an adult, he would serve six months at the Plymouth House of Corrections. He chose the latter. As he said later, "I felt like everybody in my neighborhood was in the same house of corrections, and my brother [Jim—on a ten-year sentence for armed robbery] was doing time, so I figured there was nothing to worry about." After forty-five days at Plymouth—where he spent much of his time working out—the strapping, five-foot, eight-inch Wahlberg was released.

Once out of the slammer, Mark did not have an immediate, total rehabilitation. In summer 1990 he had a scuffle with a police officer that occurred in front of his family's home. The assault and battery charges were later dismissed.

By 1992 Mark had followed in brother Donnie's musical footsteps, forming Marky Mark and the Funky Bunch. (Unlike Donnie's squeaky clean band, Mark's ensemble had street grit.) The group's debut album, *Music for the People*, full of raw rap, was released in July 1991 and did very well. A year later, as the Funky Bunch was peaking with the fickle juvenile set, the still hot-tempered Mark had a run-in with a security guard at the Savin Hill Park tennis courts in Dorchester. After settling a civil lawsuit, the criminal charges against Wahlberg were dropped.

Before Mark of the chiseled body and baby face chilled out as the A-list movie star of such entries as *Boogie Nights* (1997), *The Perfect Storm* (2000), and *Planet of the Apes* (2001), and *The Truth About Charlie* 2002, he had a few more antagonistic encounters of the strange kind. These included a charge of verbal assault in front of a Los Angeles gym and in the summer of 1993 a head-on collision with Madonna. At the time, the Material Girl held a grudge against the fast-rising, handsome Wahlberg for off-the-cuff remarks he had made about her looks in a magazine interview. The two adversaries came face-to-face at a Hollywood Hills party and words flew between

Spunky Mark Wahlberg out and about in Tinseltown. (Photo by Albert L. Ortega)

the pair. Each of the celebrity's followers got into the act and before long the contretemps had moved outside. "The semi-rumble" (as *Time* magazine called it) saw punches exchanged between members of the rival contingents. The skirmish eventually tapered off, but the hosts' garden was a mess. So much for life among the Hollywood set.

More recently, Mark was absorbed by the establishment, hanging around with pals such as actor George Clooney and dating the likes of actress Jordana Brewster and then model Rhea Durham. The trouble-prone days of the onetime juvenile delinquent seemed to be as long gone as his former incarnation as Marky Mark—once famous on stage for baring his butt and grabbing his crotch. Movie star Wahlberg was now saying such things as "I think happiness is around the corner. . . . You just gotta shift those gears and get around the corner." Then, in December 2001, one of the star's former bodyguards reportedly sued Mark for $2 million. The plaintiff alleged that a few weeks earlier he'd been assaulted and beaten by the performer outside a restaurant in lower Manhattan.

Such is life in the world of a still untamed Hollywood celebrity.

John Wayne

[Marion Michael Morrison]
MAY 26, 1907–JUNE 11, 1979

Decades after his death, Wayne remains a major icon. His elevated superhero status goes far beyond being just a colorful pop culture symbol: a famed movie star who made more than 160 films in fifty years and won an Oscar for 1969's *True Grit*. In fact, long before his passing, this bigger-than-life man emerged as a universally recognized archetype of the rugged and resilient American spirit. Most of his many fans were unfazed that this outspoken, ultraconservative individual was a big booster of the anti-Communist witch-hunt and black-list in Hollywood during the 1940s and 1950s, or that Duke produced and starred in the strongly pro–Vietnam War film *The Green Berets* (1968) at a time when most (young) liberal Americans were loudly protesting the war. His enthusiasts also glossed over the man's frequent right-wing political incorrectness. For example, it was Wayne who said about the winning of the American West: "I don't feel we did wrong in taking this great country away from [the Indians]. There were great numbers of people who needed new land, and the Indians were selfishly trying to keep it for themselves."

If today, in retrospect, Wayne emerges as an outspoken private citizen full of glaring prejudices and simplistic, outmoded concepts, he was also quite human in other facets of his off-screen life. Unlike the paragon of manly virtues he generally played on camera, his personal lifestyle certainly did not qualify him to be placed on any pedestal. Nowhere was his Hollywood bad-boy behavior more evident than in his extracurricular romantic activities.

The first of two boys, Marion Michael Morrison was born in Winterset, Iowa, in 1907. His father (never a business success) was a druggist and his domineering mother came from County Cork, Ireland. In 1913, because of the father's ill health, the family relocated to Southern California, eventually settling in Glendale. There Mr. Morrison opened a drugstore where Marion helped out. (During this period, the future movie star received his nickname "Duke" because that was the name of his Airedale dog.) Granted a football scholarship, the six-

John Wayne and Maureen O'Hara in a dramatic moment from *Rio Grande* (1950). (Courtesy of JC Archives)

foot, four-inch Morrison enrolled in 1925 at the University of Southern California as a prelaw student. However, a gridiron injury halted his sports career and ended his scholarship by his sophomore year. He found work at the old Fox Films studio in Hollywood as a prop boy. Soon he was doing bits in films (1926's *Bardelys the Magnificent*) and, after leaving college in 1927, worked full time as a movie stuntman, extra, or bit player.

He got a tremendous career break when director John Ford cast him in the lead of an epic western, *The Big Trail* (1930), in which the handsome, rugged actor was billed as John Wayne. The movie flopped and John was soon demoted to freelancing, mostly making budget westerns (1932's *Two-Fisted Law*) and serials (1933's *The Three Musketeers*) at poverty row studios. Gaining career experience and bruises in the process, Wayne developed a strong camaraderie with the hard-living men on the action movie sets. Thus he had a long-established carousing lifestyle when he wed Josephine Saenz in June 1933. John had initially met the aristocratic, Spanish-American beauty when he had been a college freshman. Even when their first son, Michael, was born, the actor still hung out with the studio guys after work and joined the weekend boozing and card games aboard filmmaker John Ford's yacht. Such activity was completely opposite to the refined, upscale home life and socializing that devoutly Catholic Josie wished for her growing family (which would include three more children: 1936, 1937, and 1939). The schism between the couple widened.

Wayne was rescued from a career of B westerns when Ford costarred him in *Stagecoach* (1939) with Claire Trevor. The sagebrush tale was a major hit and launched John to screen stardom. There were rumors that John and the also-married Claire, who were quickly teamed for two more pictures, were sparking together off camera. Meanwhile, in 1940, sultry screen siren Marlene Dietrich was about to make *Seven Sinners* at Universal Pictures. As legend has it, one day in the studio commissary the sophisticated German-born actress spotted Wayne striding across the room. She turned to the picture's producer and suggested, "Daddy, buy me that!" John was soon cast in the picture, which was the start of a torrid romance between these two very different movie celebrities. Before Marlene and the nearly-foot-taller he-man called it quits in 1942, they had made three pictures together and given the industry gossip mill much to discuss. During their scorching relationship, Wayne moved out of his home to a bachelor's apartment. Being Catholic, Josie refused, at the time, to give her husband a divorce.

While other movie stars were serving in World War II, Wayne, who had gained draft exemption because of his age and being a family man, became a true Hollywood playboy. With Marlene John had attempted to be somewhat discreet. Such was not the case with Esperanza Bauer, a fiery Mexican film actress and singer who was nicknamed "Chata" ("nice little pug nose"). Wayne was drawn to this tall, lithe spitfire who physically resembled Josie. Wayne and Bauer became a fixture on the Hollywood club scene. Later in 1943, Josie finally agreed to start divorce proceedings, which became final in 1945. In January 1946 John and Chata were wed at the United Presbyterian

Church in Long Beach, California. Almost from the start it was a stormy union, not helped by the attraction between Wayne and his new costar, the tormented, hard-drinking Gail Russell in *Angel and the Badman* (1947) and *Wake of the Red Witch* (1948). Even after it was over, tempestuous Chata refused to let the Russell matter be forgotten; she constantly berated Duke about this and other suspected misadventures.

In 1950 Wayne was named the most popular male star at the American box office. He became president of the ultraconservative Motion Picture Alliance, and starred in John Ford's well-received western *Rio Grande*. On the home front, however, John's life was falling apart. By 1952 he and Chata had separated and things turned nasty once she realized he was having an affair with Peruvian actress Pilar Pallette, whom Wayne had met in her homeland on an industry goodwill tour. Later, Pilar had come to Hollywood and the (secret) dating with Wayne had begun. The bitter Chata had no intentions of slinking away quietly. Instead she threatened to expose *all* of Wayne's indiscretions to public scrutiny. Thus began a battle of news headlines with Wayne accused of assorted infidelities and domestic abuse. After a media-covered battle of wills, the couple divorced in October 1953. The split became final a year thereafter, and two days later, on November 1, 1954, John and Pilar married in Kona, Hawaii. The couple would have three children (1956, 1962, and 1966).

During his third marriage, Wayne directed, produced, and starred in his overly ambitious *The Alamo* (1960) and continued to churn out mostly westerns: *The Sons of Katie Elder* (1965), *The War Wagon* (1967), and *True Grit* (1969). Now well into middle age, the still hard-drinking man was no longer a woman-chaser as before. He also had to curb another vice—his one-hundred-cigarettes-a-day habit—after he underwent lung surgery for cancer in 1964. Refusing to slow down his career, Wayne was still frequently away from home making movies. By 1973 Pilar was fed up with following him on location and the couple officially separated. However, they were still married when he died of cancer in Los Angeles in 1979 at age seventy-two.

Bruce Willis

[Walter Bruce Willis]

MARCH 19, 1955–

When Willis burst into the national consciousness, it was as smug, chauvinistic, flirtatious David Addison in the hit TV series *Moon-lighting* (1985–89). On the show—for which he won an Emmy—he did weekly battle with his aloof detective agency employer, played by Cybill Shepherd. Not long after the program's launch it became common gossip that the coleads were hardly harmonious on the soundstages, and accounts of their spats—real and otherwise—became legendary. Thus, Bruce put forth an image as a wisecracking, swaggering newcomer, someone who smirked his way through life. It suggested that perhaps he lacked humility or appreciation regarding his lucky career break. It was an impression that took Willis a long time to overcome, especially when in the mid-1980s he was seen on the Hollywood party circuit as a freewheeling playboy.

Willis was born in Idar-Oberstein, West Germany, the eldest of four children. His father was a U.S. serviceman and his mother was German-born. In 1957 the family relocated to the United States and settled in the blue-collar town of Carneys Point, New Jersey, where Mr. Willis found work as a mechanic at the Camden shipyard. At the age of eight, the future actor developed a stutter, leading the youngster to find ways to make people laugh so they might overlook his speech impediment. (When Willis later began to act or appeared before a live audience, the stutter disappeared.) He attended high school in the nearby town of Penns Grove. Bruno (as his pals called him) was a prankster in and out of the classroom, and gained fame for once streaking through town and for losing his virginity at fourteen when he was a Holiday Inn bellboy. However, he also found time to be in the drama club, learned to play the harmonica, and was elected student council president.

In mid-1973 the high school graduate was working as a driver at the E.I. DuPont plant in Deepwater, New Jersey. He quit his job as being too hazardous when another employee was killed in a plant explosion. After other work and playing harmonica with a band, he enrolled at Montclair State College, focusing on drama. When he landed an off-Broadway role in early 1977 he quit college and moved to New York where he lived in the rough section of town known as Hell's Kitchen. (One of his roommates for a time was actress Linda Fiorentino.)

When not making casting rounds, Bruce worked as a bartender, particularly at Café Central, a pub that boasted a large show business clientele. At work and around the city Willis wore baggy trousers, a torn T-shirt, and earrings—a man ahead of his time. Behind the bar, he often entertained the customers with his harmonica playing, singing, and racing down the bar length on roller skates. He got a cash bonanza when he was hired for a Levi Strauss jeans commercial and earned his Screen Actors Guild union card when he played an uncredited bit in the Frank Sinatra vehicle *The First Deadly Sin* (1980).

Willis's career escalated in the early 1980s, including taking over a key role in off-Broadway's *Fools for Love*. In 1985 he played a wife-beating weapons smuggler on a *Miami Vice* episode. By now he was dating Sheri Rivera, the ex-wife of talk show host Geraldo Rivera, and with her many contacts she helped him to network further in the industry. This led to his test for *Moonlighting*, one of three thousand actors considered for the part.

Once ensconced in Hollywood with *Moonlighting*, the almost thirty-year-old Bruce started a "fun seeking" period that included an escalating consumption of alcohol and other substance abuse as he partied through Tinseltown on his hipster nights out. With his improved TV series salary and revenue from his record albums that he had made over the years, TV specials, TV ads, and movies like *Blind Date* (1987), Willis could afford his plush house in Nichols Canyon situated in the Hollywood Hills. On Memorial Day weekend of 1987 Bruce gained notoriety when neighbors called the police complaining (again) of the loud music reverberating from the holiday partying at his house. During the commotion after the law arrived, he and four of his friends were carted off to jail. The charges of drug possession, disturbing the peace, and so forth were dropped once Bruce agreed to apologize to his neighbors. He did, but then moved to new digs by the ocean and became suspicious of the media. Meanwhile the tabloids nicknamed Willis "Hollywood's Bad Boy."

Later that year, however, Bruce abandoned alcohol and drugs. He got married that November in Las Vegas to actress Demi Moore, seven years his junior. She'd been previously wed to musician Freddy Moore. Demi had been one of the Hollywood Brat Pack and, for a time, had a serious relationship with one of its members, Emilio Estevez. Once Bruce and Demi were wed, the supermarket publications delighted in presenting them as the quarrelsome duo, he allegedly jealous over her current leading men or her past involvements. The twosome would have three daughters (1988, 1991, and 1994) and for a time in the 1990s would be considered Hollywood's most powerful couple.

A "cautionary" Bruce Willis interacts with the press. (Photo by Albert L. Ortega)

The action saga *Die Hard* (1988) paid Willis a $5 million salary, and the hugely successful feature gave him a franchise with new installments in 1990 and 1995. That allowed him to do small pictures such as *Mortal Thoughts* (1991) in which he played opposite his wife. Meanwhile both he and Moore acquired an $8 million triplex on Manhattan's Central Park West in 1990. They had already made their home base in Hailey, Idaho (population, 4,506), far away from the Hollywood glitz and craziness. Before long, they had turned an old launderette in town into a chic office and shop building and opened a retro diner there. They bought a decaying movie theater and redid it in lavish Art Deco and converted a crumbling bar into a trendy nightclub. On the outskirts of Hailey, they had their own $7 million, eighteen-acre ranch.

The good times in Hailey came to a halt when Bruce and Demi's marriage—long predicted to be on the rocks—disintegrated in the late 1990s. The movie stars stopped their investments in town and closed down some of their prior operations. The couple separated, with Willis purchasing his own home not far from his original Idaho spread. The divorce proceedings took two years, not only so the three girls could adjust to the domestic change but also to work out the split of Bruce and Demi's estimated $150 million holdings (which included several homes, many cars, and a private jet plane, not to mention an entourage of twenty-two bodyguards, maids, cooks, masseuses, and so forth). While this was occurring Demi dated a martial arts teacher some years her junior, and Bruce, star of the enormously successful thriller *The Sixth Sense* (1999), was romancing an attractive Spanish ex-model named Maria Bravo. (Their high-profile but wavering romance broke up in summer 2000, by which time Maria had suffered an alleged overdose of prescription pills, an act supposedly triggered by her losing Bruce's baby in a miscarriage.) Later Willis dated model Emily Sandberg and then Alisha Klass, a former adult-film actress. He also coped with the death of his younger brother who died of pancreatic cancer in 2001 at age forty-two.

Now an unfettered bachelor, Bruce had abandoned trying to hide his badly receding hairline. When not making movies such as *Bandits* (2001) or *Hart's War* (2002) or spending quality time with his three children, he divided his living time between Los Angeles, Hailey, and his $15 million Trump Tower apartment in Manhattan. Said Willis, "I like having the dough to come and go as I please." He also noted, "I'm staggered by the question of what it's like to be a multimillionaire. I always have to remind myself that I am."

HOLLYWOOD BAD BOYS

Gig Young

[Byron Elsworth Barr]

NOVEMBER 4, 1913–OCTOBER 19, 1978

In show business one of the toughest acting gigs on screen is to be the main character's best friend. The role demands that the performer be an interesting adjunct to the overall production, but *never* so riveting that the focus is drawn away from the star. It requires walking a delicate creative line. The task of sustaining the right touch from one such thankless secondary role to another is all the more difficult when the supporting player is convinced that he or she has the talent and looks to play the lead. Being stuck in such a second-banana rut for much of one's professional life would be enough to drive one to drink or worse. And that's exactly what happened to Hollywood's Gig Young who made a career of playing the affable other man.

Born Byron Elsworth Barr in St. Cloud, Minnesota, in 1913, he was the third child of a hard-working Scotsman who had recently founded the J. E. Barr Pickling and Preserving Company and his ex-schoolteacher spouse, Emma. Not long after Byron's birth, she became bookkeeper for the family business. It seemed the Barrs were more comfortable working than tending to their children, and Byron, the youngest and most sensitive of the trio, felt abandoned. His sense of rejection worsened when Mrs. Barr developed nervous symptoms (perhaps imagined) that kept her confined to her room and withdrawn from her family. Meanwhile, "Aunt Jessie," the teenage adopted daughter of Emma's stepmother, joined the Barr household to care for the two youngest children. Byron latched onto this new mother figure, starting a lifelong pattern of reaching out for older women as nurturing/sexual objects.

During the Depression when their business fell apart, the Barrs and Byron (the only offspring still at home) moved to Washington, D.C. When the parents next relocated to North Carolina for better work opportunities, Byron remained in Washington. It was the young man's landlady—another mother figure—who encouraged him to follow his need for attention and his dreams by joining a local theater group.

Later, to please his stern parents he took a regular job (at a car agency) but did badly at it and was fired. He then hitchhiked to Hollywood.

On the West Coast, the good-looking, six-foot, one-inch Byron worked at odd jobs while studying at the Pasadena Playhouse and making the casting rounds of the movie studios. At the theater he met and soon married (in August 1940) a pleasant, but plain-looking actress named Sheila Stapler. That same year he was hired by Warner Bros. and began playing bit parts on camera. It was in *The Gay Sisters* (1942) with Barbara Stanwyck that Byron made an impression as the handsome and dashing young artist. (From this lucky picture, he took the name of his character, Gig Young, as his own.) During the making of *Old Acquaintances* (1943), Gig had a brief romantic fling with the film's star, Bette Davis, even though she also was married.

After serving in the U.S. Coast Guard during World War II, Young returned to supporting roles at Warner Bros. One of his studio boosters was the lot's drama teacher, Sophie Rosenstein. Although married,

Gig Young at the microphone as Al Lewis looks on in *They Shoot Horses, Don't They?* (1969). (Courtesy of JC Archives)

she (a plain but warm-hearted individual) and Gig developed a special rapport, which helped when Warner Bros. cancelled his contract in 1947. By 1949 Gig and Sheila had divorced and, the following year, he and the six-years-older Rosenstein, now single, were wed.

Young's breakthrough screen assignment—thanks to his wife's industry contacts—was as an alcoholic composer in *Come Fill the Cup* (1951) with James Cagney. It won him an Oscar nomination for Best Supporting Actor and helped to restore (temporarily) his professional confidence. In this potentially joyful period, Sophie developed cancer and died in November 1952. To cover over his sorrow and to disguise the dullness of his boring film roles, Young turned increasingly to alcohol, a substance abuse that had been going on for years. He worked frequently in other mediums: TV and Broadway. While on Broadway in *Oh Men! Oh Women!* (1953), he dated busty stripper Sherry Britton. Unfortunately each of them had a tremendous fear of intimacy and their relationship ended when she refused his bold (for him) marriage proposal. Next, Gig turned to actress Elaine Stritch, but she was interested in someone else then, plus she sensed that some great, masked frustration(s) controlled his life. The two decided to be just good friends.

Back in Hollywood, in 1956 Gig married actress Elizabeth Montgomery, who was twenty years his junior. Meanwhile, when not acting on the stage, Young continued as the screen's most debonair and adept second male lead. He reached his apex in the Doris Day–Clark Gable fluff *Teacher's Pet* (1958) for which he was again nominated for a Best Supporting Actor Oscar. By the early 1960s, Gig, a very heavy drinker, had divorced Montgomery. Feeling middle-aged and abandoned—again—he turned to increasingly younger women for distraction. By now his substance abuse included drugs. In 1963 Gig wed real estate agent Elaine Young and their daughter, Jennifer, was born the following April. By November 1966 the couple had divorced.

Thanks to his constant diet of liquor, Young, now in his fifties, appeared puffy-faced and flabby. He returned to Broadway in *There's a Girl in My Soup* (1967) and dated actress Skye Aubrey, thirty-one years his junior. She favored marriage, he said no. Gig finally won an Academy Award for being the dissolute emcee in the artistic movie

They Shoot Horses, Don't They? (1969). But, thereafter, he suffered the "Oscar jinx" and was stuck with mediocre assignments. He was further drained by fighting with his ex-wife Elaine over their property settlement, enduring backstage cast squabbles during a revival of *Harvey* (1971), and the humiliation of being let go from Mel Brooks's movie spoof *Blazing Saddles* (1974). By this juncture Gig had an industry reputation of being unreliable, making decent work difficult to find.

Young was among those hired in 1977 to shoot *Game of Death*, which utilized footage from a film Bruce Lee was making in 1973 when he died. On the set he met Kim Schmidt, a young German actress and script assistant. Their problematic romance (she was more than thirty years his junior) culminated in their September 1978 wedding in New York City. Very quickly the couple began having loud daily arguments. Already suffering from paranoia and other maladies, Gig became increasingly withdrawn. He still refused to deal with his substance abuse problems. One night, he phoned a longtime woman friend in Los Angeles, begging her to fly to the East Coast and accompany him back to Hollywood. He said his self-worth was at rock bottom because of his deteriorating relationship with Kim and his seeming inability to memorize lines when he did find work. Using tough love, the pal said "no" to Gig. This latest dismissal in a lifetime full of real and imagined rejections led Gig to immediate, desperate measures. He killed his wife in their Manhattan apartment and then put the barrel of the Smith & Wesson gun into his mouth and squeezed the trigger.

So ended the emotionally plagued life of one of Hollywood's most successful on-screen playboys.

BIBLIOGRAPHY

Publications

Biography
Classic Film Collector
Daily Variety
Ebony
Empire
Filmfax
Films in Review
Film Threat
Globe
Hollywood Reporter
In Style
Jet
Los Angeles Daily News
Los Angeles Times
Movieline
National Enquirer
Newsweek
New York Daily News
New York Observer
New York Post
New York Times
People
Playboy
Premiere
Psychotronic
Sight & Sound
StarTeen People

Time
Total Film
Us Weekly
Vanity Fair

Books

Amende, Coral. *Hollywood Confidential*. New York: Plume, 1997.

Anderson, Loni, with Larkin Warren. *My Life in High Heels*. New York: Avon, 1995.

Austin, John. *Hollywood's Unsolved Mysteries*. New York: Shapolsky, 1992.

———. *Tales of Hollywood the Bizarre*. New York: Shapolsky, 1992.

Basinger, Jeanine. *Silent Stars*. Hanover, N.H.: Wesleyan University/New England, 2000.

Belushi, Judith Jacklin. *Samurai Widow*. New York: Carroll & Graf, 1995.

Berlin, Joey, ed. *Toxic Fame*. Detroit, Mich.: Visible Ink, 1996.

Bodeen, DeWitt. *From Hollywood*. South Brunswick, N.J.: A. S. Barnes, 1976.

———. *More from Hollywood*. South Brunswick, N.J.: A. S. Barnes, 1977.

Bogart, Stephen. *Humphrey Bogart: In Search of My Father*. New York: Dutton, 1995.

Bosworth, Patricia. *Montgomery Clift*. New York: Limelight, 1990.

Brando, Anna Kashfi, and E. P. Stein. *Brando for Breakfast*. New York: Berkley, 1979.

Brando, Marlon, with Robert Lindsey. *Brando: Songs My Mother Taught Me*. New York: Random House, 1994.

Braun, Eric. *The Elvis Film Encyclopedia*. Woodstock, N.Y.: Overlook, 1997.

Britton, Ron. *Kim Basinger: Longer than Forever*. London: Blake, 1998.

Brooks, Tim, and Earle Marsh. *The Complete Directory to Prime Time Network and Cable TV Shows: 1946–Present* (seventh ed.). New York: Ballantine, 1999.

Cameron-Wilson, James. *Young Hollywood*. Lanham, Md.: Madison, 1994.

Carpozi, George, Jr. *Clark Gable*. New York: Pyramid, 1971.

———. *The John Wayne Story*. New York: Dell, 1972.

Cawthorne, Nigel. *Sex Lives of the Hollywood Goddesses*. London: Prion, 1997.

———. *Sex Lives of the Hollywood Idols*. London: Prion, 1997.

Cerasini, Marc. *O. J. Simpson: American Hero, American Tragedy*. New York: Pinnacle, 1994.

Chaplin, Charles, Jr., with N. and M. Rau. *My Father, Charlie Chaplin*. New York: Popular Library, 1961.

Cline, Camille, et al. *Famous Mugs*. New York: Cader, 1996.

Craddock, Jim, ed. *VideoHound's Golden Movie Retriever 2002*. Detroit, Mich.: Visible Ink, 2001.

Crawley, Tony, ed. *The Wordsworth Dictionary of Film Quotations*. Ware, Hertfordshire, England: Wordsworth, 1994.

Crockett, Art. *Celebrity Murders*. New York: Pinnacle, 1990.

Crosby, Gary, and Ross Firestone. *Going My Own Way*. New York: Fawcett, 1983.

Cunningham, Ernest. *The Ultimate Bogart*. Los Angeles: Renaissance, 1999.

Dalton, David. *James Dean: The Mutant King*. New York: Dell, 1974.

Davidson, Bill. *Spencer Tracy: Tragic Idol*. New York: Zebra, 1989.

Davis, Don. *Fallen Hero*. New York: St. Martin's, 1994.

Des Barres, Pamela. *I'm with the Band: Confessions of a Groupie*. New York: Jove, 1988.

Douglas, Kirk. *The Ragman's Son: An Autobiography*. New York: Simon & Schuster, 1988.

Drop, Mark. *Dateline: Hollywood*. New York: Friedman/Fairfax, 1994.

Edmonds, Andy. *Frame-Up!* New York: Avon, 1991.

Eells, George. *Final Gig: The Man Behind the Murder*. New York: Harcourt, Brace, Jovanovich, 1991.

Eliot, Marc. *Burt!* New York: Dell, 1982.

Ellenberger, Allan R. *Celebrities in Los Angeles Cemeteries; A Directory*. Jefferson, N.C.: McFarland, 2001.

Epstein, Edward Z., and Joe Morella. *Mia: The Life of Mia Farrow.* New York: Dell, 1991.

Farrow, Mia. *What Falls Away.* New York: Bantam, 1998.

Fields, W. C., with Ronald J. Fields. *W. C. Fields: By Himself.* Englewood Cliffs, N.J.: Prentice-Hall, 1973.

Fiore, Carlo, *Bud: The Brando I Knew.* New York: Dell, 1974.

Fisher, James. *Spencer Tracy: A Bio-Bibliography.* Westport, Conn.: Greenwood, 1994.

Freedland, Michael. *The Two Lives of Errol Flynn.* New York: Morrow, 1979.

Giddins, Gary. *Bing Crosby: A Pocketful of Dreams—The Early Years.* Boston: Little Brown, 2001.

Gilmore, John. *Live Fast—Die Young: My Life with James Dean.* New York: Thunder's Mouth, 1997.

Glatt, John. *Lost in Hollywood: The Fast Times and Short Life of River Phoenix.* New York: Primus, 1995.

Goldman, Albert. *Elvis.* New York: McGraw-Hill, 1982.

———. *Elvis: The Last 24 Hours.* New York: St. Martin's, 1991.

Goodall, Nigel. *Johnny Depp.* London: Blake, 1999.

Graysmith, Robert. *The Murder of Bob Crane.* New York: Berkley, 1994.

Grobel, Lawrence. *Conversations with Brando.* New York: Cooper Square, 1999.

Guralick, Peter. *Last Train to Memphis: Careless Love.* Boston: Little Brown, 1999.

———. *Last Train to Memphis: The Rise of Elvis Presley.* Boston: Little Brown, 1994.

Hack, Richard. *Hughes: The Private Diaries, Memos and Letters.* Los Angeles: New Millennium, 2001.

Hadleigh, Boze. *Celebrity Feuds!* Dallas, Tex.: Taylor, 1999.

———. *Hollywood Babble On.* New York: Perigee, 1994.

Hall, Elaine Blake. *Burt and Me: My Days and Nights with Burt Reynolds.* New York: Pinnacle, 1994.

Hardy, Karen. *The New Breed.* New York: Henry Holt, 1988.

Higham, Charles. *Errol Flynn: The Untold Story.* New York: Doubleday, 1980.

Hofstede, David. *James Dean: A Bio-Bibliography*. Westport, Conn.: Greenwood, 1996.

Hopkins, Jerry. *Elvis: The Final Years*. New York: Playboy, 1981.

Houseman, Victoria. *Made in Heaven*. New York: Bonus, 1991.

Hunter, Jack, ed. *Johnny Depp*. London: Creation, 1999.

Hyams, Joe, with Jay Hyams. *James Dean: Little Boy Lost*. New York: Warner, 1992.

Keats, John. *Howard Hughes*. New York: Pyramid, 1970.

Kelley, Kitty. *His Way: The Unauthorized Biography of Frank Sinatra*. New York: Bantam, 1987.

Kirkpatrick, Sidney D. *A Cast of Killers*. New York: Dutton, 1986.

Kobler, John. *Damned in Paradise: The Life of John Barrymore*. New York: Atheneum, 1977.

LaGuardia, Robert. *Monty: A Biography of Montgomery Clift*. New York: Avon, 1977.

Lambert, Gavin. *Nazimova*. New York: Knopf, 1997.

Latham, Caroline. *Priscilla and Elvis*. New York: New American, 1985.

Lawford, Lady. *Bitch!* Brookline Village, Mass.: Brandon, 1987.

Lawford, Patricia Seaton, with Ted Schwarz. *The Peter Lawford Story*. New York: Jove, 1990.

Levy, Shawn. *King of Comedy: The Life and Art of Jerry Lewis*. New York: St. Martin's, 1996.

MacGraw, Ali. *Moving Pictures*. New York: Bantam, 1992.

Maltin, Leonard, and Richard W. Bann. *The Little Rascals*. New York: Crown, 1992.

Mann, May. *The Private Elvis*. New York: Pocket, 1977.

Manso, Peter. *Brando*. New York: Hyperion, 1994.

McLean, Adrienne L., and David A. Cook, eds. *Headline Hollywood*. New Brunswick, N.J.: Rutgers University Press, 2001.

Monti, Carlotta, with Cy Rice. *W. C. Fields & Me*. New York: Warner, 1973.

Moore, Terry. *The Beauty and the Billionaire*. New York: Pocket, 1984.

Moore, Terry, and Jerry Rivers. *The Passions of Howard Hughes*. Los Angeles: General Publishing, 1996.

Morris, Michael. *Madam Valentino*. New York: Abbeville, 1991.

Morton, Danelle. *Meg Ryan*. New York: Time, 2000.

Munn, Michael. *Hollywood Bad*. New York: St. Martin's, 1991.

Mustazza, Leonard. *Ol' Blue Eyes: A Frank Sinatra Encyclopedia*. Westport, Conn.: Greenwood, 1998.

Nazel, Joseph. *Richard Pryor: The Man Behind the Laughter*. Los Angeles: Holloway House, 1981.

Newman, Rayce. *The Hollywood Connection*. New York: Shapolsky, 1994.

Norden, Martin F. *John Barrymore: A Bio-Bibliography*. Westport, Conn.: Greenwood, 1995.

Osterholm, J. Roger. *Bing Crosby: A Bio-Bibliography*. Westport, Conn.: Greenwood, 1994.

Parish, James Robert. *The Hollywood Book of Death*. Chicago: Contemporary Books, 2001.

———. *Hollywood's Great Love Teams*. New Rochelle, N.Y.: Arlington House, 1974.

———. *Let's Talk! America's Favorite Talk Show Hosts*. Las Vegas, Nev.: Pioneer, 1993.

———. *The Tough Guys*. New Rochelle, N.Y.: Arlington House, 1976.

Parish, James Robert, and Don E. Stanke. *Hollywood Baby Boomers*. New York: Garland, 1992.

Parish, James Robert, and Lennard DeCarl. *Hollywood Players: The Forties*. New Rochelle, N.Y.: Arlington House, 1976.

Parish, James Robert, and Michael R. Pitts. *Hollywood Songsters*. New York: Garland, 1991.

Parish, James Robert, and Ronald L. Bowers. *The MGM Stock Company*. New Rochelle, N.Y.: Arlington House, 1973.

Parish, James Robert, and William T. Leonard et al. *The Funsters*. New Rochelle, N.Y.: Arlington House, 1979.

———. *Hollywood Players: The Thirties*. New Rochelle, N.Y.: Arlington House, 1976.

Parish, James Robert, with Gregory W. Mank. *The Hollywood Reliables*. Westport, Conn.: Arlington House, 1980.

Parker, John. *Five for Hollywood*. New York: Carol, 1989.

Peters, Margot. *The House of Barrymore*. New York: Knopf, 1990.

Pryor, Richard, with Todd Gold. *Pryor Convictions and Other Life Sentences*. New York: Pantheon, 1995.

Pulver, Andrew, and Steven Paul Davies. *Brat Pack: Confidential*. London: Batsford, 2000.

Ramer, Jean. *Duke: The Real Story of John Wayne*. New York: Charter, 1973.

Riggin, Judith M. *John Wayne: A Bio-Bibliography*. Westport, Conn.: Greenwood, 1992.

Robb, Brian J. *River Phoenix: A Short Life*. London: Plexus, 1995.

Roberts, Jerry. *Robert Mitchum: A Bio-Bibliography*. Westport, Conn.: Greenwood, 1992.

Robinson, David. *Chaplin: His Life and Art*. New York: McGraw-Hill, 1985.

Rovin, Jeff. *Kelsey Grammer*. New York: HarperPaperback, 1995.

———. *Richard Pryor: Black and Blue*. New York: Bantam, 1983.

———. *TV Babylon*. New York: Signet, 1987.

———. *TV Babylon II*. New York: Signet, 1992.

Ruuth, Marianne. *Eddie*. Los Angeles: Holloway House, 1985.

Ryan, Joal. *Former Child Stars*. Toronto: ECW, 2000.

Sanello, Frank. *Don't Call Me Marky Mark*. Los Angeles: Renaissance, 1999.

Schickel, Richard. *Brando: A Life in Our Times*. New York: St. Martin's, 1991.

Schoell, William. *Martini Man: The Life of Dean Martin*. Dallas, Tex.: Taylor, 1999.

Scott, Cathy. *The Killing of Tupac Shakur*. Las Vegas, Nev.: Huntington Press, 1997.

Sealy, Shirley. *The Celebrity Sex Register*. New York: Fireside, 1982.

Seminara, George, ed. *Mug Shots: Celebrities Under Arrest*. New York: St. Martin's, 1996

Server, Lee. *Robert Mitchum: Baby I Don't Care*. New York: St. Martin's, 2001.

Shales, Tom. *Legends: Remembering America's Greatest Stars*. New York: Random House, 1989.

Shepherd, Donald, and Robert F. Slatzer. *Bing Crosby: The Hollow Man*. New York: Pinnacle, 1981.

Shipman, David. *The Great Movie Stars 3: The Independent Years*. London: Macdonald, 1991.

Shulman, Irving. *Valentino*. New York: Trident, 1967.

Spada, James. *Peter Lawford: The Man Who Kept the Secrets*. New York: Bantam, 1992.

Sperber, A. M., and Eric Lax. *Bogart*. New York: Morrow, 1997.

Spotto, Donald. *Rebel: The Life and Legend of James Dean*. New York: HarperCollins, 1996.

St. Charnez, Casey. *The Films of Steve McQueen*. Secaucus, N.J.: Citadel, 1984.

Stacy, Pat, with Beverly Linet. *Duke: A Love Story*. New York: Pocket, 1983.

Stempel, Penny. *River Phoenix*. Philadelphia, Pa.: Chelsea House, 2000.

Strait, Raymond. *Mrs. Howard Hughes*. Los Angeles: Holloway House, 1970.

Taraborrelli, J. Randy. *Sinatra: A Complete Life*. Secaucus, N.J.: Birch Lane, 1997.

Thomas, Bob. *The One and Only Bing*. New York: Tempo Star/Ace, 1977.

Thompson, Peter. *Jack Nicholson*. Secaucus, N.J.: Birch Lane, 1997.

Thompson, Verita, with Donald Shepherd. *Bogie and Me*. New York: Pinnacle, 1982.

Thomson, David. *Warren Beatty and Desert Eyes*. New York: Doubleday, 1987.

Tornabene, Lyn. *Long Live the King: A Biography of Clark Gable*. New York: Pocket, 1976.

Tosches, Nick. *Dino: Living High in the Dirty Business of Dreams*. New York: Dell, 1992.

Tresidder, Jody. *Hugh Grant*. New York: St. Martin's, 1996.

Wayne, Jane Ellen. *Ava's Men: The Private Life of Ava Gardner*. New York: St. Martin's, 1990.

———. *Gable's Women*. New York: St. Martin's, 1987.

Wellman, Sam. *Ben Affleck*. Philadelphia, Pa.: Chelsea House, 2000.

Woodward, Bob. *Wired: The Short Life & Fast Times of John Belushi*. New York: Pocket, 1984.

Young, Robert, Jr. *Roscoe "Fatty" Arbuckle: A Bio-Bibliography*. Westport, Conn.: Greenwood, 1996.

Television

A&E: *Biography*
E! Entertainment Television: *Celebrity Profiles*
E! Entertainment Television: *Mysteries & Scandals*
E! Entertainment Television: *True Hollywood Story*
Lifetime: *Intimate Portraits*
MSNBC: *Headliners & Legends*

Internet Websites

All Movie Guide: www.allmovie.com
The Celebrity Morgue: www.celebritymorgue.com
E! Entertainment Television Online: www.eonline.com
Find a Grave: www.findagrave.com/index.html
Internet Movie Database: www.imdb.com
Mr. Showbiz: www.mrshowbiz.go.com
Roadside America: www.roadsideamerica.com
The Tombstone Tourist: www.teleport.com/~stanton

INDEX

ABOUT THE AUTHOR

James Robert Parish, a former entertainment reporter, publicist, and book
series editor, is the author of more than
one hundred published major biographies
and reference books of the entertainment industry. A partial list includes the
following:

The Hollywood Book of Death
Jet Li
The Multicultural Encyclopedia of
*   Twentieth Century Hollywood*
Gus Van Sant
Jason Biggs
Whoopi Goldberg
Rosie O'Donnell's Story
The Unofficial "Murder, She Wrote" Casebook
Let's Talk! America's Favorite Talk Show Hosts
The Great Cop Pictures
Ghosts and Angels in Hollywood Films
Prison Pictures from Hollywood
Hollywood's Great Love Teams
The RKO Gals

Mr. Parish is a frequent on-camera interviewee on cable and network TV for documentaries on the performing arts. He resides in Studio City, California.